British Tastes

An enquiry into the likes and dislikes
of the Regional Consumer

British Tastes

An enquiry into the likes and
dislikes of the Regional Consumer

D. ELLISTON ALLEN

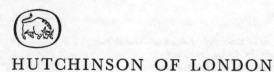

HUTCHINSON OF LONDON

HUTCHINSON & CO (*Publishers*) LTD
178–202 Great Portland Street, London W1

London Melbourne Sydney
Auckland Bombay Toronto
Johannesburg New York

First published 1968

*This book has been set in Baskerville, printed in Great Britain
on Antique Wove paper by Anchor Press, and
bound by Wm. Brendon, both of Tiptree, Essex*

09 088110 9

Contents

	Acknowledgments	vii
	Introduction	1
	Map of Standard Regions	12
	The Regions of Britain	13
I	North v. South	21
II	London and the South East	43
III	The Rural South: East Anglia and the West Country	70
IV	Wales	86
V	The Midlands	104
VI	The North West	129
VII	The North East: Yorkshire and Tyne-Tees	150
VIII	Scotland	180
IX	The End of Difference?	217
	Notes and References	223
	Index	243

To
W.L.

Acknowledgements

My grateful acknowledgements are due to the many people, too numerous to name individually, who have helped me in the collecting of the material for this book, if only by patiently bearing with my questions on matters that must often have seemed to them trite, tedious or irrelevant. I should like to pay tribute, especially, to those whose dual backgrounds (Welsh-born Midlanders, London Yorkshiremen, exiled Scots) provided them – and me – with insight into points that would otherwise have been missed altogether. To colleagues and friends in the worlds of marketing and market research I owe innumerable debts, for information, for shared interest and for often stimulating discussion. A few who have supplied me with particularly extensive unpublished data are thanked in the Introduction; the rest will, I trust, accept an overall assurance that their contributions were warmly appreciated and have not been forgotten.

I must specially thank those friends who undertook the task of reading the book in draft: Mr. J. S. Downham and Mr. Edward Moar, whose care and knowledge have rescued me from many errors; Mr. and Mrs. B. R. S. Megaw, who with some of their friends and colleagues very kindly perused the chapter on Scotland; and Mr. C. F. Greenlaw and Miss S. B. Raphael, who have tested my arguments and tidied up my English. While the book is immeasurably better for their efforts, they are none of them, I must stress, in any way responsible for the views that appear in it, and such faults as it still possesses are wholly and completely my own.

D.E.A.

Introduction

Since the later 1920s the public of Great Britain has been subjected, year in, year out, to increasingly fierce bombardments – by questionnaire. That central technique of the modern social scientist, the large-scale interviewing known as the 'sample survey', has gradually percolated into almost every aspect of our national life so that today the census-taker, the market-research interviewer and the opinion pollster must be more familiar figures on the average housewife's doorstep than even those hardy perennials the Jehovah's Witnesses and the 'Man from the Pru'. Irritating the busy, cheering the lonely, flattering the downtrodden, infuriating the reticent, this gallant army of buttonholers and bell-ringers has wormed its way into the private lives of the nation and emerged with an array of facts and figures all too little known in their tremendous extent and variety. Some of these are patently important – to those who plan the nation's welfare, to businessmen faced with million-pound decisions – but the majority are seemingly trivial and hold meaning only to those who sit in back rooms with slide-rules, calculating where to fit the countless little pieces into the larger pattern.

In most of these surveys, by long tradition, the answers to almost every question, reduced to numerical form for tabulation on punch-card machines or computers, are cross-analysed by a number of standard categories such as the age, sex, social class and regional location of each person interviewed. In the business world much of value is normally extracted from the first three of these; but the regional variations, unless very pronounced, have for years been given little more than a passing glance. For this there are several reasons.

First and most obviously, a general though largely unspoken idea has long prevailed that regional differences in habits and tastes are commercially unimportant, merely awkward creases in the overall national pattern that for some reason or other – backwardness, obstinacy, unevenly distributed sales pressures – have just temporarily failed to be ironed out. They are interesting, it is allowed, even quaint and intriguing, but all the same almost entirely 'academic'; for it has long been held that there is little one can do about them, at least in ways that make economic sense. The peculiar strength of the national press in Britain, blanketing the country efficiently and, for advertisers, relatively cheaply, has helped to sustain this view, permitting media buyers in the advertising agencies to ignore these inconvenient regional minutiae, and in the process has caused local newspapers to languish.

The arrival of commercial television bringing for the first time regionally based media of great marketing influence and sophistication might have been expected to kill this myth of nation-wide uniformity almost overnight; but for various reasons, chiefly the exceptionally long freedom enjoyed by rival stations from the need to compete more vigorously for advertisers' wares, their beneficial influence on behalf of regionalism has only recently started to become apparent. For this we mainly have to thank the spread of the concept of 'test marketing': choosing a limited area in which to sell and advertise a new product as an experimental precaution before risking far greater resources nationally. The commerical television areas offer excellent examples of test markets, and their lead in promoting themselves in this role has been copied by the more progressive groups of provincial and local newspapers. In this way, by accident more than design, a regional counter-revolution is now developing – and facts and figures that were dismissed as trivial or irrelevant will surely begin to take on a far greater importance.

A second reason for the neglect of the regional differences is, I suggest, a psychological one. 'Geography', as E. C. Bentley has assured us, 'is about maps.' Unfortunately, very few people in Britain (and perhaps anywhere) have minds like maps; and unless thinking like this is a habitual mental reflex with strings of place-names immediately arranging themselves in their proper locations on being fed into the brain, the geographical circumstances of a taste or habit are likely to be a tedious added complication, even indeed a meaningless bore. Add to this the fact that knowledge of the geography of his own country on the part of the average educated Briton – unless his work has involved him in constantly travelling the length and breadth of it – can only be described as utterly deplorable, and it is hardly surprising that an anti-geographical bias appears to prevail very generally.

Thirdly and lastly, regional differences have been played down just because they make little sense when seen in isolation. To be properly evaluated, they need to be viewed *en masse*. This at once involves working through a great mass of surveys and extracting every regional fact of apparent significance. Yet the very people who have ready access to the greatest numbers of surveys are almost without exception also the people with the least time and energy to devote to marginal tasks of this character. An academic specialist might conceivably work up enthusiasm to ransack the government publications for survey data of this type, but without adding to this the far more extensive and varied information dredged up and put out by commercial organisations, he would be likely to end up not only with a very lopsided picture, but with some singularly meatless dry bones.

In compiling this work over the past ten years I have been fortunate to be employed in positions which have involved what must be several hundred surveys, of all shapes and sizes and on an almost unimaginable range of topics, passing through my hands. A surprisingly high proportion have been of a non-confidential nature – a proportion which, happily, has grown even larger in the last year or two. Before 1959, published surveys, even in duplicated form and circulated privately on a limited scale, were frustratingly few and far between. Since then the scene has changed almost miraculously. We now have the numerous marketing surveys commissioned and published by the television companies and newspaper groups; the welcome and growing release of private surveys, in whole or in part, for public-relations purposes; and the spread of the subscription system in market research, which allows the results of a survey to be offered, on a non-exclusive basis, to anyone prepared to subscribe a requisite proportion of its cost. All these have combined to produce a cascade of information, available to all comers, so great that it is not only difficult to keep pace with but has even conveniently removed all necessity, in undertakings of the present kind, to press for the release of figures still treated as confidential.

Although, accordingly, none of the information cited in this book comes from confidential sources, I have had the benefit of being able to draw on a very large amount of data of this type to help me in reaching my broader conclusions. Thanks to this I have been able to tread much more firmly in several places where the published information on its own left the ground statistically rather shaky. And further, by laying alongside one isolated item from one confidential source with one from another, it has in some cases proved possible to arrive at useful new 'aggregate facts' – that is, large-scale truths that can be cited freely without betraying the confidential character of the particularised lesser facts out of which they have been conceived.

Excluding confidential data has been both a gain and a loss. On the one hand, in good scholarly tradition, every fact in the book can be readily run to earth should anyone in some respect or other later wish to do so. There is thus no risk of factual statements proving uncheckable (which would be most undesirable in a compilation of this kind) due to the banging shut of private files. On the other hand, the range of subjects which chance to have been covered by published surveys is, inevitably, much more limited. As everyone who has ever tried to unearth and compile information on markets will have found, the amount available varies quite extraordinarily. There is almost too much published on cigarettes, for instance, yet next to nothing on sweets or toys. If you should want to know what kinds of dresses women buy you will be hard put to it to discover much but you will be swamped with information on their cosmetics or stockings. Most of the surveys that are published are aimed at the pockets of advertisers spending sizable budgets to promote individual brands. Therefore if a market has been neglected in this respect it is probably because it appears too small or too static to be an interesting prospect for substantial brand promotion; or because it is tightly shared between two or three giants who do all their own consumer research to the point of satiety; or because by its very nature, as in the case of sweets or patent medicines, it is much safer to rely on measuring sales over the retailers' counters than on shoppers' memories—and retail figures, partly because of the generally much higher sums spent in acquiring them, tend to be guarded from competitors (and the public eye) like bars of gold.

To fill in the crevices, or sometimes just to add colour to the more mundane information drawn directly from surveys, I have incorporated the odd *trouvaille* from articles in the Press or from books or derived from badgering the more seemingly reliable regional expatriates among my friends. In all such cases I have been careful to cite the source (not, unfortunately, always the primary one) in the list of references at the end of the book. The geographer, however, like the historian, is not expected to cite authority for his every statement; and as this book is intended also for the general reader, I have purposely confined further references to those surveys that might be considered rather more obscure. The remaining sources from which the principal mass of facts has been drawn are surely familiar to everyone closely enough engaged in this field to want to refer back to the originals: the various regular government surveys, ranging from the Censuses of Population and Distribution to the Family Expenditure Surveys and the even more invaluable National Food Surveys; the marketing surveys of the newspaper and television companies; the standard books reporting on particular major projects such as *The Foods We Eat* of W. S. Crawford Ltd. (Cassell, 1958) and, in many ways the most useful of all, the long series of surveys circulated over the years by Odhams Press Ltd. For a considerable amount of non-confidential data till now never published, or at least freely released, I am particularly indebted to the Research Manager of Odhams Press Ltd. and to the directors of Contimart Ltd and Fashion Trends.

Culling information in this way from a very large range of sample surveys, many of them covering the same topics, provides one at the same time, quite incidentally, with an uncommon opportunity of assessing the consistency of data collected by this method. There are – it has to be accepted – many unbelievers still among the laity: many people still who once, perhaps, lied quite deliberately when they happened to be interviewed and hold that everyone else must, of course, invariably do the same; or who dismiss out of hand the validity of all sampling – and maybe all statistical technique as well – on the strength of temporary aberrations in the (normally very accurate) published opinion polls. To these doubters one reply only is possible: the results of these surveys are, on the whole, impressively consistent – always provided that the persons conducting them behaved with a proper professionalism, taking every care to frame the questions sensibly, to draw the sample to be interviewed with unswerving randomness and to build in appropriate checks to minimise the effects of cheating (by the interviewer no less than by the respondent). That interviewing is the weak link in the long chain of survey processes few people would deny, and indeed there is an ample repertoire of horror stories on this topic that regularly go the rounds. Yet time and time again, one finds, one firm's figures concur more or less exactly with another's – including, most convincingly of all, those cases where both chanced to investigate the same novel subject simultaneously. The miscreants, one is forced to assume, are few. Most members of the public, on the contrary, seem only too delighted to be asked to air their views and revel in the experience of having what they say carefully attended to and noted down in writing. Only a small minority, at the best of times, can have the necessary sharp-wittedness to make up all the answers – and compared with the effort involved in this, to state the truth is ordinarily far simpler. Deception, when it occurs, mainly comes at worst half-intentionally, in answer to questions that are ambiguous or embarrassing or to the forty-third item in a half-hour standing session.

While this compilation clearly has most immediate relevance for the world of marketing – and is addressed in the first instance, accordingly, to the sales representative and the advertising man – I hope it may also prove of value and interest within a wider context. Regional planners may perhaps welcome it as a means of varying their normally rather starkly over-statistical type of diet. Conductors of surveys may find it convenient to have listed in one place some of the various regional distortions that need to be taken into account when devising samples. Migrants from one region to another may find it helpful to be forewarned of the surprising range of differences in daily living that they are still likely to find confronting them upon resettlement.

Of more general interest still may be the larger proposition put forward in this book: namely, that all the myriad isolated facts to be gleaned about any region are, in one way or another, interrelated; that there is, in other words, a much greater degree of connection, albeit often subtle and not at once apparent, between such seemingly very different fields as illness and leisure interests, crime and aesthetic tastes, or electoral behaviour and shopping patterns, than we normally suppose. For it is my secondary purpose to suggest – but no more than suggest (for the evidence is still insufficient for any more confident assertion) – that each of the regions of Britain has at bottom a detectable set of interwoven attitudes, a distinctive trend in its underlying psychology, which is long-enduring and which imparts a certain special look or direction to virtually every kind of human activity carried on by its inhabitants. For this reason I make no apology for the often startling juxtapositions of subject matter in the pages that follow. I believe we have much to gain by considering attitudes to oranges, say, in the same glance as suicide rates, or by regarding the incidence of apple pies as no less potentially significant than the incidence of asthma. The telltale signs that help us to identify the deeper traits in a region's character are just as likely to be located in the trivialities of shopping as in more earnest aspects of human behaviour. Moreover, by intermingling for once so many apparently quite incongruous facts it is always possible that we may chance to spot some unsuspected correlation, which might lead us towards a solution, for example, of some long-outstanding medical puzzle.

The notion that we can distinguish different regional

'cultures' (in the social scientist's sense of this term) is, of course, far from new. Till now, however, it has lacked precision. We have had to be content with vague impressions and nuances captured by more observant natives and travellers, or with the largely antiquarian reporting of local folk beliefs and styles. Because we have been able to take in only one area at a glance at any single time, we have tended to spotlight the bizarre and the curious – the practices very often of the tiniest of minorities – and to disregard everything that seemed dull, humdrum, commonplace and ordinary.

The sample survey has now arrived to confer on this study of regional cultures a new and extra dimension. Like the aerial camera which reveals to the archaeologist a whole array of clues invisible on the ground, simultaneous interviewing of the population on a nation-wide scale gives us the overall perspective that till now we have sadly lacked and so greatly stood in need of. For, unfortunately, the regions of Britain do not differ from one another in ways that are normally at all clear-cut. Midlanders do not wholly, or even largely, wear blue suits and Lancastrians brown: 42 per cent are liable to wear the one colour in one region and 52 per cent the same colour in the other. Almost every fact cited in this book is a matter of a trait being relatively rather more or rather less frequent in the region in question than in the country as a whole. We could scarcely discern gradients as subtle as these by ordinary observation, even by rushing rapidly through region after region – and even supposing we could observe them we could never satisfy the world of their existence in the absence of clear statistical support.

The very slightness of these differences, nevertheless, makes for a certain insoluble problem of distortion when we come to compose a portrait of each region out of such survey data. For as in the portrayal of some living person, we have to highlight, lay emphasis on, even dramatise, the particular points that constitute the individuality so that they stand out with a quite unnatural sharpness when viewed against the drably monotone background. Let it be confessed at the outset that the regions of Britain resemble each other, alas, a great deal more than they differ. But our search is for idiosyncrasies, not for traits shared in common: it is inevitable therefore that our attention should go to the detecting of slight differences in the noses and that we should pass over the fact that the faces as a whole are virtually those of twins.

By concentrating in this fashion on the points of difference between each region, not on the points of resemblance, we find ourselves with lists that seem at first like shapeless spoil-heaps composed of numerous fascinating but quite unrelated facts. Yorkshiremen, we find, eat very little cheese, smoke pipes the most, have a remarkable fondness for carpets. . . .

On closer scrutiny, however, most of these can be seen to group themselves more or less naturally, with the minimum of forcing, into larger clusters (or 'configurations') each of which exemplifies some broader theme of behaviour: a tendency to parsimony, perhaps, or a liking for spicy foods. These clusters, in turn, as they grow in evidence, prove to stand in a meaningful relationship to one another and gradually coalesce into a single, logically consistent whole. This whole, therefore, we may legitimately term the regional 'personality'.

This is, I readily admit, back-to-front social research: trying to build up a picture of personality from a random assemblage of trivial facts collected for a thousand different and unconnected purposes. Far better to carry out a single, specially conceived psychological study and measure the full range of attitudes of each region in appropriate depth. Unfortunately, no one shows the slightest signs as yet of doing just this. Meanwhile the regional facts and figures mount and mount, crying out to be rescued from dusty shelves and waste-paper baskets and worked into some kind of more serviceable order. Better, surely, a stop-gap at once, however imperfect, than have in a few years a quite unmanageable flood?

England and Wales, showing Standard Regions, conurbations and county boundaries. (*Reproduced by permission of Her Majesty's Stationery Office*)

The Regions of Britain

There is no single, ideal way of subdividing Britain. The very uneven spread of the population renders a purely geometrical solution absurd; but almost any other approach would find its proponents and detractors, ready with reasons for separating one area or for not recognising another. The invitation to carve up the country somehow brings out the butcher in people, causing pens or crayons to be wielded with the ruthlessness almost of knives.

Fortunately, certain areas have a natural unity that no one can deny. Scotland and Wales are universally admissible as still, to a large extent, separate countries, with anciently different traditions reinforced by a considerable measure of political autonomy. As for England, everyone recognises a North and a South; and, if pressed, they might concede a Midlands, perhaps a different way of life between the South East and the West Country, and just conceivably know sufficient of the North to admit that lumping Lancashire with Yorkshire may be risky. It is in deciding what to do with the portions that are left that the arguments really start.

It is not altogether surprising, therefore, that a considerable variety of schemes are current. Quite apart from the many commercial firms that have grouped their sales territories into larger areas by drawing apparently arbitrary lines across the map – often oblivious of the fact that such things as local government boundaries exist and that working out their populations will thus be impossible with any kind of precision – almost every nationalised industry has separate regional divisions of its own. The British Rail Regions bear no resemblance whatever to the Regional Hospital Areas; the gas and electricity industries each relate their work to different geographical bases; and – just to make things easy for the uninitiated – there are twelve regional electricity boards but only nine electricity generating divisions. The Post Office has its own set of regions, the Ministry of Agriculture another and the Ministry of Transport yet another. And now that each has been allowed to go on collecting all its figures in its own special way for so many years, any change-over to a single standard system would entail a nightmarish expense in time and money, to say nothing of the temporary administrative chaos that would certainly accompany it.

In spite of these anomalies there is, thankfully, one system that has long commanded fairly general adherence throughout the Government and commercial circles: the Registrar General's Standard Regions.

The Registrar General first began dividing up the country regionally for purposes of statistical analysis with the Census of 1931. Those regions, however, were substantially different from the ones that are now in use; though in some ways they were considerably more meaningful, notably in recognising a much wider South Eastern Region that took in the entire Home Counties.

The present Standard Regions had their origin, rather romantically, as the Civil Defence regions instituted in 1939. One idea behind their creation was that each should be large enough to function independently should it become isolated from the rest by enemy action, enjoying self-government under Regional Commissioners – a replica of Cromwell's system of rule by major-generals. The whole wartime administration subsequently worked through these regions, which thus became so familiar that with the coming of peace they were retained (despite the dissolution of the administrative system that they had embodied) and given precise definition in a Treasury minute. Since then a large proportion of all statistics published by the various ministries have included analyses by these twelve Standard Regions and varying combinations of them have similarly formed the basis for the geographical treatment of data in most commercial sample surveys.

Throughout the period covered by this book the Registrar General's Regions were:

Northern: Cumberland, Durham, Northumberland, Westmorland, the North Riding of Yorkshire.

East and West Riding: the rest of Yorkshire.

North Western: Lancashire, Cheshire, the High Peak District of Derbyshire.

North Midland: Derbyshire (other than the High Peak District), Leicestershire, Lincolnshire, Northamptonshire, Nottinghamshire, the Soke of Peterborough.

Midland: Herefordshire, Shropshire, Staffordshire, Warwickshire, Worcestershire.

Eastern: Bedfordshire, Cambridgeshire, Isle of Ely, Essex, Hertfordshire, Huntingdonshire, Norfolk, Suffolk.

London and South Eastern: Kent, London Administrative County, Middlesex, Surrey, Sussex.

Southern*: Berkshire, Buckinghamshire, Hampshire, Oxfordshire, Poole M.B., Isle of Wight.

South Western: Cornwall, Devon, Dorset (other than Poole M.B.), Gloucestershire, Somerset, Wiltshire.

Wales I: Breconshire, Carmarthenshire, Glamorgan, Monmouthshire.

Wales II: the rest of Wales.

Scotland.

The subdivision of Wales has not normally been followed in market-research surveys. Instead, making up the deficiency, the Greater London conurbation is often treated as an extra region in its own right.

* In 1959 Dorset (except for Poole M.B.) was transferred from the Southern to the South Western Region.

An annoyingly high proportion of government surveys are limited to England and Wales for administrative reasons. Market-research surveys when mounted on a national scale normally cover Scotland as well. On the other hand, even more often than government surveys, they tend to ignore Northern Ireland. The Isle of Man and the Channel Isles, politically outside the United Kingdom and in any case absurdly expensive to include in a national sample, are very rarely covered by either. This book accordingly only concerns itself with Great Britain: that is to say, England, Wales and Scotland.

At the time of the last Annual Return (mid-1964) in which the Standard Regions appeared in their traditional form, their estimated populations were:

		%
Northern	3,301,000	6·3
East & West Ridings:	4,241,000	8·1
North Western	6,665,000	12·7
North Midland	3,760,000	7·1
Midland	4,926,000	9·4
Eastern	3,969,000	7·5
London & South Eastern	11,273,000	21·3
Southern	3,043,000	5·8
South Western	3,547,000	6·8
Wales	2,676,000	5·1
Scotland	5,207,000	9·9
Great Britain	52,608,000	100·0

Thus, apart from the irremediable discrepancies of London's population and Scotland's great area, the Standard Regions offer probably as reasonable a balance as we could hope to find in terms of territory and numbers of people combined.

In 1965 the Standard Regions were extensively altered, to bring them into line with the regions now in use for economic planning. However necessary this is greatly to be regretted, as comparisons with past data will be rendered that much more difficult. The main changes are:

The addition to the East and West Ridings of the north half of Lincolnshire, to form a new region, *Yorkshire and Humberside*;

the Eastern Region, after losing Bedfordshire, Hertfordshire and Essex to the South East and acquiring the Soke of Peterborough, becomes *East Anglia*;

the Southern Region disappears on being absorbed by a much-enlarged *South East*;

and (at long last, and very sensibly) the Midlands and the North Midlands become what they always more truly were, the *West Midlands* and the *East Midlands* respectively.

Except for the use of 'West Midlands' and 'East Midlands', which have so much more meaning geographically, these changes have been ignored for the purposes of this book.

Apart from the Standard Regions the only other important subdivisions of Britain in widespread use for surveys are the eleven commercial television areas. These are defined by surveys carried out by Television Audience Measurement Ltd. (TAM), which establish the territorial coverage achieved by each transmitter. Inevitably, different television areas overlap each other at certain points, in some cases very considerably. Since their inception most of the programme companies have commissioned and published sample surveys, which provide a great wealth of additional regional information. Several of the areas covered coincide, more or less, with Standard Regions; but in other cases – most notably Anglia, Tyne-Tees and the north and south halves of the Television Wales and West area – these surveys form the main source of knowledge about the lesser regions, which are too small for most market research surveys mounted on a national scale to be able to provide data about separately. Apart from the companies' own surveys, however, the commercial television areas have not yet come into general use. It is earnestly to be hoped that they will not be allowed to displace the use of the Standard Regions in commercial circles altogether, for among the many casualties would be the ability to make comparisons with government surveys on consumer matters.

NOTE

To save much tedious repetition, the words 'relatively' and 'proportionately' have been used as little as possible throughout this book. Their addition should, however, be understood wherever one region is compared with another or with the country as a whole, in its level of ownership or heaviness of consumption of any product in question. Thus, 'East Anglia has most cycle-owners' has to be read as meaning that this region has a higher *percentage* of persons owning cycles than the other regions of Britain, not that there are greater actual numbers (even though this might be true as well, were the percentage to exceed that of all the other regions by a high enough margin). In other words, cycle-owning is to be seen as more characteristic of East Anglia than it is of other regions. Those who may wish to translate statements such as these into raw terms for use in marketing must convert the original percentages back into actual numbers, so that the underlying differences in population size between one region and another can be taken into account. It will then often prove to be the case that some traits of great interest in illustrating the distinctive nature of a region have less significance for marketing, because of the very small numbers of persons so involved. The aim of this book, let it be stressed, is to highlight the *character* of each region, not to serve as a straightforward guide to market potential.

I

North v. South

Most discussions on the subject of regional differences begin (and frequently end) by broadly contrasting North and South. We shall do the same. For though the customary stereotypes are often crude and overdrawn, none the less, as will be seen, they have a certain solid substance of truth to them. In more respects than we normally realise the British way of life does indeed alter as one gradually progresses up or down the length of the country.

'The length of the country' is written advisedly, for it is the length that shows the differences much more than the breadth. Quite a number of traits exhibit a neat geographical gradient in their occurrence from one end of the country to the other (equivalent to what biologists would term a 'cline'), but of these surprisingly few rise or fall in frequency latitudinally between East and West; and of those that do, most display the pattern somewhat obliquely. Many of the examples so far known are medical ones, suggesting that, in some cases at least, the root cause may eventually prove to be racial. The incidence of epilepsy, for example, appears to increase rather steadily from North East to South West. In contrast (to take two non-medical instances), serving onions – other than the spring variety – for meals[2] and naming oranges as one's favourite fruit[3] increase no less steadily in precisely the reverse direction. The other diagonal, from South East to North West, shows itself in the death-rate from strokes;

in the incidence of certain anaemias[4, 5] (possibly reflecting the pattern of iron deposits), in deaths of babies at or around birth and in the amount of illness among men causing more than the statutory four days off work.[6] In this last case the Scots, as not infrequently happens, prove an exception to spoil the neatness of the picture by keeping their incapacity rates down to Midland levels. Indeed we should probably find far more of these gradients, were it not for the odd region that in so many instances departs from the overall pattern.

That the differences between regions should display such broad and regular country-wide trends, instead of always occurring haphazardly, is perhaps at first sight somewhat unexpected. A closer look will show, however, that most of them merely reflect the distribution of some fairly obvious underlying social or physical characteristic. Much ill-health, for example, gradually rises to reach a peak in the North West because of the concentration in that corner of so many ill-paid, unskilled workers with the poor living conditions and diet that this generally seems to imply. Many another pattern owes its origin to the climate and terrain, particularly to that classic division of Britain much emphasised by geographers: the Highland Zone of the North and West contrasted with the Lowland Zone of the South and East. The Highland Zone, because of its much greater hilliness, discourages bicycle ownership quite drastically. For the same reason motor-cycles there tend to be more powerful. The Lowland South and East, for the most part composed of younger rocks, produce harder water which promotes (at least initially) high sales of synthetic detergents[7] and a lower demand for electric immersion heaters; it also influences the type and amount of tea that is used. The much wetter North and West exact a heavier toll in rheumatism[6, 8] and demand, especially from women, a much greater investment in mackintoshes and, marginally, in rubber boots.

The basic distinction between the oatlands of the Highlander and the barley- and wheatlands of the Lowlander is still as immutable for farmers as the climate that is its cause, but the patterns of consumption that have traditionally arisen from this have now become a good deal blurred. Beer, of course, still prevails in the barley zone, but it has made great inroads in Scotland and the West at the expense of whisky, cider and even milk – this last a pure relic of pastoralism, with a reputation for unmanliness foisted on it over the centuries, quite ruthlessly, by the beer-drinkers of the East. Oven-baked bread, similarly, has now spread more or less universally ousting the thin quarter-circles or 'farls' made without yeast that once prevailed in the West. Even so, the old oat culture still ordains the Scotsman's porridge and his biscuity confectionery just as his soups and his liking for pulses spring from the ancient stewing, steaming and gentle simmering of the permanent pot on the hearth – a tradition that still lies behind cooking methods throughout the North, where pressure-cookers are much more popular; where potato types like Epicure are held in special favour because they boil without first breaking up; and where vegetables are more often steamed and more often shredded before being tossed into pans.[9] In 1797, in his remarks on *The State of the Poor*, Sir Frederick Eden pointed to the better diet enjoyed by labourers in the North of England due to 'the great variety of cheap and savoury soups' compared with their counterparts in the South, who were never in the habit of boiling meat for stock. Today the Northerner still prefers to boil where the Southerner roasts or grills: the cooking-pot, as always, resisting the advance of the oven.

The agriculturalists of the Lowlands, accustomed to the back-breaking toil of ploughing and harvesting, were inevitable ancestors of the people who today most intensively cultivate their gardens. Rose-growing, most English of pursuits, still loses popularity northwards and westwards.[10] In the Highland Zone cattle were prized and crops disregarded; tillage was a matter for small plots, and green vegetables featured only very sparingly. So today in these areas carrots, swedes and turnips – the last two specially suited to poor, upland soils[11] – enjoy a popularity unparalleled in the South and East. Another relic may be the raising of geese: concentrated today in the Fylde and in much of Wales and the West Country.[11]

The hearth was the focal centre for the household in upland, pastoral Britain, as opposed to the kitchen-table in the lowlands. Tables in the 'Celtic' parts still tend to be small, preferably folding away, and sometimes they are lacking altogether. It is the English who have made the cult of 'the board', the place where the bread was taken from the oven and carved. With their business-like ways they preferred to sit up and face each other – preparing themselves for 'board-rooms' and a lifelong dedication to committees. The 'Celts' perched dreamily by their firesides, turning their scones and oatcakes on a griddle or tending their simmering pots. The dresser, which we still nominally connect with the Welsh, took the place of the table as the most important piece of kitchen furniture, its exact position prescribed by custom.[12] Pottery-making, too, was never a tradition in the North and West (a loan-word has to do duty for 'potter' in Gaelic), and to this day a line can be drawn through Britain sharply separating those parts with teapots predominantly made of metal (nowadays normally aluminium) from those where the teapots are usually of china or earthenware.[13] Metal teapots similarly prevail in Ireland and the Isle of Man. The making of tea is one of the most deep-seated British rituals, impervious to change, so the apparently lineal descent of two-fifths of all the teapots in the country from the ancient, semi-sacred pot on the hearth – perhaps even going back to the prized cauldrons of the Bronze Age – is only fitting.

But it is all too easy, in treating of a country like

Britain, to start excavating and burrowing into the ancient past at almost every turn. Enough has been said to stress that more, much more, than we normally care to think is deeply and firmly embedded in antiquity and likely to prove uncommonly difficult to dislodge, however powerful the commercial promotion. The very fact that a trait is to be found widely established over any large part of the country, and has moreover shown itself evidently long-lasting, clearly indicates its quality of permanence.

In contrast, the straightforward North–South gradient is much less likely altogether to be resting on the bed-rock of physical geography. As far as can yet be made out, the great majority of the broad, overall patterns that are detectable running up and down the full length of the country are more or less purely social in their origin. This inevitably means that they are likely to be looser, and perhaps even transient. Even so, despite the massive drift in recent years from Wales and the North to the prosperous Midlands and South (about half a million people in the 'thirties, and over 600,000 as recently as 1951–61), the differences between the two opposing ends are still strikingly persistent, very numerous – and the cause of much misunderstanding on either side.

They are misunderstood because the pattern of their occurrence shows, at first sight, little obvious logic. In fact, the only group that can be ascribed quite unambiguously to wholly natural causes – thereby removing them from the arena of regional bickering – are what may be termed the 'temperature traits': those characteristics whose distinctive patterns arise from the simple fact of geography that as one goes northwards in Britain the climate becomes steadily colder. These are more various than one might at first imagine. The further north one goes, the thicker the weaves of cloth, for example, and the heavier the fabrics generally; the more cardigans and full-length coats, the thicker the linings to rainwear,[14] the more numerous the layers of bedclothes. Conversely, the smaller the number of sleeveless dresses, diaphanous slips and nightdresses,[15] short jackets, sandals, summer-weight suits (or, at least, customers demand for these) and men's ankle-length socks.[16] The hotter summers in the South tend to drive out soup, ordain more ice-cream and salads and make refrigerators more necessary and usual; they also mean more home-grown fruit and require far heavier use of insecticides by gardeners.[10] More households in the South live all the year round in caravans and houseboats. In the North, however, much heavier stocking of cough and cold remedies indicates, not (as one might think) more colds, but evidently more severe bouts of sneezing and spluttering.[8] Yet, paradoxically and ironically, Britain's central heating is heavily concentrated at the warmest end of the country – just as the ownership of umbrellas is densest at the driest.

In these last two facts we have the first hint of a conflict between social realities and geographical requirements. For this both North and South are to blame almost equally: the one for preferring conformity to comfort, the other for indulging quite superfluous needs.

Here we are, already, making sweeping generalisations about North and South. All too easily it becomes a kind of game, 'Happy Polarities', like those endless over-tidy theories on the different mental make-up of men and women. And yet, incredibly, as the sample surveys only too amply confirm, the popular pictures are indeed true to a very considerable extent. Some of the more extreme assertions, admittedly, take some swallowing – like a recent one characterising the South as 'a part of the country whose very nature is based on all that is gay, superficial and transitory'. That appeared, very typically, in *Yorkshire Life*.[17] Yet Southerners' denunciations of the North can be even wilder, springing usually from an even greater ignorance – for most Northerners tend to visit at any rate London some time in their lives. For probably all too many Londoners 'The North' is merely an obscure, grubby hinterland of smoke, shawls, cobbles and clogs that begins (thanks to the unfortunately worded signposts) somewhere just the other side of Hatfield.

One can only hope that the recent barrage of propaganda on behalf of the more 'benighted' parts of Britain has at last destroyed some of the cruder distortions. Certainly it seems to have had one effect: it has made the true facts so familiar by now that they can safely be raided for humour. In one recent novel,[18] for example, the hero's feelings on leaving the North are depicted with an intriguing new note of irony: 'Behind, now, lay decency, plain speaking, good feeling; ahead lay the southern counties, all suède shoes and Babycham.'

Let us now turn to facts. Of these, by far the most important single one is that, compared with the South, the North is far more preponderantly working class, both in actual numbers and in outlook – which are by no means necessarily coexistent, as we shall see when we come to consider the West Country. Not only are there, relatively speaking, many more manual workers, but the professional and managerial groups are much more thinly represented. The North contains, in fact, only 30 per cent of Britain's professional population against 43 per cent of her semi-skilled and unskilled, the proportions in the South being reversed.[19] This means, at once, a far sharper distinction between 'Us' and 'Them'. The middle classes feel more exposed, more self-conscious about their status, seeing the consequence of economic failure in starker terms. The working classes, without the challenges to their solidarity that occur in the socially much more heterogenous South, adhere more confidently to their traditional behaviour and values. The narrower variety of jobs serves only to increase the uniformity of tastes and interests on either side of the social iron curtain. The predominance of industry, with its abrupt division between workers and management, tends to encourage the different classes to live apart so that a particular district of a town becomes a reservation or ghetto to an extent less often encountered further South. The general lack of experiment and initiative that results is both cause and effect of the smaller range of that great assortment of societies and organisations and interest-groups technically termed the 'infrastructure'. The thinner the infrastructure, it seems to be the case, the lower the dynamism in the society, the less the creativity. Where the social boundaries are tightly drawn, as in the North, it is harder for people not only to strike out in new directions but to persuade others to follow. A lifetime spent cosseting one's respectability develops blind, deeply rooted habits of conforming, so that even a trivial departure from the common mould can take on the appearance of a social enormity, amounting to a betrayal of a whole way of life.

These brakes hold all the firmer in the North for the added reason that people there (except, of course, in Scotland) are much more likely to have grown up with each other. Families there have been far less uprooted for generations. Children, by long tradition, have seldom left the neighbourhood on marriage; parents have not made a habit of retiring to the country or the coast. There have not, of course, been the economic temptations that exist in the South, but the very homogeneity[20] of Northern society – to outside detractors, its cloying quality – has in itself made those born into it more disinclined to leave. The family itself, as an institution, thrives more in the North and stretches further; partly because its larger average size makes it more real, partly because of the greater history of poverty which has developed its strength for mutual help, and partly, perhaps, due to echoes of the ancient lineage system that once prevailed throughout the pastoral Highland Zone. Whatever the cause, it is probably this cult of the family that has given the North a warmer heart than the South, a natural underlying kindliness that has been less soured by class.

Living more frequently among old friends and relations,

people in the North are less likely to marry a comparative stranger.[21] Weddings are made far more of; an alliance between two old-established local families needing to be proclaimed to the world as grandly and as emphatically as possible. The couple receive more presents, thirty photographs are taken compared with the national average of twenty-five, and even the bills for hire-cars are noticeably heavier.[22] Should they fall ill, the family can be counted on to help – while the Southerner commits himself much more to sickness and accident insurance. And even when they die, a formal family gathering is more likely to occur as one of the rites accompanying their funeral.[23]

This sense of family spills over, unnoticed, into a more engulfing sense of community. Brought up in larger families, employed for the most part in factories, inured to overcrowded housing, Northerners have a greater matey-ness and altogether less liking (or respect) for privacy and personal reserve. This is most of all true of the Lancastrian, who can be so oblivious of barriers that he becomes not merely matey, but nosey, and is carried away by an inquisitiveness that almost lands him inside his next-door-neighbour's skin. In the Yorkshireman this same natural urge to be direct tends to bluntness, if not brusqueness, and can on occasions appear offensive. This artless quality in Northerners comes, one must suppose, from their need to streamline themselves to fit into their more constrictingly uniform social background. They cannot, unlike so many Southerners, permit themselves to sprawl, experiment with their likes and dislikes, give their individual tastes and whims free play. And even if they could, their stronger Nonconformism, with its Puritan traditions, would certainly make their consciences twitch. As the psychologists find from attitude research, thanks to Puritanism Northerners tend to see life in harsher, more black-and-white terms, have generally more positive reactions and opinions. The fact that they favour earlier

29

toilet-training for children,[21] whom they are also readier to punish with beatings,[21] gives this certain suggestive Freudian undertones. They buy harder brushes, coarser suitings, foods that they can crunch. Northerners tend to be chewers of sweets, Southerners suckers. In the North they demand for their money simpler, more straightforward effects: stronger beer, because they drink beer for what it does to them rather than to ponder the nuances of flavour; floral perfumes;[24] Gorgonzola with little or no mould[25] – 'good, old-fashioned' things that make immediate sense, plain, homely fare without suspicious-sounding ingredients or fancy names, food to 'stick your ribs together' and plenty of it. They have fewer meals than in the South, but eat far more on average at a sitting. In the South there tend to be fewer courses, more between-meal snacks, and elevenses and afternoon teas are both more common. The Northerner, particularly the York-shireman, likes gigantic blow-outs, eating for the sheer hell of eating – and worries more about constipation, keeping laxatives handy, while the Southerner (inclined to bolt his snacks, or talk too much) buys indigestion remedies.[8] The Northerner likes to think all his food must do him good and looks for nourishment value in what would scarcely occur to the Southerner as more than just tasty variety. Soup, for him, is very much a food, so – apart from nationally-shared tastes like tomato – he keeps to safe, familiar flavours like chicken, kidney and celery, leaving the obscurer, 'fancier' ones to the Southerner. Any soft drink that can be shown to have health-giving properties will sell more in the North, the mere refreshers best in the South. Even the drinking of liquor will be justified for its tonic benefits if these can be asserted without overstraining credulity. And as if all that were not enough, it is clearly the North, ever-anxious about its sustenance, that is the more addicted to those safety-first cure-alls, vitamin pills.[8]

Large meals incorporating too much carbohydrate tend

to end up as excessive obesity. Northerners, inevitably, are plumper on average. Yet slimming – or at least the buying of slimming products – is a more popular pursuit in the South, where a higher proportion of husbands take their wives' efforts to slim seriously and give them encouragement.[26] Northern women, particularly in Lancashire, consequently have to lever themselves into heavier types of corsetry. At the same time they are shorter: stature in Britain[5, 27] (and, correspondingly, the size of English, though not Scottish, feet[28]) progressively increases southwards, probably due to a complex interaction between racial inheritance and diet. This means that the average Northern woman has a dumpier appearance and the greater number of short-waisted figure types in consequence means greater sales in the North of to-the-waist girdles.[29] But while vertically she may be more or less inelastic, having to content herself with the height that nature bestowed on her, the same cannot be said for her horizontally: for on bereavement, the somewhat macabre fact emerges, it is precisely Northerners (though not Scots) who most tend to find themselves losing weight.[23] The Northern girth thus has a greater element of impermanence: it is largely a voluntary stoutness, due to eating much too much – or at any rate much too much of the wrong sorts of food.

The puritanism also has its black side. The Northern character, simpler and franker in its responses and with fewer of the behavioural tripwires that so complicate life for the Southerner, is altogether less safe when the barriers come down. Crimes of violence, heterosexual assaults and offences of drunkenness have all long been higher in the North than in the South.[30] More people, especially women, are slaughtered on the roads. There are more bookmakers and betting offices per head and more men who play cards (presumably for money)[31] – even though substantially fewer people declare themselves pro-gambling than in the South.[32] Accordingly, the North is more sternly repressive. There are fewer public houses in proportion to population, drinking being banished on a far greater scale to the decent privacy of licensed clubs; only half as many as in the South agree that contraceptive advice should be available to the young, whether married or not;[33] and, perhaps reflecting the same general attitude, women in labour are given analgesics to a noticeably smaller extent.[5]

Perhaps this also helps to explain the fact that many types of food and drink – not just clothing, as one might expect – grow darker northwards. Treacle toffee is well known, but the North goes in for a wide range of other black sweets besides. Icing sugar tends to be darker, crimsons and purples rising to a peak of popularity.[34] Darker ales are drunk as well as darker (Demerara) rum, and a marked taste has lately developed for brown sherry,[35] possibly, however, because a deeper colour is often associated in drinks, whether rationally or not, with greater sweetness – and sweet wines are a Northern speciality. Or perhaps there is even an idea of more body in darker products: certainly, more people in the North subscribe to the belief that the deeper the colour of the yolk, the better the egg.[36] It could be that this taste for darkness is not necessarily a taste for the sombre, but springs from a variety of unrelated causes.

Detectable in the Northerner there is also a streak of something almost childlike, to be seen not merely in his artlessness, but in the more miniature scale of some of his tastes and habits: 'fairy' cakes, for example, which almost look as if they came out of dolls-houses, or that endearing multiplicity of tiny bags in which purchases are wrapped – a world away symbolically from the all-in-one bag of the ultra-sophisticated supermarket. Ingenuous, too, is his preference for taking things in turn one by one and gulping them down in larger doses: his pattern of meals has already been noted, but what he eats on his plate is no less suggestive, food being served up solo and unadorned which in the South would generally rate some tasty accompaniments.

The Northerner eats as he lives, plainly and even starkly, without attention to décor or side-issues. Even at the cinema the North specialises in simple single-feature programmes, films running more often full-length;[37] the South, more restless, demands more variety for its money and finds less objection to cutting.

Southerners, by contrast, untrammelled by quite as many doubts about what-will-the-neighbours-think, living in any case less on top of one another and often relative newcomers to their area of residence, enjoy much more freedom to escape from the bonds of background and to discover themselves as individuals. More complex people, formed by a more complex society in which class divisions are usually more blurred, their approach to life in a thousand different ways is more tentative, more questioning, less sure. Their intentions are more elusive because they are less convinced of what they want. It is not just that, being in the main better-off and engaged in less exhausting work, they are better equipped for the savouring of nuances that goes with any reasonably leisurely style of life. It is also, more basically, a matter of personality, a consequence of existing within a pattern of society that hangs less tightly and throws its members, more ruthlessly, on to their own inner resources. One could say, speaking very broadly and generally, that where the North is collective, the South is individual and self-contained.[38] Yet when the Southerner exerts his right to his much-needed privacy he is liable to be misunderstood. The Northerner sees this as mere stand-offishness and labels him 'up-stage'. But the very nature of life in the South requires more space around the soul; greater self-sufficiency breeds greater social distance and mutual respect for personal autonomy; the crudities of contact have to be more discreetly sheathed. The Southerner's responses need a longer launching-pad, but they are none the less powerful for all that. In his subtler society, composed of far more refinements and gradations, he needs more time to orientate and has to bring out his instruments of feeling from deeper down.

As a shopper, he tends to be a stickler not so much on price as exactly the right match or cut. His palate, equally, is more finely tuned. He goes for rarer flavours: saltier bacon that is generally smoked, very different from the Northerner's more ham-like 'green' types;[39] peppery sausages (at least pre-war);[40] more cheese of all kinds, but especially the more pungent sorts, Cheddar rather than Cheshire[25, 41] and Gorgonzola with plenty of mould.[25] The South prefers saltier New Zealand and Australian butter, the North the Danish variety.[39] Under rationing, bitter Seville oranges, specially imported, were pounced upon in London for making marmalade, but in Liverpool were virtually ignored.[42] Dry sherries,[35] savoury spreads in general, even spinach,[43] are all essentially Southern tastes. The North, in the few respects that it displays anything pungently distinctive, goes in for harsher sauces, for more vinegar and onions, for malted milk and malt bread, and for flavours like liquorice, aniseed and sassafras.[34]

The Southerner's insistence on delicacies of flavour have often, one suspects, no real basis in physiology, but are merely ploys to enable him to express his individualism yet more variously. This can be carried further by cultivating mixtures of more or less abstruseness, to serve as a personal signature as much as a gesture of high sensibility. It is significant that the South contains more gin-drinkers, for the gin-based drinks have long offered unending scope for just this kind of quirkish originality— and a fine way of 'placing' new acquaintances at their exact point in the pecking order of sophistication. On the same pattern, food is combined more imaginatively: serving blancmange and jelly together as a single dish instead of separately is, for example, more of a Southern peculiarity; so are mixed flavours in jams.[44] The greater variations on clothing themes obtainable from separates have a greater appeal in the South, not only to women,[13] but even to men, who buy more sports trousers to combine with jackets or sweaters, while the Northerner tends to concentrate on suits. Larger purses southwards allow, admittedly, larger wardrobes, but fashion is more compelling and more pervasive, penetrating into layers unthought-of further north. Women in the South, to take a rather bizarre example, buy many more brassières, almost certainly not because they discard them more quickly, but because they keep a wider selection, happy to pay a high price from time to time for a style that will exactly hit off the nuance of some special occasion. The greater pressure of fashion, the greater hunger to look and feel different, also accounts for the – at first sight surprising – fact that more home-dressmaking takes place in the South.

On the whole, the South is just as keen as the North on making things in the home, but it tends to be in more of a rush; it pours less of itself into tasks of this kind and wallows less in the feelings of virtuousness that result. Housewives in the South are fonder of all the speeded-up ways of cooking. Even when they boil, many more of them turn the heat full on, use less water and, leaving off the lids, then stand over their pans impatiently. Far from averse to taking short cuts, they often heat up water for boiling vegetables first of all in a kettle, before turning it out into a pan.[9] Packet mixes are used with less compunction and made-up dishes served more often. They worry less about the 'goodness' in what they eat and are more concerned about providing, and enjoying, a proper variety. Food is more often fun, less often a mundane matter of nutrition. For under less compulsion to raise wifely skills to the level – it almost seems – of a cult, they find day-to-day cooking more humdrum, even a chore, preferring competence to virtuosity. Their expertise in the

35

kitchen is an expertise in width, rather than in depth: they expect to be praised for the extent of their repertoire, not for their flair in interpreting a traditional mystique. Ever readier to cast around for novelty and less likely to have inherited a back-supply of family lore, their shelves are altogether more likely resting-places for Mrs. Beeton and her seemingly endless progeny of today.[45]

It is symptomatic that the two traditional bakery specialities alone mainly confined to the South are both dubiously of domestic (as opposed to commercial) origin. These are Chelsea buns,[46] now almost hybridised out of existence by the usually misnamed 'Danish pastries'; and Swiss rolls, which never in fact came from Switzerland and to which they are now exported in pleasingly enormous quantities. For some reason neither has penetrated the North in anything more than a singularly half-hearted manner. Perhaps people up there find their whorl-like structure too out-of-keeping, too nicely mirroring the Southerners curled up in private, deep inside their shells. Tarts[45] and flans also find their principal appeal in the South, the North preferring pies, which are more substantial and more demonstrably nourishing.

If there is one single word that seems to sum up the South it is 'specialisation'. Life here has evolved more distinctions, sprouted more branches and twigs. It is the South that mainly insists on separating dining-rooms from sitting-rooms, the South that least regards the kitchen as a place for living and eating in[47] – due in part, of course, to its much wider tradition of keeping servants. It has more specialist types of shops, and its larger middle class permits the support of a far greater range of service trades, particularly of the more unlikely forms of personal assistance. Even the products it buys tend to be, as the Americans say, more 'personalised': bacon sold in ready-cut strips, rather than sliced on the counter from a communal roll; butter in separately wrapped slabs, rather than, as so often in the North, chunks 'off the lump'.[39] It wants its goods dressed up more, given fancier names to conceal their dreary ordinariness. It shares none of the North's distrust of the more recondite varieties and flavours, for it likes to give these things a try and in this, as in everything else, seeks to forge distinctiveness out of the generalised, anonymous mass.

This drive towards 'personalisation' can also be seen, perhaps, as an outcome of the Southerner's craving for identity. One way in which he can succeed in differentiating himself, in perceiving himself in bolder outline, is by holding himself apart. Hence 'the silent Southerner': his house is far more likely to be detached from its neighbours and to have a back garden but no front garden, and he will seldom use it, unlike the Northerner, to advertise bereavement by drawing the blinds or inserting a card in the window.[23] It is the Southerner, particularly, who refuses to answer questions in sample surveys. Deploring crowds, he prefers to spend his leisure in relative isolation; even in that most solitary of popular pursuits, angling, preferring to fish on his own rather than copy the 'match anglers' of the North and sit in a queue-like line with his fellows. 'Live and let live' is the eternal motto of the South. And it produces a gentler, more tolerant type of society, more readily shared in common by both sexes.

Office-work, so much commoner in the South, somehow typifies this greater overlap between the man's world and the woman's world and contributes in no small measure to the greater mingling of social classes. The conveyor-belt, by contrast, is strongly divisive. However much altered by the advent of television, the typical Northern pattern is still basically one of segregation: the husband downing pints with his mates in his club or the local, the wife busying herself in the kitchen. More shops in the North combining the sale of men's and women's clothing is hardly the exception to this widely held rule that it might at first appear, for the tendency for wives to buy

37

most of their husband's clothing is much more common in the South.

More office work in the South has, naturally, wider implications still. The absence of overalls and the need to convey an impression of 'quality' to clients, buyers and bosses, enforce higher standards in dress. More is spent at hairdressers', as these are within easy, lunchtime reach of women office workers. More, too, is spent at laundries and dry-cleaners. Above all, secondary education is, of necessity, more widely intensive in almost all respects. On average, children in the South leave school later and a far higher proportion of leavers enter employment involving twelve months' training or more.[48] Higher expenditure at booksellers and stationers implies more reading and writing, and this is confirmed, indirectly, by the larger number of table and standard lamps per household.[49]

More educated people around means, in turn, more choosiness, more assertion in claiming one's rights. Consumer complaints are much commoner in the South; people have more finesse, more *savoir faire* (appropriate words for those who feel more at ease with foreigners and foreign ways), and are altogether less tolerant of bumbledom. It is easier for the man with a grouse in the South to go straight to the top and he is more likely to have friends or relatives in high places – higher, at any rate, than the purely parochial world of the borough or urban district council. He likes to aim at being rational; and, just as he is far more vocal as a shopper, he is more likely to alter sides between elections. He looks more closely at what he is offered and likes to be sure of what he is buying, which probably explains why mail-order shopping has been less than half as popular as in the North,[50] and why self-service caught on so much faster.

The Southerner, it must be admitted, has a gentler way of life because his life is also in many minor respects more luxurious. Less likely to have to clock in at work, he leaves his bed later and so has more chance there for early cups of tea.[12] The Northerner, going to bed earlier, has to bring his whole evening forward, having his main meal and starting to view television a good hour or two before the South. Because office jobs are traditionally more secure, the Southerner also feels more secure in making plans ahead. Moreover he has better facilities in general. There are more general practitioners per head in the South (despite more illness in the North) and proportionately more dentists. There are more new schools, more 'A'-level passes, more state scholarships to universities. And there are, only too plainly, far, far fewer slums.

Nevertheless, the North is more to blame for its poverty of privilege than it usually cares to admit. Distrusting and spurning the transient, it has clung instead to solidity – and found itself overtied to heavy industry in a world that wants mainly consumer goods, which it has known little about and cared less for. The fickleness of the average consumer it finds repugnant. Even in textiles, the one great Northern industry geared to fashion, a blithe unconcern with taking the pulse of the public prevailed for generations. Trade shibboleths have flourished, the old ways have been deified, the urge to experiment frustrated. All because, at heart, the North half-disapproves of change, of new-fangled ideas that would undermine its comforting, monolithic uniformity. The insistence on plainness has produced a bareness of amenity; self-denial has brought life-denial. And as the gap between the North and South has become visibly wider, defiance has turned to resentment.

The Northerner has probably never, in modern times, felt wholly at ease with Southern ways. Used to a slower pace, to slower speech and reactions, he could never quite keep up. The South dazzled him and confused him with its slickness – yet it is from the South, by long tradition, that new ideas have largely come. 'What Manchester thinks today London will think tomorrow' was a fine-sounding boast, but it never had much substance in the down-to-earth matter of consumption. A tradition of ideological radicalism does not necessarily betoken material receptiveness; more often than not it seems to imply the reverse. Almost every kind of novelty achieving national currency, especially anything invested with an element of fashion and without any prior connotations of social class or geography, has arrived first in London, spread from there through the South and Midlands, and only then reached Lancashire, the gateway to the North (because of all the Northern cultures the Lancastrians' sits least tightly). This historic corridor of innovation is much more than the mere reflection of decreasing affluence that proponents of the popular 'Golden Circle' theory[51] would apparently have us believe. Basically it is an ancient, enduring pattern of decreasing receptiveness. The more closely woven the community, the stiffer its sinews, the more resistant it is, and has to be, to new ideas. The North finds it harder to assimilate newness simply because, to a much greater extent, it is all-of-a-piece. Take one brick out to replace it with another and you risk bringing the whole venerable edifice toppling down in ruins. The North accordingly is wary and condescending in its dealings with the South, willing to sample its wares, maybe, but slow on the whole to accept and absorb them. Which is all to the good, so long as this remains a process of critical sifting and not of sheer negative obstructiveness.

The North's more rigid texture, the prime cause of this conservatism, also brings about a pattern in consumption that appears at first sight paradoxical. Because of its greater resistance to the more deep-rooted types of innovation, those types which demand adjustments of emotion or complicated shifts in custom, it is mainly the 'froth', the inessentials of varying degrees of triviality, which percolates most easily through the ordinary social filters and constitutes the most obviously visible movement northwards. Trading stamps,[52] fruit juices, filter-tipped cigarettes, electric shavers and pre- and after-shave lotions, men's shampoos, mohair coats, brightly coloured anoraks,[53] bikinis,[54] women's leather jackets, plastic sandals, tumbler driers, aluminium garden chairs,[10] aerosol hairsprays, 45-r.p.m. records,[55] amateur flash-photography,[56] table wines – the list of novelties that in recent years have steadily spread northwards region by region is almost endless; a high proportion of them luxury or sophisticated products that are natural candidates as status symbols. But, just for this very reason, their adoption in the North, with its far smaller minorities both with the wherewithal to be discriminating and the necessary social boldness not to be deterred from flaunting fripperies that might be rated effete, is altogether slighter and more restricted.

The more sober innovations, by contrast, make slow headway. Even a compelling rationale can scarcely help; for the rate of progress northwards is just as arduous for products like the medical profession's fashionable new drugs,[5] if there is something acceptably valid already in use that has to be displaced. The North is highly sceptical of change just for change's sake. Indeed, by studying what it rejects or the relative speed at which it accepts, we may provide ourselves with remarkably faithful instruments for gauging the ups and downs of its prejudices at any particular period. Old fashions that linger on in the North and take an unconscionably long time a-dying may betray, by this very fact, a special emotional or functional value in the regional context over and above their original innocent expression. Why else, for example, would the North choose to cling so long to high heels, to pink corsetry, to large non-filter cigarettes, to patterned carpets, or to ankle-length wedding-dresses with trains, long sleeves and high necks?[57]

Not all fashions arise in London and ripple outwards, however, as writers in the national press so blandly tend to assume. Ultra-extreme fashions seldom survive outside the Metropolis. Others spring up spontaneously in different centres in the provinces and succeed, to a greater or lesser extent, in colonising their home territories. But for a provincial fashion to reverse the normal pattern and sweep the entire country, including London, is distinctly rare – and sufficiently against logic to suggest some extra dimension of super-utility or symbolism. Of this, two classic examples exist: the adoption of potatoes and 'Beatlemania'.

Potatoes became a standard food in the North at least a century before the South, as the Southerner's attachment to expensive, pure-white wheaten flour, with its complex considerations of social class, allowed him less chance of incorporating them into his regular diet.[58] According to Sir Frederick Eden, writing in 1797, labourers in the South rejected soup made from potatoes even in times of famine, protesting that 'this is washy stuff, that affords no nourishment; we will not be fed on meal and chopped potato, like hogs'. Against such prejudice the southward march of the potato was a far more considerable feat than it tends to appear in retrospect.

The other example, 'Beatlemania', proves that this phenomenon of crashing the national barriers is just as possible today, given certain circumstances. Of 100,000 copies sold of the Beatles' first record, released in October 1962, the great majority were snapped up at once by the North.[59] The conversion of the South followed only some months later. The Beatles were, and maybe still are, essentially Northern idols, the very epitome of Merseyside; and part of their extraordinary success has lain, surely, in their role in personifying the North's now resurgent self-confidence.

II

London and the South East

The natural starting-point for a tour of Britain is, inevitably, London. The central focus for the arts and for fashionable living, the home of the Press, the progressives and the politicians, the capital is where the great majority of novelties begin.

'London and the South East', so often harnessed together without further thought, is really two distinct regions living in a curious symbiotic relationship with each other. Londoners, a very high proportion of them now non-British in origin, tend to like the bright lights and typically remain incarcerated in the city or its suburbs; the South East, in the broad sense of that wide belt of smaller towns and villages ('exurbia') to which so many of those who work in the Metropolis return to sleep, shares many of its tastes and much of its sophistication but at heart detests city life and is rooted emotionally, if not always physically, in the country. The distinction is not, of course, clear-cut and the boundaries between the two are blurred further by a third, sizable group, the week-end commuters: young unmarrieds who return home to their parents every Friday (often with a weekly tribute of washing in their cases), or affluent couples with a second home in the country or on the coast who leapfrog the dormitory belt altogether. Such people have split allegiances and in the values they subscribe to often display a fascinating mosaic of city man and exurbanite. The critical difference seems to reside in how far one can rest content to spend most of one's week-ends amid bricks and mortar. Those who are content devise for themselves a completely different way of conserving those forty-eight precious hours than those who insist on migrating. They remain far less conscious of the seasons, take far less exercise and on the whole pass more of their time indoors. And although the advent of television has evened up the score in the matter of commercial entertainment, Londoners still tend to seek the outside diversions of the theatre and the cinema. When a Northerner speaks disparagingly about the South it is usually London and the Londoner's highly specialised way of life that is uppermost in his mind. London is the South wildly exaggerated, almost to the point of a lampoon. It is, at one and the same time, the prototype of all its failings or advantages and a part of that life peculiar to itself and utterly distinctive.

The Greater London conurbation contains approximately eight million inhabitants, or almost one Briton in every six. These are merely the inhabitants. The figure excludes the vast army of daily commuters from outside its boundaries, of whom up to half a million pour through the London termini every weekday by train alone. It also excludes the tourists, who nowadays swamp the city every summer in tidal waves: some two million overseas visitors – about a quarter from the United States – almost all of whom pass through the capital and most of whom stay at least the odd night, to say nothing of the very large numbers who come to London for a holiday from other parts of the kingdom. But as soon as the tourists arrive, Londoners start to leave on their own annual holidays. The city becomes like a bath with both taps on but no plug. The mathematics of drain and counter-drain are complex in the extreme, but it is probably a fair guess that at lunchtime on an average weekday at the height of summer the city holds more like nine million people than eight.

44

About three and a half times the size of any other British conurbation, London is the only one that can reasonably claim to be considered a region in its own right. This makes it, however, the only region that is exclusively urban; and this exaggerates its peculiarity, for in every other case where cities constitute a substantial proportion of the whole their distinctive contribution is diluted by the sharply differing ingredient of small town and rural characteristics. Even so, London is the city of cities. And as far as urban patterns of life are concerned it is very far indeed from the pale average.

Having said this, it is perhaps ironic to have to point out that one of London's most famous traditions, as a city, has now virtually ceased to exist. Thanks to the Clean Air Act of 1956, fogs have gone – or at any rate the old, dense, choking 'pea-soupers'. In the ten years up to 1963 the amount of smoke in the London area declined by about 60 per cent (though there was an offsetting 32 per cent rise in sulphur emission). In time, perhaps, the highest percentage consulting doctors for chronic chest conditions[1] will cease to be London's special contribution to the national statistics of illness. Already, indeed – such is the greater cleanliness of the air after only ten years – a perceptible increase in the numbers of wild birds feeding partly or wholly on insects has occurred in Inner London, which is believed to be possibly due to this cause.[60]

A good deal of the credit for such speedy results is doubtless due to the blessedly wide expanse of parks in the west central district, which not only makes the capital a much greener and pleasanter city to live in than most of its sisters, but also allows it a considerably better airing. The fact that hospital admissions for asthma are much higher for each sex in the north-eastern sector than in any other part of the Metropolis[61] certainly seems to indicate a forceful prevailing wind – which blows in from the South West (thus showing, too, that the wealthier classes who originally selected the S.W. postal districts because

45

of their relative freedom from fumes and filth had a more substantial reason for this choice than we nowadays tend to credit). Even so, for all the recent improvement and for all its special endowments, London is still, like almost every other city in Britain, undeniably dirty. Vacuum-cleaner ownership, that incomparable yardstick, is as high as anywhere and so, too, are cleaning bills, though these also owe much to the stringent standard of grooming required of those most typical of Londoners, the office workers.

After the dirt: the heat. This is a less remarked-on feature of the natural environment, yet one rather more special to London. It can be oppressive, in different ways, at opposite seasons of the year. In winter, a high proportion of the shops and offices are nowadays centrally heated, but the heating is far from always aptly attuned to the ups and downs of the temperature outside. Shoppers enter from the streets muffled up, only to encounter a microclimate evidently designed for sales assistants in flimsy dresses. The agony is worst of all for visitors from out of town, accustomed both to dressing for life in generally colder and draughtier buildings and to a more rigorous atmosphere outside – for London is a 'heat-island', normally warmer by several degrees than the surrounding hinterland (mainly due, experts believe, to the heat retained by so many tall buildings and road surfaces being released more slowly during the night[62]). In summer, in a heat-wave, the pavements almost blaze and the crowds compete for the little fresh air that penetrates through the built-up acres. Not surprisingly, refrigerators are unusually widespread, large quantities of ice-cream are consumed, salads are popular at all levels, and there is the highest demand in the country for shellfish. It may be the heat, too, that helps to produce the capital's high milk consumption. During the war milk-drinking was found to be about as above average in popularity among London dockers as it was below

average among dockers in Liverpool.[63] Clothes, too, have
to be adjusted accordingly if their wearers are to escape
being stifled. London women buy far more sandals than
elsewhere, and even the men have to bow to the climate
by taking to lightweight suits or, still more desperately,
to thin cotton jackets.

Then there is crime. London is distinctive in its crime
pattern and the stereotype not altogether in agreement
with the facts.[30] It has more crime as a whole, true, compared with the rest of England, but this in itself tells us
very little, for a high percentage of all crime everywhere
is only petty and an excess in London could merely be
due to greater chances of exposure and greater vigilance,
both by the police and by the public. In some respects, as
it happens, the capital is a remarkably safe place to live
in. For a start, there is less haphazard violence. Contrary
to popular belief, police statistics (assuming these are
reasonably reliable) show that crimes of violence as a
whole are no more common here than in the remainder
of England; if anything, indeed, they appear to be
somewhat below average. London has fewer indictments
for wounding than the provinces and even its homicide
rate, after an increase peculiar to itself in the 'fifties,
could hardly be termed outstanding; its sole claim to
special notice being that more of the victims of killings
here (at least at the moment) are teenagers. The steep,
upward trend in violence that has been so marked a
phenomenon of post-war Britain, so far from starting in
London and radiating outwards – like any ordinary
fashion – actually made its appearance here considerably
later: London only caught up the rest of England in this
in the course of the 'fifties. Instead, the capital easily leads
the country in offences against property: its speciality,
appropriately, is quick grabs and surreptitious snatches.
London crimes are more carefully planned and are less
often the outcome of flare-ups of passion. London crim-
inals tend to stalk their prey, employing care and cunning;

47

their actions are much less often the products of random social collisions, much more often criminal by intent from the start. They thrive, in fact, on the capital's worst affliction: its atomisation.

The same might be said of London's social ills in general. The most typical ailments, for example, seem to be the product of too much morbid introspection and isolation. Far more people than elsewhere consult their doctors for neuroses or depression,[1] though comparatively few are forced off work by their nerves.[6] Psychoanalysis, relatively speaking, is popular and virtually all the qualified analysts in Britain have their practices in London. Suicide is consistently and strikingly high among women under 35 (but not among men), significantly highest of all in the eight boroughs in the inner western districts that constitute 'bed-sitterland'. But while doing away with oneself is primarily a solution of young women, the less drastic method of drowning one's sorrows is common in both sexes at later ages: middle-aged drunkards are one of London's more regrettable specialities.

Such is the price, it seems, that has to be paid for the luxury of self-sufficiency. Less hemmed-in by social pressures and convention, able to indulge his interests, however obscure and eccentric, and find like-minded, equally unusual people to share them, able to select his friends, the Londoner has more chance to exercise the subtler facets of his personality. In the process he grows specialised and complex. Accustomed to freer self-expression, less ironed-out by conformity, he begins to expect more of everyone and everything; and insists on standards in his friends, in his tastes and in his entertainments that run ever nearer the risk of being self-defeating.

This, perhaps, as a description of 'the Londoner' bears little enough semblance to what most people would conjure up if asked to say what they understood by this term. The majority, very probably, would plump for the

Cockney. But Cockneys now are in a decided minority. As early as 1951 less than half of the county's inhabitants were Londoners born and bred; now, sixteen years later, this proportion may be even lower. Overseas immigrants apart, over a quarter of the capital's present-day population can claim to be intruders in so far as they were born well outside the qualifying earshot of Bow Bells. The crucial point that we must realise about London, therefore, is that for many, perhaps already for the majority, its way of life represents something that its inhabitants have opted to share in – or, at worst, voluntarily stranded themselves in, with their eyes wide open – not, as in all other regions of Britain, something that they have shared in and been shaped by in consequence of a common birthplace and upbringing. No longer is there any real matrix of racial stock or conditioning history. Instead of the normal moulding forces of a natural region, there is now only an artefact for an environment; in place of a natural community with a shared set of habits and reactions, there is now only an unordered mass with little conscious identity or purpose. The new London – or at least the larger part of London that finds its reflection, inevitably, in the sample surveys – is essentially a fortuitous product, the result of the drifting together of many diverse types. We cannot therefore expect the ways of its inhabitants to hang together with quite such convincing inner logic as we can be confident of encountering in other regions. In so far as there *are* common, widely exhibited patterns that we can distinguish as London's culture, these are the outgrowths – some might say the excrescences – of largely reasoned choices more consciously adjusted than elsewhere to conform with the dictates of the city's geography and the demands of individual economics.

This very lack of the underlying harmony of a collective sense of direction is reinforced in London by the natural reserve of Southerners, itself compounded in turn by the other isolating mechanisms seemingly inseparable from

49

all such vast agglomerations of human beings. So many people who live here have come to escape and forget. No mean proportion are foreign nationals, or at least of foreign birth, many of whom insist on staying in essence foreign and maintain contact solely with fellow-country-men. The Census of 1961 turned up half a million persons of non-United Kingdom birth in the County of London alone, equivalent to 16 per cent of its total population – as against only 10 per cent ten years earlier. In four boroughs (Kensington, Hampstead, Paddington and Westminster) no less than a third of the population came into this category. The great distances between one district and another, and the time and expense involved in trying to bridge them, are further complicating obstacles to a wider social life. Still another is the cellular pattern of society-in-depth: the temptation to self-imprisonment in a circle largely confined to one profession (like the actors, the politicians), or in specialised taste-sets (like the music-lovers), or in tight, little, self-hugging cliques of handfuls of old friends of great permanence.

Except in the East End and in some of the outer suburbs true communities therefore can scarcely be said to exist; in their place there are only warrens, tenanted by individuals or families each separately immured in a single deep-running burrow and perhaps encountering one another only where their respective exits converge. And this is not just a feature of the better-educated, as one might at first be inclined to suppose. As one careful observer[51] has lately noted, there is 'a staggering lack of community, even of elementary contacts', among working-class people in at least some parts of London. Not all the inhabitants of the city at this level, by any means, have that warm-hearted ebullience that we traditionally associate with the Cockney.

There is another side to this coin, even so. City life is blessedly anonymous. For all who want to flee from gossip, or refresh themselves with a roll in the mire, the great rubbish-heap of humanity that constitutes the Metropolis offers concealment exceptionally difficult to rival. One aspect of this is contained in the figures for illegitimacy: almost exactly double the national average. At least a quarter of the unmarried mothers who help to give London such an alarmingly high rate in this respect are newcomers already pregnant on arrival – some running from local scandal or censure, others apparently scarcely caring. The most imposing rates are in the catchment areas for immigrants: socially amorphous boroughs like Paddington, where illegitimacy adds up to a quarter of total live births. Indeed, because of the huge increase in the numbers of immigrants, it is difficult to derive from London's soaring rates for illegitimate births in recent years any evidence of greater immorality in the capital in general. Nevertheless, laxer morals are only to be expected where social visibility is so greatly diminished – though, not unnaturally, there are next to no figures to give proof of this. All that we do know for certain is that many more youths aged 15–19 in London than elsewhere in the country claim to have had intercourse with more than one partner,[64] and that deaths from syphilis are notably high in both sexes.

One further factor making for a lack of cohesion in the social fabric of the city is that for so many of its inhabitants life here is at best only transient and provisional. For such people true homes are nonexistent; they shake down, rather, in billets. By long tradition the capital is a place where people go for a while, to train under big names or to broaden their experience. In this capacity it still contains many more students in total, both full-time and part-time, and an unparalleled variety of courses and classes. Close on 40,000 are currently here from overseas alone, enrolled full-time at universities, for training with professional bodies and, above all, at technical colleges.

Since the war Inner London has also become, ever-increasingly, a place for the young to congregate and mix in, before marrying and beating the now conventional retreat to the suburbs or the outer country. A major cause of this, without a doubt, is the heavy concentration in London of professional and clerical jobs available to women, and particularly to middle-class women, many more of whom now work for a living than was customary pre-war. This has had the important side-effect of seriously overbalancing the sex-ratio. In the 20–24 age group in the County of London in 1961 women out-numbered men by no less than 13,000: a surplus of 11 per cent. Just over half, some 73,000, of these girls were still on the hunt for husbands. As so many of them abandon the central districts on marriage, and as men marry on average somewhat later, between the ages of 25 and 35 the scales become smartly reversed – though not quite so unfairly – and it is the men, for a change, who find themselves in a most uncomfortable majority. After 40 the women, once again, resume their preponderance, evidently due to an increase in widows, for the proportion of spinsters remains just about constant. London marriages, common observation would suggest, have a greater propensity for ending up in the divorce court; less well-known, but probably even more influential (for un-remarried divorcees comprise only 1·3 per cent of London's female population), is the tendency for London men in abnormally large numbers to die while only in their forties and fifties. A noticeable surplus of older single women is, in fact, one of the marked features of London compared with the other major cities in Britain. It helps to account for the much higher proportion of pensioners here – 39 per cent against about 30 per cent normally – who live entirely on their own; at least four out of five of these being women. The explanation may partly lie in the many more jobs of standing here open to better-off women aged over 40, encouraging them to make their homes in the capital or else discouraging them from leaving; and partly, and much more certainly, in the lower proportion of London women who marry at all than in the more conformist atmosphere of the provinces. Even when they do marry, those who continue to live on in the centre more often than elsewhere stay childless. The career woman and the 'bachelor girl' are both very much London animals – and not seldom the same animal. The career possibilities are far more numerous and, on the whole, altogether more enthralling; and the social pressures on the single are blessedly far slighter.

The unmarried are doubtless wise to cling to the centre, for two reasons. In the first place they are far more likely to find a partner there than if they moved out to the periphery, for the suburbs and the dormitory belt are almost total preserves of married couples, almost all of them with children and with a social pattern that can hardly admit single people without slight problems and difficulties. In the second place, most of the property best suited to their state, namely flats and bed-sitters, is largely restricted to the central area. Single women, in any case, have long had more trouble in securing mortgages from building societies; and while just over three-quarters of all the dwellings in London are rented, better-class housing outside the city's boundaries normally has to be purchased.

Young middle-class couples, on the other hand, have begun to forsake the centre more and more for the suburbs or further out, when the first child arrives and the urge arises for a garden. As a result, and because of more numerous childless marriages, there is a marked deficiency in the central boroughs of children over the age of four. More prosaically, if young couples want a home of their own – and steadily appreciating property values and a tax system heavily weighted against renting make it increasingly foolish not to aim for this – the choice in the central parts is either wildly beyond their means or limited to more or less renascent slums. Those who cannot afford a mortgage, and so cannot contemplate

53

moving further out, have to resign themselves to the insecurity of renting a home or living with parents or in-laws. An analysis by one of the larger building societies of the age and status of those who borrowed from it during the first half of 1963 showed that only 15 per cent from London and the South East were under 25 compared with 25 per cent in the much less prosperous North West,[65] a discrepancy which must far outweigh the later average age of marriage in the Metropolis. In consequence only 16 per cent of all the households in the County of London are owner-occupiers – the average for England and Wales is 44 per cent – and the private landlord continues to flourish, whereas elsewhere he is fast disappearing. In poorer boroughs like Bermondsey, Shoreditch and Stepney the proportion of owner-occupiers is so low, even, as to be almost non-existent, ranging from one to three per cent at most.

The threefold post-war influx into the overcrowded centre, first by the great surge of displaced persons from Central and Eastern Europe, then by the young un-marrieds and students, finally by the Irish, Cypriots, Pakistanis and West Indians, has completely swamped the accommodation available and made subdivision of single homes in that area all but universal. In the inner ring of boroughs that comprises the Administrative County of London, which holds 40 per cent of the Greater London population and constitutes its more typical core from the point of view of environment, nearly one house-hold in every three now has to content itself with sharing a 'dwelling' (that is to say, according to the Census definition, living in a room or rooms within a single building but deprived of a separate front door). Glasgow, by comparison, has ten times fewer households doubling up in this manner – thanks to far fewer single people living on their own. Thirty-one per cent of all households in the County in 1961 were entirely without the use of a fixed bath and a further 19 per cent were forced to share one. Thirty-seven per cent entirely lacked piped hot water. Only 45 per cent had exclusive use of all the basic domestic amenities. These figures are actually more appalling than they appear even at first glance. Two out of three of the households condemned to share a dwelling, for instance, consist of two or more people: nearly a quarter of a million cases of bed-sitter sharing, in other words, or of couples or even families squashed into a small set of rooms which fails even to rise to that euphemistic description 'maisonette'.

Over 100,000 people in the County of London are one-room-only dwellers. This represents about one household (defined as a separate catering unit) in every ten. Just over half of all households live in no more than three rooms, not counting a bathroom or a kitchen not used regularly for eating in. The latter, of course, must include the great majority of London's flats, some of which even in these terms must rank as quite luxurious. Every other London home, more or less – a convenient statistic, this, for carrying around in the head – is a flat or a room, as opposed to a house. Flat-dwelling is the rule, as one would expect, in the central and inner western areas, where land values are at their highest and where tall, cliff-like edifices somehow seem more comfortingly fitting. But in the last few years, as well, it has burgeoned all over erstwhile slum areas, where the councils at last have been forced to the inevitable and begun to build upwards.

With all these extra flats London has come much more to resemble the cities of Scotland or capitals on the Continent, and the distorting effects of high-living have become that much more apparent. Far fewer people here than elsewhere, for example, can garage their cars – and the general takeover of the public streets for all-night parking has far-reaching implications for sellers of various kinds of equipment to motorists. Hauling coal up several floors is hardly a popular activity, and in past years a high proportion of London householders failed to draw in full the ration to which they were entitled, having in any case often little or no room in which to store it.[47] Electricity, oil and, pre-eminently, gas accordingly take the place of coal very largely. London spends much more on gas per household than any other area of Britain and gas fires, gas refrigerators and gas geysers for heating water are all noticeably more widespread here than elsewhere. Living in flats also means few people garden – and, therefore, far less buying of everything from seeds to lawn-mowers, wheelbarrows and greenhouses. It also means far fewer dogs, the bulkier breeds in particular. The lack of space too, and the popularity of the capital with relatives and friends, seeking a bed for just the odd night or so, presumably accounts for the heavy investment in convertible divans.

The rarity of home fruit and vegetables helps to explain the high incidence of greengrocers and the high patronage of market stalls and barrows,[2] though these also owe much to the cheapness and freshness of the produce made possible by the existence of Covent Garden. The inestimable value of the system of distribution that brings such daily benefits is only properly appreciated by Londoners on moving to other cities less well blessed in this respect. It is also much older than most of them appear to imagine. As long ago as 1839, for instance, it was possible to pronounce quite boldly and categorically that 'in London every one expects to see a good potato on his table as a matter of course. . . . Every vegetable is better in London than in any part of the United Kingdom'.[66] The picture has changed amazingly little since. Londoners still spend a lot on green vegetables, and in a survey in 1958 complaints about the quality of potatoes (probably merely reflecting the degree of consumer fussiness) turned out to be much more numerous in London and the South East combined than anywhere else in Britain.[67] The capital also continues to consume more of all kinds of fresh fruit (with the single notable exception of rhubarb) than the rest of the country. Even canned fruit finds its best market here. Fruit and custard as a dessert, in place of stodgier puddings, is far commoner in London than elsewhere and perhaps represents a typical compromise with the ways of Continentals – the presence of so many of whom must, in any case, raise the level of fruit consumption abnormally. Londoners go abroad for their holidays more than any other Britons and this, for a start, must make them more receptive to foreign modes of eating. So many settlers from overseas around them every day, too, so many foreign students and visitors, so many restaurants and cafés serving exotic foods must all have a further cumulative influence on their palates. Indian and Chinese food, in particular, has less of the out-of-the-ordinary connotations that it has in the provinces and, because of the large numbers of resident nationals who provide a regular and knowledgeable clientele, is often – most unusually for anything metropolitan – cheaper than elsewhere in the country, at least outside the tourist- and gourmet-ridden West End. Italian pastas, principally spaghetti (commonly accompanied by chips), are very popular and sales of the tinned varieties reach colossal proportions in the East End especially. Other imported tastes include French bread, rye bread, crescent rolls and creamy Continental-type gateaux, these last often serving as a dessert. This is the only part of the country, too, where books on foreign cookery are owned in any significant numbers.[45]

The cosmopolitan nature of the metropolis, however, needs little stressing. Capitals tend to have more affluent inhabitants with more opportunities for travel; they also tend to be the centres for the arts and for the creative professions, which need to keep awake to trends abroad. London's obvious function as the first point of entry and as the crucial proving-ground for fashionable novelty afford almost unlimited opportunites for many people. Men (in particular) with artistic leanings gravitate here from the provinces. Acting, advertising, journalism and publishing, the fine arts, the world of high fashion, broad-casting – all of these are heavily concentrated in London, in some cases almost exclusively. In consequence, the taste of London men is far sharper and far fussier, in general closer to that of women. Symptomatic is the frequency with which husbands, not wives, choose the colour schemes for certain rooms.[68] Men are much more finicky about their personal appearance and – outside that redoubt of fossilised uniform, the City – more confidently adventurous in their clothes-buying, not only for themselves but also when buying presents for their women. This is a general tendency, it must be stressed; the many male homosexuals in the capital (allegedly, at least 100,000[69]), which some may be tempted to invoke in explanation, are proportionately far too small to produce survey figures of the magnitude that one tends to encounter.

As far as women are concerned, the important fact is not that London is more fashion-conscious and generally ahead in this respect – in any case, with the inception of teenage fashions its influence has become sensibly less certain – but that standards in general are so much more demanding than in the provinces. In a smaller place a woman can count on a comparatively insignificant ward-robe not betraying her into wearing the same clothes as six other people in the same street or office. But in London the chances of this happening are sufficiently great to demand either larger wardrobes or a faster turnover – and preferably both. In any event, as we have seen, the numbers of unmarried women in London are greater, both relatively and absolutely, and they have on the whole more money, more sophistication and more opportunity in which to choose the things on which to spend it. Sophistication, above all, decrees more care in wearing the right clothes for the right occasion, and in the complicated social life of a capital city the occasions are not only unusually varied, but often quite unpredictable in character. Matching of co-ordinates is a perpetual source of worry, and it may be as much for this reason as for any other that the choice of black for outerwear is so distinctive of London women. In the provinces black tends to be regarded as funeral wear, yet in London it has a strong following even at comparatively low price-levels.[70]

The formidable *depth* of fashion reveals itself, especially, in the outstandingly high expenditure on cosmetics. London women, compared with those in the provinces, probably deploy the common types with no greater intensity, but relatively more of them have joined the battle and their range of weapons is awe-inspiringly far wider. We find here easily the highest use of eye shadow, mascara and eyebrow pencil, of nail varnish and depilatories, of toilet water and deodorants. All this and, maybe, more baths too: 1·8 per person per week as against 1·4 over most of the rest of the country[47] (and even though such figures, inevitably, must be of doubtful reliablity the very fact that Londoners make such higher claims testifies to the greater social importance that they attach to constant cleanliness).

London women have the highest ownership of sweaters, the lowest of cardigans – those frumpish garments. Suits are popular, providing plenty of scope for niceties of cut and even the nylon stockings purchased have a thinner denier on average.

There is more knowledge of brands of all kinds and a greater tendency to specify them when shopping. There is more familiarity with trends in furnishings and more expertise in buying and using the latest domestic appliances. There is greater readiness to accept consumer innovations, like self-service and *laundromats*, and less inhibition in pressing for and using officially provided facilities, like maternity beds in hospitals.[61, 69] Londoners expect good service, and are quite prepared to pay for it. Before the war twice-a-day milk deliveries were notably more common here than in other cities in Britain.[71] Some years back, too – for all one knows, it may still be true – far more people than elsewhere regularly sent their bulkier items to laundries, instead of washing them at home.[72] Made-to-measure suits have long been, and still are, a specially metropolitan indulgence. The customer here has grown used to being wooed, in smart, luxurious surroundings and, most typically of all, in huge, palatial department stores; and assistants, to keep pace with them, have to keep on their toes – with an excessive number of varicose veins[61] to show for this. London is the home of the *Which?* reader, of the emancipated, ultra-rational shopper, just as it is also the home of the challenger of all received beliefs, with the highest proportion of professing agnostics[21] and the lowest proportion of those who express approval of spanking for children.[21]

There is the sophistication of the smooth and trans-atlantic: extensive drinking of rum as a cocktail by both sexes. And the sophistication of the eccentrically anti-quated and traditional: a special fondness for vintage cars. There is elegant conversation, stimulated by the most wine-drinking at home and much the heaviest consumption of ground coffee. There is, to put it very briefly, a sense of style: that finer gloss summed up in the one word 'urbanity'.

Capping all this, almost at times caricaturing itself, an older, upper crust of taste still continues to thrive. In the snug, superlative little world of the high-class store the customer is king as he always has been and is nowhere else. He demands 'The Best' and can expect to be given it. He confers his patronage on establishments (founded 1683 or 1732); he inherits a tailor; his barber is 'By Appointment' almost from babyhood. Here is the aristocracy of consumption. It is expensive; but unlike most things aristocratic, it can be purchased.

Rarefied tastes imply, automatically, money to indulge them. The Londoner has this money and he takes pleasure in spending it – but steadily, not in wild sprees like

Lancastrians, not with the awesome, breathless groping and grabbing of the Midlander. In 1959–60, the last time the Inland Revenue analysed its figures geographically, London and the South East, with just under a quarter of the country's taxable population, held 39 percent of all incomes of £5,000 per annum and over, the City of London, in particular, having almost as many incomes at these higher levels as the whole of Scotland and Wales put together. The same disproportionate national share spreads all the way down to medium incomes throughout London and its satellite dormitories. Even teenagers have substantially higher wages: in 1959 the 16–24 age-group in London and the South East spent on average fifty-two shillings per week compared with barely forty shillings over the rest of Great Britain.[73]

These high wage rates, it has recently been argued,[74] do much to encourage the national spiral of incomes and prices. London, it is held, is the country's 'inflation leader'. London levels of earning and spending, whether consciously or not, influence the fixing of national wage and salary agreements far more than they rightly should. Goods and services that emanate from London tend to have to carry the high labour or real-estate costs of the capital in the form of higher prices. More generally still, the affluence and huge population of the London area make it easier to base charges on whatever the market will carry. With more pennies in their pockets, the argument runs, Londoners are likely to spend more carelessly than Britons in general. And people at head offices, seeing at close hand every day what Londoners are prepared to spend, conclude all too glibly that national prices can be edged just that little further up with perfect safety.

There is obviously much truth in this. At the same time it is important to remember that the average Londoner, in relative terms, is far from being all that preposterously well paid. Very surprisingly, the salaries of middle-range executives have recently been shown to be no higher in the South East and London than in the industrial belt of Yorkshire. They are only marginally higher than in South Wales or the West Country.[75] Yet the London executive earning this kind of salary is typically weighed down with much heavier mortgage repayments than elsewhere and the crippling cost of long journeys to work and back. In purely economic terms he would evidently be far better off in the provinces. The trouble is he would probably then have to endure a much more humdrum job and would find it hard, if not impossible, to satisfy the more exalted tastes that living in London had fostered. A survey by the Location of Offices Bureau has only recently turned up the fact – perhaps surprising only to non-Londoners – that two out of every five who work in the capital would like, in theory, to move out of this overcrowded corner of the country altogether, if only jobs and houses were available. Of the regions preferred instead, the heaviest vote goes to the South West.[76] Not very startling after all: people disgruntled with London life nurse dreams of living not in other cities, but closer to the countryside of Southern England. Those who least like working in central London are those who use private transport for travelling[76] – at first sight paradoxical, until one realises it is precisely such people who have already gone to the greatest lengths to escape the suffocation of crowds.

The unusually hard burden borne in London by the young married executive only throws into sharper relief the affluence of the teenagers and the young unmarried. Girls, in particular, draw much higher pay than they receive for similar work elsewhere in Britain, due to the voracious demand for shop assistants, secretaries and clerical workers of every type. One school-leaver in every five goes into clerical work in London and the South East; everywhere else the figure is hardly more than one in ten. A predictable consequence is a high rate of abandoning school at the earliest age permitted, a rate only matched in the Birmingham area. Very often the girls draw higher wages than their brothers or boy-friends, whose terms as trainees or apprentices confine them for several years to what, by comparison, must seem a mere pittance. While the boys, moreover, sweat away in overalls on oily factory floors, the girls are preening themselves in ever-brighter and cleaner offices and spending their lunch hours looking around expensive shops. In this way, increasingly, the girl from a humble home imbibes tastes and standards alien to the males of her own age and background; tends to expect more material luxury from marriage than can in the normal scheme of things be hers; and, more often than ever before, manages to side-step the whole problem by marrying upwards – thus increasing still further the amorphousness of the capital's social pattern. It was this great concentration of relatively highly paid young girls that set the pace for the nation-wide teenage boom that began in the mid-1950s, a boom which first revealed its strength in fields where girls' purchases were pre-eminent, like blouses and skirts, cosmetics, and pop records. The boys, in the early days at least, had far less to splash around on fashion items like these. For one thing, so much more of their money, as always, went on cigarettes: 15-year-olds in London who are regular smokers smoke over one and a half times as much as their equivalents in Edinburgh or Oxfordshire.[77]

London's teenagers typically live at home with their parents. But for a high proportion of the city's population spending on rent or on mortgages and rates takes a painfully large slice out of earnings. As in the 1930s, expenditure diverted to housing, in one form or another, is roughly 50 per cent higher than in Britain in general. At the same time, compared with the rest of the country, the amounts spent on public transport and on meals away from home are more or less double. The very character of London life also renders a telephone more essential – about one household in three possesses one, which though

63

high for the country as a whole, is still seriously deficient. So, all in all, the Londoner with a home of his own needs a higher income merely to keep his head above water, let alone up with the Joneses. In many occupations, fortunately, he can count on one; but otherwise he tends to be hard-pressed, and in this segment of the population, with more taste than money yet surrounded by others who seem enviably free of their problems, the gap in sympathy with teenage affluence widens to a chasm. The result is that quiet suburban desperation that erupts politically every now and then, which we have come to see personified in the well-known shape of Orpington Man.

There is one saving, even so, that Londoners can make more simply than elsewhere, provided they feel inclined. They can deny themselves a car. The Underground supplements the buses to render public transport unusually comprehensive (its inadequacies made to sound worse than they really are by typical big-city impatience); and hiring taxis to take one to and fro may even make more sense in the long run economically than troubling to drive around oneself. In 1961 London's share of the country's cars almost exactly matched its share of the population,[78] but as it is so much more wealthy, many more than this might have been expected. Clearly, more people than is generally supposed find motoring a superfluous luxury in London, not an indispensable necessity. Even those who do run cars spend relatively little on them, despite high rates of insurance, average mileage being significantly lower than elsewhere.[78] Distances to work (though by no means always journeys) are mostly not very lengthy, and a great many make use of their cars only at week-ends or in the evenings.

The rhythm of London motoring is decidedly jerky, made up much more than elsewhere of short dashes; and in this it resembles the rhythm of London fashion: the endless round of recurrent enthusiasms for swiftly jaded ears, eyes, noses and throats. It is typical of the general

64

restlessness of the capital. The fast, nervous tempo is inescapable, above all in the madcap centre, insinuating its pulsations almost everywhere: in the rattling speech, in the greater speed of operatives in factories,[79] in the very high incidence of ulcers.[61] Housewives cut corners, very noticeably, in their methods of cooking and baking, and in the bed-sitter belt the cramped conditions make moves in this direction even more desperate and drastic. The high proportion of men here who fend for themselves altogether perhaps reveals itself in the excessive reliance on boiled eggs for winter breakfast and on fried eggs and bacon for summer suppers – both, significantly, peculiar to London men but not to London women. Quick-frozen vegetables, also, find much their greatest sale here. And what, finally, could be more in keeping with the Londoner's character than that his special fruit[3] should be that superbly unzippable time-saver, the banana?

The mad rush ends at the boundaries of London. Once outside, in the ring of dormitory towns and villages, the tempo begins to slow down, almost visibly. The Green Belt calms and soothes; and life becomes, progressively, more and more rural.

Just short of nine million people, or rather more than in the Greater London conurbation, inhabit this rather vague area that is what we normally, and rightly, regard as 'the South East': three million in the misleadingly named South Eastern Region, composed of just the three counties, Kent, Sussex and Surrey; another three million in the equally misnamed Southern Region, a nebulous entity half-way to the West Country in fact and in outlook; and almost as many in the prosperous parts of the Eastern Region that lie outside that true East Anglia so conveniently equated with the area of Anglia Television. This wider South East has an obvious basic unity, in that so much of it is populated, and certainly dominated, by the wealthier type of commuter. It is the half-in-half land so unbeloved of the late Professor Joad, neither city, nor true country, but a rustic compromise between the two: the England of mock-Tudor frontages, crazy paving and terracotta gnomes. It has the highest proportion of intensely-cultivated gardens – the townsman's crops – and, uniquely in Britain, just about as many women gardeners as men.[10] In a region with many retired single women and where few mothers with children go out to work the housewife's role spills out-of-doors, and she ends up – or so she claims – by doing the greater share of the work in what is normally the husband's domain. It is she, no doubt, who wields much the highest percentage here of secateurs, itching to prune and to tidy up. Sawing logs, however, is a task for husbands, who must also sweat away pushing the frighteningly large number of garden rollers.[10]

Unlike London, this is very much a home-centred society. Husbands and wives potter about doing faintly rustic things, like carpentry[31] or making jam.[44] Cinemas are neglected and dance halls[2] are less popular than anywhere else in Britain. There is a great deal of home entertaining – but, unlike London, not just in the evenings (the prevalence of children makes for baby-sitter problems), but at midday and especially at afternoon tea, which here becomes a full-scale meal of bread and butter or sandwiches and cakes in place of the meagre cup of tea and a biscuit which is what the Londoner understands by the term. Even so, curiously little tea is drunk. Perhaps alcohol helps to take its place: Kent, Surrey and Sussex have more public houses per head than anywhere else in Britain, and drinking at home is also sufficiently heavy (and expensively indulged in) to cause an equally high density of off-licences, many more than usual of them licensed grocers. Cocktail parties are frequent, but in atmosphere quite different from those in London: 'bare shoulders and skin-tight brocades are inappropriate twenty miles from the statue of Eros'.[80] People dress to blend with the scenery, social and physical, not to stand out. High fashion is frowned on and even in the grandest circles considered slightly fast. It is smart to be unsmart, for the emphasis in everything is on comfort.

This is, indeed, a comfortable region. 'Live in Surrey, free from worry, Live in Kent and be content', in the words of the pre-war railway advertisements. Perhaps too comfortable, even. While the husbands grow thin and worn in the city struggle, the wives relax – and grow fat. The South East is the slimming centre of Britain. Here women receive the greatest support from their menfolk in the battle of the bulges, and one husband in every four claims to be positively anxious that his wife's efforts should achieve success.[26] Consumption of all starchy foods is strikingly low: few potatoes or suet puddings are eaten and little rice or bread. Salads, in contrast, enjoy the highest popularity.

Perhaps this care over diet, along with the fresh air and the unhurried pace, helps to explain why in this region women outlive men on such a scale. Sussex has long had a more preponderantly female population than any other county in England, and Surrey follows close behind. Elderly people settle here – or maybe just survive here – in disproportionate numbers, and the town that jointly holds the record for the highest percentage of pensioners is in Sussex: Bexhill. This stretch of the South coast constitutes one long geriatric belt, full of widows, but its distinctiveness from the marketing point of view is generally concealed, unfortunately, within the broader regional figures. We do know, however, that this is the best area in Britain for lavender water,[24] and there must surely be other special features of this type.

Above all, the South East, or at any rate the non-retirement areas, is extremely prosperous, very English and strongly upper-middle class. Significantly, many more of its houses than elsewhere are detached. People are less on top of their neighbours and accordingly have few

67

complaints to make about them.[21] This is a tolerant, easy-going way of life and governed, after the rural fashion, by a code of friendliness and hospitality between people who in larger towns and cities would probably never find occasion to meet and mingle.

The numerous large houses explain the heavy expenditure on coke and electricity, the high ownership of paraffin stoves (for heating draughty halls and so many more remoter corners), perhaps the very large number of furniture shops per head, and certainly much the highest incidence of servants both living-in and daily. Telephones are as well distributed as in London – though still only among a third of households or thereabouts – and cars as plentiful as one would fully expect, a particularly high number of them with radios, perhaps because of the distances people here tend to drive to work. The outlay on rail fares is, inevitably, extremely heavy. Even so, the region has by far the highest level of saving in the country – even down to Christmas and holiday clubs. In this cult of thrift, alone, it could hardly be more different from its neighbour, London. There are, of course, far fewer expensive distractions and the more relaxed pace doubtless encourages more stopping to pause and reflect before rushing into new purchases. There are also much heavier educational expenses to save for, in an area that rivals Wales in the proportion of children who continue at school until after 15. The popularity of private schooling, involving unusually late ends to summer terms, presumably explains why so few families in this region take holidays in July and so many more in September, contrary to the normal national pattern.[81]

Almost everything else that remains to be said of the South East can probably be safely ascribed to its highly unrepresentative class composition. Most middle-class publications, for example, are devoured much more avidly here than in London. Jewellers are thick on the gound. Toilet requisites match medical goods in attracting

68

extra-lavish levels of expenditure, making this the best area in Britain to set up in business as a chemist. Much the most is spent on professional services, including those of solicitors and undertakers. Almost all of this, one may fairly reasonably claim, can be put down to quietly comfortable, cosily expansive, above-average incomes.

However, in the last analysis, taste, as always, must be expected to override the simple dictates of economics. Greater affluence, on its own, can hardly explain, for example, this region's special vagaries at breakfast: a great deal of fried bread, which Londoners largely neglect; and a curious passion for herrings, which Londoners, ever-keen on the conspicuously exotic, tend to replace with kippers. Greater affluence, too, can hardly account for the heaviest demand here, year after year, for wholemeal loaves. Every region has such anomalies; and in due course, no doubt, the reason for each one will gradually become clear. Before that can happen, however, the reserved South Easterner will have to let us into his confidence and allow us a glimpse of his more than usually private life.

III

The Rural South: East Anglia and the West Country

An hour and a half's train ride north or west from London and we are out at last into the open country, free of commuters and the capital's gravitational pull. To the north: East Anglia, just over two million people sleepily corralled in a still distinctive region, miraculously preserved from modern blights by bad trains and roads that lead nowhere in particular. To the west: three and a half million people in that giant triangular slab, the South Western Region – or, more familiarly, 'the West Country' – to which the Southern Region, though generally assigned to the South East, is really a half-sister just beneath the skin. In truth, all the way from Norfolk and Suffolk to Cornwall and Devon 350 miles of green fields and hedgerows form one long, continuous stretch, unbroken by anything more urban than Bristol and Oxford. To think in terms of the Far East and the Far West is highly deceptive. The two have a basic pattern of life in common, and this spills over into their neighbours' territories almost emphatically enough to sever the narrow umbilical cord, from St. Albans to Northampton, by which the towns and cities of the North and Midlands receive a precarious sustenance from the Metropolis.

East Anglia, as we have already seen, tends to be grouped with the South East in the majority of surveys. Its special character is consequently lost to sight. Were it not for two extensive surveys published by Anglia Television Ltd, we should still know no better: we should continue to copy the Registrar General and tack on the much more crowded southerly fringes to turn it into that bogus entity, the split-minded Eastern Region. If we do this, we add at once a large slice of the dormitory belt and a high proportion of the post-war New Towns, grafting most uncomfortably a somewhat somnolent rural backwater on to one of the primary boom areas of the 'fifties. In age-structure, attitudes and habits of consumption two more different areas could hardly be found. The southern, immensely prosperous part led the country for years, characteristically, in acceptance of television; it has far more telephones than East Anglia proper and many more motor-cycles and scooters; its inhabitants take holidays abroad much more, take far more photographs, keep fewer cats and go to church comparatively seldom.[82] Luton, only too typical, has virtually doubled in population since 1931 and at least three-quarters of the workers in its bustling car factories are estimated to be newcomers to the town. This whole way of life belongs, unarguably, to the South East. East Anglia in the true sense, on the other hand, is isolated from London – mentally as well as physically.

That the rural South still remains relatively immune from urban influences is not due only to the physical distance from the Metropolis. The newspapers, the radio, the television, the teaching in the schools: all the processes of standardisation that annihilate distance are there on every hand. It is, rather, the essentially different concerns that occupy the minds of people in these mainly farming areas, the very difference in the pace and rhythm of life, that somehow seem to give them extra powers of resistance. Rural habits, in any case, last generations and die uncommonly hard. Housewives who have toiled for years to win praise for their baking, or learned to judge the finer points of each variety of local fruit and vegetables are hardly likely to surrender to the onslaught of canned and frozen foods without a fight. Smaller communities mean fewer people to try out new things and far fewer incomers to introduce them – always excluding holidaymakers, who are too alien to count. Nor can the shopkeepers safely take risks, for wages here tend to be lower than elsewhere and prices have to keep in step. Small stocks and small shops stifle impulse buying.

Most decisively of all, a high proportion of households are childless: the West Country, in particular, shelters the retired in unparalleled numbers, and this tilting of the age scales only serves to stress the lack of liveliness for young people already swept into self-conscious *Angst* by fashionable teenage convulsions. Little industry means high competition for never particularly well paid, or even interesting, jobs; and the glamorous new professions, boosted in magazines or heedlessly idolised in the schools, mainly demand training that the home towns are unlikely to be able to offer. So it is to the cities that the young people are drifting, in ever larger and larger numbers. Sixty per cent of all grammar-school leavers in Devon, for example, now move to other counties to take advantage of grander employment. And with them goes the demand, and much of the wherewithal, for the new-fangled, expensive toys: the electric razors and electric toasters, the radiograms and record-players, the car radios and cameras.

Even television has made headway more slowly than the lack of alternative diversions might suggest, and commercial television even more slowly still. The *Radio Times* sells supremely well here, the *T.V. Times* worst of all. There is blindness to advertising, to Continental cookery, to contemporary design. Clothes, for the most part, are merely covering for the body: the sense of fashion, elsewhere so lusty, here remains rudimentary. East Anglia is the only region where, almost universally, women wear vests[83] – the absolute nadir of unfashionableness. Sales of women's slacks, in contrast, are the lowest of anywhere

in Britain.[83] The country folk look primarily for clothes
that will wear, the elderly retired for those least likely to
date; and this means, as in Scotland, higher prices on
average in the interests of good quality, a tendency
extending from clothes down to shoes and nylon stockings.
In East Anglia, departmental stores actually have to
trade *up* to prosper. Dress chains and department stores,
of the kind one associates with the larger towns and
cities, have seldom found struggling for sales here worth
the effort, for merchandise turns over far too sluggishly
to yield a normally acceptable profit. Even girls' clothing
sells noticeably poorly, perhaps because of the slighter
obsession with conspicuous display and the fewer oppor-
tunies for parties.

There is one further reason why all these things should
be. The rural South still has massive confidence in its
traditions and beliefs, with none of the anxious nagging
that now increasingly intrudes in the North. Unlike the
North, its values are less vulnerable for not being woven
into the fabric of urban living; and it has scarcely, if ever,
felt them under serious challenge. The ethos of the old
professional middle class still reigns on here, and most of
all in the West Country with its solid ranks of ex-colonials
hugging the sun in Sidmouth, Budleigh Salterton and
Cheltenham Spa. This is the new Arizona of England,
Britain's garden of rest, the proud but prim place of
refuge from all the squabbles and squalls, from the strum-
ming and yelling; the stronghold of old-fashioned
Englishness and of everything summed-up by those
vaguely emotive words 'Country Life'.

The retired can rarely afford to travel much, even
should they want to; and the country-dwellers who can
afford to are all too often stranded. Little industry and
low densities of population throw up very low rateable
values; and although councils do their best, no amount
of goodwill can overcome the basic shortage of money,
without which self-help can only look like amateurish

expediency. For years the provision of essential amenities like sewerage and plumbing has lagged deplorably behind the national pattern: East Anglia as recently as 1951 had almost twice as many houses without a water-closet as any other English region. Bus services are bad and trains increasingly non-existent. Private transport is therefore almost obligatory, and we find here, despite the generally low incomes (but helped by some of the lowest motor insurance premiums),[84] the highest numbers of cars owned per head in the whole of Britain. The figures rise with increasing remoteness, Cornwall being a county particularly well blessed in this respect. Necessity pushes ownership further along all the standard scales, so that more working-class people run cars here and more people over 65. A high proportion of the cars, as well, are unusually elderly. There are even more multi-car households than elsewhere, for the farmers tend to need a run-about for rough work and another, smarter model for ordinary drives – or even two of the latter.

East Anglia, exceptionally, has a large concentration of affluent farmers (on the rich soil of the Isle of Ely, above all) who enjoy what must be the highest standard of living in Britain of any sizeable social group with a clear geographical identity, thanks to ample security, sun, servants and that rarest of commodities, space. In the absence of cars, mopeds and bicycles – rather than motorbikes or scooters – are most popular, the flat lands of East Anglia being happily suited to the latter, though ownership rises nowhere near Dutch or Danish levels. And failing even these, people can – and do – walk, which is why heavier leathers are preferred compared with the South East.[85] It may be more than coincidental that Bristol gave birth to Tuf footwear.

The catalogue of poor facilities can go on and on. Little cable-laying means fewer telephones than there should be and few rediffusion radio sets. Coal is expensive, especially in Devon and Cornwall, due to the distance from pitheads, and mains gas uncommon, so more and more homes are forced to rely on that higher-priced fuel, electricity. Electric cookers, electric kettles and electric water-heaters are all owned relatively very widely. Cinemas are few and the low borrowing of library books, too, suggests that the trouble of going into town never allowed them to gain a soundly based popularity.

Instead of going out, therefore, the tendency, as in the South East, is to stay at home and bake or garden. Home baking is particularly strong in East Anglia, resulting in heavy purchasing of flour, cooking fats, currants and raisins, and nuts. And virtually everyone has a garden: in East Anglia, at any rate, there is an almost complete absence of flats. Expenditure on seeds and plants is the heaviest in Britain, similarly on insecticides and fertilisers; greenhouses are plentiful, and, in good rural style, there are more wooden ladders and wrought-iron gates, more sickles and scythes than anywhere else.[10] Vegetable plots are particularly common and the fresh produce from these contributes a healthy share of the diet: 58 per cent of West Country households, for instance, obtain vegetables in an average week from their own garden and more must come in the form of presents or through barter deals with friends or neighbours. East Anglia stands out for the masses of tomatoes and cauliflowers it consumes, and jointly with the Southern Region claims the highest liking for asparagus[43] (Breckland is one of the two main areas in Britain where this is grown as a crop[11]). The West Country specialises in spring cabbage and in the various kinds of beans.[2] Only onions languish.

Fruit, too, is available free in enviable quantities and going so far as to buy any is likely to be rated extravagant,[3] which injures the sales of oranges, grapefruit and bananas. Fresh fruit, in fact, is something of an obsession, at least in the West Country: a lot of it is eaten even for breakfast, and when choosing fruity flavours, housewives distinguish themselves by going for the more *outré* ones like greengage for jellies or blackberry for jam. There is a mystique about fruit here, which could well be extremely ancient. Certainly apples have produced the dominant drink of these parts since time immemorial and the folklore surrounding the cider orchards (of which Somerset and Devon have rather more than half of the nation's total acreage)[11] is undeniably impressive. Until quite recently – and for all one knows the custom still persists – on a certain date in the year, properly January 17th (Old Twelfth Night), many of the orchards were ceremonially toasted in cider from a communal bowl and special 'wassailing' ditties sung in their honour. The crop could only be harvested when the moon was on the wane. Apple juice was thought to have magical powers and was used for sprains and smeared over faces, hopefully, as a kind of cosmetic; while eating the fruits was considered a sovereign remedy for depressions. It all has the weird deliberateness of a long-forgotten religious cult. Small wonder, therefore, that cider has proved so obstinately resistant in the West to the advancing tide of beer – which in this part of the world becomes a notably weak type of brew. (Cider-drinking also reappears on a considerable scale in the East, but here the orchards are much more modern).

The very abundance of so much free produce may perhaps explain why mobile shops are relatively few in both areas and have low sales per head compared with, say, the Lake District or the Highlands.[86] Furthermore, English villages are much more likely than the tiny hamlets or clachans of the upland zone to have general stores: those primeval supermarkets of legendary versatility, capable of retailing everything and anything, from a tin of shoe-polish to a bin, a set of deck-chairs to a box of crackers – to say nothing of most of the gossip. Delivering by tradesmen is, nevertheless, more common than in more urban regions. One effect of this is that bread, being brought to the door and made more by small local bakers, tends to be unwrapped (and, of course, unsliced) more frequently than elsewhere, thus impeding still further the march of the big multiple bakeries – which depend on the wrapping for advertising their brands.

Other local activities benefit from the countryman's isolation apart from his garden. Women's institutes, for example, flourish in this region above all others.[21] The Church of England is equally vigorous, the dioceses of Bath and Wells (Somerset), Exeter (Devon) and Ipswich (Suffolk) being among the top three or four in average attendances on Sundays, in proportion to population.[82] Even so, there is, as one might suspect, a negative side: social life is too introverted, and one result is an excessive amount of friction and quarrelling between neighbours.[21]

There is much else that may be listed, stemming from this primarily rustic style of living. There are the free eggs and butter, in mouth-watering quantities (yet a remarkable disdain for chicken); the tied cottages free of rent, accounting for as many as 7 per cent of all homes in the West; the wild larders, heavily raided, of game and rabbits. There is the popularity of pipes, filled with cheap tobacco, and the prevalence of clothing clubs. There are the very few burns to men and the high incidence of that apparently more rural affliction, cerebral palsy.[61] There are the large numbers of homes with cats, as also in Wales – though not nearly as many as in the Channel Isles or France, with their more numerous peasant smallholdings. Finally, and most far-reaching in its effects on behaviour, there is the farming pattern of mealtimes; a hefty breakfast – shown by the high consumption of cereals as well as toast and marmalade – followed by a substantial midday meal; then a tea of bread-and-butter, jam and numerous cakes; and lastly a nightcap at nine or ten of cocoa or some other milk drink (the branded milk drinks find their best market here, relative to population, for this reason) with bread-and-cheese, or sandwiches, as a necessary filling accompaniment. This is the diminuendo pattern of people who rise early and go early to bed: quite the opposite of the pattern in London, which at its most extreme is no breakfast, a beer and sandwich at midday and a latish, gargantuan dinner. For the Londoner the best time of day is traditionally the evening, the precious margin of leisure reserved for the excitements that form the *raison d'être* of life in a capital, and he therefore opens gently, timing his climax of eating to coincide with the period that tends to make most demands on his stamina. Just as his real day is often starting, the countryman is already on his way to bed. In East Anglia there is little viewing of television later than half past ten.[87] Even in a regional city like Bristol the rural pattern still prevails, and night-life in consequence has a difficult task to flourish.

So far, in everything that has been described, the West Country and East Anglia resemble each other sufficiently closely to constitute a single, larger region. But in a good many other ways they differ, betraying a loyalty to a broader, underlying Western or Eastern nature respectively.

East Anglians, for example, have certain characteristics in common with Yorkshiremen. Big, burly people of probably similar racial stock, they share the same reputation for dourness, a strong disinclination to accept orders or kowtow to authority, an equally sharp class division in their voting behaviour, and a general distrust of frills and 'fancies'. They have the same liking for bulk in their diet, producing a huge consumption of suet; the same liking for both sweet and savoury puddings and for dumplings, these last eaten as a first course with gravy as Yorkshiremen once traditionally ate Yorkshire pudding – a good, solid foundation on which to construct a meal. Aggressive eaters, they like to bury the appetite, not titillate it. Like the rest of the East, they stuff themselves with fish-and-chips and their diet has traditionally leant rather heavily on pigs. The ratio of pigs to other farm livestock is high in general almost throughout East Anglia,[11] but despite the background of the Suffolk ham and the Dunmow flitch the only pig products now eaten in excess of the country as a whole are pork sausages. In Yorkshire, in contrast, these are not particularly popular, nor is much pork itself eaten; instead, York hams have retained their hold, supplemented by Spam in unusually large quantities.

Havelock Ellis, in a now forgotten work based on an analysis of the places of birth of the grandparents of every Briton listed in the *Dictionary of National Biography*,[88] found East Anglia was one of the three great foci in England of intellectual ability. This ability, moreover, was of a distinctive type. The careful, patient, judicious, cool-tempered people bred by this region in well above-average numbers won distinction above all as brilliant mediators, particularly as statesmen or ecclesiastics, like Walpole and Wolsey. They had, he concluded, no aptitude for abstract thinking or mathematics: solid and down-to-earth, they shone in the accumulation of facts, as classifiers and collaters. These are unexciting qualities, and we should expect from this region accordingly neither shocks nor surprises. Attempted suicides here are thankfully unusual occurrences.[61] And even the marriage rate is consistently low, 12–15 per cent below the national average, which likewise can be put down perhaps to the prevailing phlegmatic character. Serious disorders of pregnancy and childbirth,[61] a good test of general inner calm, are easily the lowest in the country. So, too, are most of the rates for deaths in infancy, including those due to congenital malformation.[5] These in turn permit an unusually high rate of maternity deliveries at home,[61] which, though in any case more convenient in such a rural region, is believed to be aided by a general reluctance among doctors locally to recommend expectant mothers to resort to hospital. The healthiness of East Anglians is proverbial among those familiar with pharmaceutical statistics (though, unfortunately, none have been published to date divided into categories so fine as this) and attested by at least one set of medical statistics;[89] but whether this is due to genuinely better health, thanks to a good diet and country life, or just simply to a more ascetic strain leading to less fuss and less use of remedies is one of those impenetrable points that crop up at every turn when dealing with such a multi-factored field as disease and illness. Let us be content to marvel that in one part of Britain, at any rate, hypochondria appears to perform no service at all to industry.

Just as East Anglia resembles Yorkshire, the West Country, in turn, in certain respects resembles Wales. Most notably, from their common pastoral background the two Western regions have inherited a passion for dairy products, in particular for fresh milk and cream. Devonshire cream and Cornish cream, so inseparably linked with the West Country in the minds of all visitors, are merely the picturesque lava-flows from an all-consuming fervour beneath the surface. Cream, like fruit, seems to have taken on an almost magical aura, poured into and over as much as possible like a kind of sacred libation. Even vegetables fail to escape this indiscriminate anointing, kidney beans with cream being one particular farmhouse favourite. In parts of Cornwall, it is reliably reported,[90] almost all families, regardless of income, buy a quarter to half a pound of the local clotted cream each week – or, alternatively, make their own – without the slightest feeling of extravagance. It is not so much the taste that appeals, one suspects, but the colour; for cream is a favourite choice in this area for household goods and, significantly, for bedroom walls,[69] almost as if it had some intense symbolic meaning. Could it be more than coincidence that it is the West Country too, above all other regions of England, that lays most stress on the need for marital purity?[21] Has purity, perhaps, become a kind of diffuse obsession, requiring whiteness on every hand?

80

The West Country also differs sharply from East Anglia in the large numbers of holidaymakers who drive through in summer. As a result there are proportionately many more cafés and a conspicuous excess of garages and filling-stations, which, despite the high local level of car-ownership, could scarcely thrive in such numbers without the benefit of this substantial seasonal traffic.

Another difference, rather baffling in view of the apparently similar rural background, is the elaborateness of the precautions taken in connection with childbirth, which makes the East Anglian approach seem almost slap-dash by comparison. Attendance at ante-natal clinics and delivery of babies in hospitals[61] are both particularly pronounced here, and of all regions there is the widest provision of analgesics for women in labour.[5] One possible reason for all this is not, unfortunately, hard to find: the exceptional number of infants dying from congenital malformations[5] – again sharply different from East Anglia – which might have built up a preference for playing safe among local doctors. Such an excess of congenital troubles (a feature, also, of Ireland) might in turn be the outcome of too much rural inmarriage, of which the notable frequency of mental defectives[89] is another, more forcible reminder.

Another explanation which might well be true, at least in part, is that the draining away of young people from the region means that the maternity facilities available are less swamped than elsewhere. To this could well be added more middle-class determination – to ensure that the facilities exist in the first place and to be active in making use of them. For, as has been mentioned already, this is a region, like the South East, ruled by ways of thinking that are essentially those of the professional middle class but, unlike the South East, a professional middle class of sternly traditionalist views which have undergone little of the post-war reinterpretation that has radiated outwards from the cities. Geoffrey Gorer, in his

Exploring English Character,[21] appears to have been the first to draw attention to this fact and to document it extensively. The West Country, he found, has much the highest proportion laying claim to middle-class status, which in itself is symptomatic of the still unchallenged sway here of the 'old' middle-class scale of values. In this region, as electoral studies have shown, the Conservative Party wins relatively more votes from the working class than elsewhere: the strong dissent of the undeferential East Anglian is conspicuous by its absence. Those who completed Gorer's questionnaire – and they were mainly readers of the *People* and so representative of the readership of that paper – differed from the rest of the country in the extent to which they argued from the standpoint of ethics, expressing strong disapproval of pre-marital intercourse, unfaithfulness in marriage, drunkenness and divorce. They laid more stress than elsewhere on the importance of respecting the innocence of children; at the same time they most approved of caning for boys. Privacy, 'keeping oneself to oneself', was seen as an especially praiseworthy attribute.

In the West Country, accordingly, we find abundant evidence of 'old' middle-class tastes and customs that have filtered downwards, to an extent quite unknown today in regions overwhelmingly affected by the new, post-war mass society. In this quiet siding, almost unnoticed, there has calmly continued to take place that very gradual kind of social transformation that in most other, more exposed parts of England, had now been short-circuited. Whether this can continue indefinitely, however, must be open to serious doubt. Day by day the insidious new influences creep nearer, and it scarcely seems likely that even this cosy enclave will prove so self-sufficient as to resist their blandishments, to the extent of keeping its social and cultural distinctiveness intact.

One sign of danger already is that, ever-increasingly, the native population of the region is drifting away from the villages to the towns and from the towns to Exeter Bristol and Plymouth. The urban infections in this way draw steadily closer to hand. All the more reason, therefore, to welcome the strong counter-movement of recent years that has brought so many retired people, particularly from overseas, to settle in the houses and cottages progressively vacated by the local countryfolk as well as in the many newly built seaside bungalows and in caravans – a one-storeyed way of life which, on so large a scale, represents a radically new departure and which promises to have as far-ranging implications for manufacturers as the profusion of flat-dwellers in Scotland and in London. The tastes that have accompanied these new arrivals, being predominantly those of the 'old' middle class, have merged with remarkable facility with those that pre-existed; and the access of newcomers, so far from proving disruptive, has rather served to bolster the region's self-confidence. So numerous has this retired element now become that its special characteristics peep up more and more over the top of the ordinary West Country ones in sample surveys, so that we find now in this region, to take just three examples, the widest prevalence of grey hair, a heavy consumption of invalid foods, and a marked tendency to consult doctors for sprains or fractures.[1] There is a great deal of knitting,[91] a surprisingly high outlay on both wines and spirits and on quality cheeses (for of all expensive tastes, those of the palate are the last to be dropped), but, in compensation, little smoking and almost no betting or gambling. Tight budgets and pleasant, relaxing surroundings discourage much holidaying; but when holidays do happen, May, the month when the country is looking its best, is twice as popular a choice as elsewhere in Britain.[81] Journeys away are usually eastward or northward (rather than abroad), for of all regions this is the one containing most people separated from their families.[21] This is, one might say, the grandparent zone: married sons and daughters tend to live in the suburbs or commuter country and *their* children, when out of school, increasingly in the city centres. In this way Southern England is coming to show a marked replacement pattern, from West to East, in the dispersal of the generations, reflecting in a most appropriate way the successive ages of the underlying strata in the rocks. In the far West, due to this sparsity of relatives as well as to the distances imposed by rural life, family gatherings, after funerals[23] for example, are necessarily less usual; and people spend a daunting amount of time writing letters – an invisible local industry – as revealed by the heavy expenditure on postage and the greatest density of shops that specialise in stationery.

So few children around means marie biscuits take over from chocolate assorted, fish-paste from sweets. Washing-machines become superfluous luxuries and laundries are resorted to instead. Hard goods and furnishings are bought with less freedom and on fewer occasions, for families here more often contract than expand, and decking out extra rooms as children grow up can be less relied on as a constant factor helping to create demand. Replacement sales, in turn, are hardly helped by the generally conservative atmosphere and apathy about design – or by the complete housefuls of treasured pieces that the retired so commonly arrive with (any further acquisitions being confined for the most part to china or glass). Much the same holds true for clothes. The retired pay little heed to fashion and expect their wardrobes, with unimportant exceptions, to see them out. What little they are prepared to spend goes, quite literally, to their heads: mainly on morale-boosting visits to hairdressers, on which their outlay is quite disproportionate and as high as in the prosperous South East.

Nevertheless, retail sales as a whole in this region are high relative to population. Since fewer purchases are made overall, this suggests that people pay rather handsomely for the comparatively restricted range of items that they choose to purchase, though this may be due, in part, to considerably less price-cutting. The shops, which tend to be small, also need to charge for providing a more than ordinary amount of service – which is still an effective way of winning custom in a traditionally small-scale, face-to-face society, especially when reinforced by so many members of the professional middle class with particularly exacting standards. More people, proportionately, are employed in retailing than in any other region, yet the shops here have the lowest sales per person. An economist would argue from this that they are over-staffed. But shopkeeping is a way of life here and to condemn merely for lower efficiency would surely be over-harsh. Probably a high percentage of those who run or assist in shops earn disgracefully little, but who can blame them when other work is so difficult to find? Or for choosing to eke out a comparatively meagre existence, if this alone ensures they can continue to live in this region, which remains, still, so contented, so tranquil and so undemanding?

IV

Wales

Unlike the other areas so far described, Wales is indisputably a region of its own, a foreign country even as far as England is concerned, with absolutely no argument about where it begins or ends (once we have agreed, as surely we must, that it also takes in Monmouthshire). Nevertheless, for practical reasons, it does not always enjoy separate treatment. Its population of rather more than two and a half million – one Briton in every twenty, or roughly half a Welshman to every Scot – is too small to bear separate analyses in most commercial nation-wide surveys, trimmed as these usually are to conform to budgets that permit of no such statistical luxuries. In these circumstances its conventional bedfellow is the South Western Standard Region. This is a better choice than the alternatives – the Midlands or the North West – for, as we have seen, the two have certain basic tastes in common. They share, too, one and the same I.T.V. station. Furthermore Bristol, the capital of the West Country, is just down the road from Glamorgan and Monmouthshire, which between them hold well over half of the Principality's total population. For this last reason the Wales revealed by sample surveys is essentially South Wales: the North, in many ways so different, is altogether too slight in numbers for its individuality to be thrust forward by this means on our attention. For 'Wales', therefore, nationalists who wish to be pedantic should read 'the greatest number of Welsh people' in all that follows.

The first point to bear in mind is that the region is somewhat anomalous geographically. Although, in a spatial sense, it links itself naturally to the South and to England, it is of course quite different from these in spirit. Its roots are 'Celtic', and over a wide range of characteristics its affinities are essentially with Scotland. Some of these, legacies of the pastoral Highland Zone, we have seen already. There are plenty of others: a heavy consumption of bread, eggs and salt, a pronounced distaste for fish-and-chips, salads, coffee, liver and chocolate blancmanges; little spending on hairdressing or on seeds or flowers; little interest in most kinds of household gadgetry. The two share a strong allegiance to kinsfolk and a low proportion of childless marriages (relics of the lineage system, or simply due to a greater fondness for children?), little home-dressmaking, a blithe unconcern with cricket, comparative freedom from the English obsession with class. They also share that little-known phenomenon, the 'Celtic' bed. Shorter and wider than the normal English bed, typically 4 ft. by 5 ft. 9 ins. (though the length now tends to be extended, to keep pace with the larger size of the people), this traditionally matched the bed-space, a chest-like hole, found in farm cottages and reproduced in tenement flats – for the Scots, in particular, have always believed in saving space. One by-product is that in British mattress factories, for years, an extra production-line has had to be kept in being specially to cater for 'Celtic' demand.

In other respects, however, Wales diverges sharply from Scotland. A much warmer climate melts the consumption of the two great Scottish standbys, soup and porridge, down to South English levels. Cakes and biscuits are curiously unpopular; beef gives way to lamb; made-up meat products tend to be avoided; and both linoleum and carpets come in for high esteem, a trait shared with the North-easterners but certainly not with the Scots. There is also less pipe-smoking – but then pipes, the natural resort of the phlegmatic, could hardly look more incongruous than in the mouths of excitable Welshmen.

Though they have the same dogged earnestness as the Scots, the Welsh in other ways rather resemble the Irish. Spellbindingly voluble, both are fine talkers – yet visually unaware: they wander around, it almost seems, oblivious to line or colour, as though glimpsing the world through ill-focused lenses. Numerous writers have remarked on this. Some have blamed a long history of poverty – yet there has been no comparable stunting of the Italians, or the Spaniards. Others have blamed Nonconformism, with its general hostility to painting and architecture – yet, while this may apply to the Welsh, it can hardly apply to that equally non-visual people, the Irish. The truth, probably, is that the deficiency has always been present and forms some deep-seated expression of the national sensory make-up.

One result of this strange visual trait is that the Welsh are notorious for their poor response to new styles in fashion. Over the last ten years a wave of prosperity has surged all through the south of this region, average earnings in industry from 1960 to 1964 having been consistently higher than in even the Midlands or London – admittedly inflated by the very high wages in the steel industry and in the manufacture of domestic appliances. One would have expected from this a notable improvement in standards of dress. Nothing of the sort, however, seems to have happened. South Wales, apart perhaps from Cardiff, still retains its reputation as a wilderness for fashion, among manufacturers of women's clothing[83] no less than among manufacturers of teenage shoes[92] and this despite having the highest number of shoe shops per head in the country.[93] Colours tend to be drab – grey, navy blue, beige – and, unlike the rest of Britain, plain monotones are preferred almost exclusively to tints.[83] Both tendencies hold good for furnishings as well as for clothes. Styles, too, are mainly 'safe' and slow to change; and nothing could be more typical than the exceptionally small proportion of women in South Wales who consider vests old-fashioned.[85] Spending on women's outerwear is low in general and spending on cosmetics and millinery, the less essential top-dressing, lower still. It is almost as if Welsh women wanted to hide themselves, fading into the background in order to leave the centre of the stage to the men. As if to make up for neglecting their own persons, they attend to their menfolk's wardrobes to a quite exceptional extent, accompanying them into shops to buy suits more often than elsewhere in Britain and revealing their hand, unmistakably, in the disproportionate amount spent on men's underwear and socks.

This is merely part of a wider and more general build-up reserved for the male in Wales – almost as if the wives fail to find their husbands substantial enough and feel a desperate need to enlarge them, if only in their minds. No doubt the volatile nature of the average man in Wales robs him of a certain reassuring solidity. Were it not for the fact that relationships are so habitually full of warmth and the home and homely virtues so emphatically applauded, Welsh wives might well feel insecure and find themselves, like so many Midland wives, taking out their frustrations on their men. As it is, they operate from a firm base confident of their womanliness, and if they have a fault it is in smothering the men with almost too much attention. Father's room, father's chair, father's slippers, the biggest helping for father. . . . The male ego is relentlessly flattered, his manliness pandered to by the wife to the point of motherliness.

In return, as in Lancashire, he commonly entrusts her with his wage-packet, even leaving her to pay all the household expenses, contenting himself with a mere portion out of it which constitutes his pocket-money. The scene that traditionally took place on pay-day in the mining villages was well portrayed by Richard Llewellyn in his classic *How Green Was My Valley*:

'As soon as the whistle went the wives put chairs outside their front doors and sat there waiting till the men came up the Hill and home. Then as the men came up to their front doors they threw their wages, sovereign by sovereign, into the shining laps: fathers first and sons or lodgers in a line behind.'[94]

The home is the woman's world to an extent only rivalled in Scotland and Yorkshire, reflecting that greater distance between the sexes apparently found in Britain wherever the severer forms of Protestantism hold sway. Only here there is a slightly false ring. Somehow it is harder to cast the Welsh husband as an out-and-out man's man; he lacks the essential grittiness of the Yorkshireman, or the cragginess of the Scot. There is a vague, uncomfortable feeling that he is playing a part. Give him half a chance, one suspects, and he might allow himself to be enveloped by the home and the woman's world, a fly enticed into the spider's parlour. The charade has only lasted so long and so completely, surely, because of the overwhelming importance of mining in the regional pattern of employment. Only one Welshman in nine is now a coal-miner, but twenty-five years ago the ratio was one in four. The pit-face glowered over the landscape, socially no less than physically. Mining was man's work, and the dirt and danger conferred an almost glamorous halo of virility. Conversely, to lose such work was to feel helplessly emasculated and this, perhaps, helps to explain the quite exceptional bitterness felt by the Welsh miners in times of unemployment.

One relic of the old way of life, surely about to disappear, is the still strikingly low proportion of wives who go out to work, as in the Tyne-Tees area, reflecting the traditional predominance here of heavy industry. This shows up even more starkly in the fact that, of all regions, Wales has the lowest percentage of women working in manufacturing part-time, nicely illustrating the shortage of jobs ideally suited to the married. But would there not perhaps be more, if wives only showed eagerness to go out to work on anything like the same scale as in the Midlands? From all we know of the Welsh wife she is likely to prove uncommonly reluctant to come right out of her nest – a nest, in any case, usually overflowing with children in a region where paid domestic help is rare. She is still too cosily entrenched in treasured wifely functions. Wales, like Yorkshire, is one of the last strongholds of home breadmaking, and though, as we have seen already, this is not a land of cakes and buns, there are nevertheless high purchases of flour and raisins to suggest that a fair proportion of what is eaten must still be baked by the wife herself. She is also accustomed to a heavy burden of washing, due again, no doubt, to the prevalent background of mining. As in all the mining areas of Britain, acquiring a washing-machine or wash-boiler has taken high precedence and the level of ownership of these has long been most impressive. One result of this has been effectively to stifle in this region the development of *launderettes*.[95] In most other respects, however, Welsh houses are noticeably under-equipped and un-cluttered. A high proportion, something like three-quarters, were built before 1914 and far too many of them, especially in the rural areas, still lack the cardinal amenities. The percentage possessing a fixed bath, in particular, is much lower than in any English Standard Region. Turnover per head at shops selling household goods is consistently depressed, which suggests that in spite of the new prosperity there is still considerable resistance to the introduction of new methods, particularly if these mean converting the home from a nest into anything remotely resembling a mere machine for living in. The labour of housework, in all probability, is clung to as a fetish; and it may well be that the extraordinary focus of purchasing-power on tiles, linoleum and carpets that we meet with here is to be explained by the very toil and trouble required in keeping such highly susceptible surfaces clean, which makes them supreme advertisers of perfect spotlessness: a source of pride to the housewife, not only in itself but in its comforting contrast to the griminess of the man's world outside.

A further reason for a certain sparseness in furnishing is that the main living-room, as in Scotland, is so often the kitchen, the half-sacred place where the fire burns longer in the hearth without being allowed to go out – thanks in no small degree to the low cost of coal and, even more, to the free supplies enjoyed by the miners. A high proportion of Welsh families eat all of their meals there,[45] and the room is redecorated, frequently with new wallpaper, far more regularly than in any region in England.[68]

Like their beds, the 'Celts' have preserved their kitchens from their age-old rural tradition. The average townsman in Wales or Scotland is still at heart a crofter, yearning for a 'Little Grey Home in the West'. The new status symbol for young Welsh working families is accordingly, it is reported,[96] not a house but a bungalow, lushly furnished – in other words, an ancestral cottage. In such matters the special 'Celtic' sense of timelessness, of dwelling in a continuum with the dim, distant past, can be seen to be in action, bringing in its wake a deep-seated conservatism.

Welsh homes also present an appearance of bareness due to their lack of some of those ritual accessories so particularly dear to English hearts. Strikingly few of them, for instance, contain a cage-bird and hardly any a tank of fish. The Welsh are not a nation of petkeepers; they scarcely share the English empathy with animals, reserving their sentimentality much more exclusively for childhood and children.

Another aspect of Welsh home-centredness is the greatly reduced amount of travelling. Admittedly, jobs tend to be close at hand and the mining communities are comparatively self-sufficient, huddled in their separate valleys. But besides the low use of trains and buses[97] the habit of leaving home for holidays has remained stubbornly underdeveloped, even in the affluent South of the region. There is little spending on meals out or on hotels. Private transport, less essential as a means of getting to work in the mining areas than almost anywhere else in Britain, has progressed more slowly. Motor-cycles, mopeds and scooters were each to be found in fewer homes in 1960–1 than in any of the ten English Standard Regions. Only car ownership, in recent years, has kept abreast of the national average, as if the very absence of previous transport allowed the Welsh to leap several rungs at once up the conventional ladder of mobility. In turn, this general dearth of vehicles must have hardened the stay-at-home custom, enabling the salvage of a positive virtue out of a purely negative necessity. It has also meant that fewer people in Wales than anywhere else are run over or die in crashes.

Outside entertainments, too, have suffered for the very same reason. The cinema, alone, has managed to develop a strong following with a weekly patronage in South Wales as late as 1961 about half as extensive again as the British national average. But like Scotland and Tyneside, the two other areas with a similarly marked addiction, Wales is a land of large families; and it could well be that the medium survives here unusually robustly due to the substantial excess of its loyalist hard core, the teenagers and just-marrieds.[98] The greatest outside activity of all, however, the licensed club, refuge of thousands of husbands, is not formally classed as 'entertainment'. If it were, figures for spending under this head would surely rise up, for one husband in every four belongs to one of these clubs in South Wales. They are exactly as frequent, relative to population, as in the West Midlands or Yorkshire, and as in these regions they owe much of their popularity to the repressive influence of Nonconformism, at its most spectacularly successful in Wales in securing the closing of public houses (still, in many areas) on Sundays. Teetotalism at the same time claims an impressive total of adherents (if those who assent to questions on this subject in sample surveys are to be believed). One of its most drastic effects is a very marked reduction in 'marginal' drinking: only one adult in every five in South Wales admits to being an occasional drinker of beer, for instance, as against one in three over the whole of Great Britain. Spending on wines or spirits, at least for drinking at home, is also outstandingly low and there is the same proportional scarcity of off-licences that one finds in Scotland. To balance this, however, there is a heavy consumption of soft drinks.

The cult of abstinence by no means stops at the bottle. For years women in labour have less often received analgesia than in England or, at one time, even in Scotland[5, 59], as if the Welsh find stoical endurance easier to accept. Children, too, are kept on a tight rein, though here the very size of the average family must put a strain on budgets: girls have noticeably little spent on their clothes (but, as we have seen, the Welsh female has a blind spot in the matter of finery) and sales of pocket transistor radios, typically status toys of schoolchildren, have been persistently sluggish. Growing up here is an earnest business. The Welsh expect their offspring to take life seriously and be studious. Never light-hearted people they bring a natural fervour to learning, rooted in their feeling for words and for the past, as well as a deeply committed seriousness; which finds reflection in their television programmes – on the whole too earnest for the tastes of the English – as well as in their exceptionally high turnouts at both local and national elections. The general respect for education brings its just rewards: for more pupils go on to grammar schools and on to universities than anywhere in England apart from the South East, and even of those who leave school early a very high proportion attend evening institutes. Before the war Swansea had more manual workers, in absolute numbers,

enrolled as members of three-year University Tutoria
Classes (the most disciplined form of extra-mural education) than were to be found in the whole of London.[100]
Like Scotland, and unlike most of England, Wales
considers higher education worthwhile even for girls, a
notably large proportion of whom have long attended the
Welsh universities and, in turn, helped to feed back a
higher all-round standard into their native system. But
perhaps just because of the solid public approval it enjoys
(and the Welsh unfussiness about social class), remarkably
little of the education is paid for directly from private
pockets. And, oddly enough, spending on books and
periodicals is low: for all their love of learning the Welsh
are certainly niggardly in supporting its eventual production.

A side-effect of later school-leaving is the low extent
of teenage marriage and, to judge from the figures, the
exceptional chasteness of the girls. Deaths from syphilis
among Welsh women are well below the levels met with
in England and, somewhat less exotically, there continue
to be extremely low rates for illegitimacy, especially in
the rural districts – though this could of course be a
statistical illusion, if stronger parental pressure merely
produces more 'cover-up' weddings to legitimise babies
already on the way by mistake. But somehow this seems
unlikely. For one of the most striking facts about Wales
that appears to emerge from the mass of survey data
is that the country, even more than the South West, has
a powerful obsession about purity. And the effects of this
on shopping habits, no less than on behaviour in general,
seem likely to be both profound and extensive.

This obsession suggests itself in three main ways. First,
in the insistence on having medicines made up, instead of
depending on dubious patent brands. The dispensing
trade is far larger than elsewhere in Britain in consequence,
and the custom of 'going to the chemist for a bottle', even
more marked in Lancashire, still survives here and there.

95

Once again, we have something that looks extremely old. The pharmacists, it would seem, are the descendants of the old herb doctors, and have had the luck to inherit unmodified the veneration once given to makers of magic potions by a people over-fond of mystiques – and, as we shall see, over-prone to illness in general as well. As the modern guardians of purity, their profession has none of the mundane, only-too-secular aura normal throughout England: here it has an extra dimension, as though half-sanctified. As a result it is quite exceptionally respectable, and, not surprisingly, grossly overcrowded. Wales produces far more pharmacists than she can ever hope to use and many therefore have to emigrate; and that is why, throughout Britain, behind the counters of a remarkably high proportion of chemists' shops and in the laboratories of all pharmaceutical firms in industry we seem to encounter, almost everywhere, 'the inevitable Welshman'.

Next, we have the unexpected preference – unexpected, that is, in a region that prides itself on home skills and unexpected, even more, in view of its insistence on specially made-up medicines – for artificially preserved food and drink. Like the Scots, the Welsh have a poorly developed tradition of eating fresh fruit and vegetables, which, if available at all, have normally tended to be expensive. They therefore had fewer ingrained habits to overcome as modern processing methods arrived. This alone, however, is insufficient to explain the grand scale of the welcome that they have seen fit to extend to them. The heaviest consumption in Britain of quick-frozen foods, especially fish, turned out soon after their launching, to general surprise, to be among families of miners in South Wales.[101]. The region eats easily the most canned meat, a great deal of canned salmon and canned peaches, pears and pineapples, and drinks all the canned milk and cream it can afford. It also drinks canned beer in great quantity. As in Scotland, cans are certainly more convenient for a people that has to do so much more of its drinking perforce at home. Even so, this consideration may well be merely secondary. It is significant, surely, that the Welsh reason for preferring Guinness in cans is that only the cans, it is popularly supposed, come fresh from Dublin, the bottled variety being dismissed as an *ersatz* brew brought in, suspiciously, from England.[102] Furthermore, Welsh beer has to be clearer than in England precisely because – or so Welsh acquaintances assure one – the Welsh like to see exactly what they are given to drink. The can, in other words, one is driven to suggest, is seen as endowed with the purity of intactness; it is fresh from the mint, virginal, uncontaminated. As if to bear this out, the Welsh housewife, when out shopping, tends to be extremely pernickety, a stickler for tried-and-trusted brands and prepared to pay top prices as a guarantee of perfect freshness. This is well shown, for instance, in the choice of fish. Though the Welsh eat little fish (much of it hake,[103] less than usual cod), their expenditure is disproportionately heavy; Grade I salmon is demanded, Grade III often rejected.[104] This suggests more than an ordinary pride in the wifely skills of shopping: it suggests, very possibly, a dread of being surreptitiously injured. If this is true the Welsh will presumably be the last of all to accept interference with their water and to submit to fluoridation.

The third symptom of this apparent cult of purity is the great emphasis in the diet on dairy products. We have already noted signs of this in the West Country; but in Wales it is, if anything, even more generally entrenched. Welsh prejudices, however, slightly vary the pattern. Fresh (unpreserved) milk is rather unpopular – less is spent per head with dairymen than elsewhere – but canned milk and cream are bought profusely enough to more than make up for this. Sweetened condensed milk, indeed, enjoys much the strongest following in Britain. Once more we are up against something extremely ancient. Wales, by long tradition, is a pastoral country, a land of grazings in place of field-crops. Pastoral peoples, all the world over, judge a man's status by the size of his herds. Cattle are killed for meat therefore as sparingly as possible, with the result that the successful, with far more cows than they need for subsistence but without any proper system of export, accumulate milk till they are almost flooded out by it. But poor farmers, on principle, do not destroy their surpluses. The Welsh, like the Irish before the potato arrived, had to drink all the milk that they could – leaving little or no room for beer or spirits – and convert what remained into curds, cheese and butter. It is recorded that when the Welsh leader Llywelyn ap Gruffydd went up to London in 1277 to pay homage to the King of England, his considerable body of Welsh retainers startled their hosts at Islington by spurning the London beer – and demanding milk.[105] Presumably they were disappointed.

The Welsh seem to have been renowned for their cooking based on milk, since early times. The English word 'flummery' is in origin the Welsh *llymru*, a sweet dish made with milk, flour and eggs, a sort of Celtic *zabaglione*. 'Welsh cakes', made on a bakestone, required the use of sour milk. *Tatws-slaw*, a slop of mashed potatoes and buttermilk, still remains a farmhouse favourite. Even today this is a region of innumerable milk puddings,[45] producing in consequence a strong demand for rice. The Welsh Rarebit, properly a thick slice of cheese spread over a buttered slice of bread and then grilled, is another delicacy that has swept across the border – with proper *élan*, for the Welsh have always known more about cooking with cheese than the English. Their cheeses are mild and preferred milk-white,[25] best exemplified by Caerphilly, which naturally finds here its widest following.[41] The Welsh also share with South England and the Midlands a liking for Double Gloucester.[41] Butter, however, is the Welsh food *par exellence*. The consumption of this is quite colossal, rivalling that in Ireland. It is mainly eaten on bread, in place of margarine, which in Wales has never become well accepted or popular. More housewives than in any other part of the country never buy margarine at all; and those who do deign to use it relegate it much more than elsewhere to cookery exclusively.

Welsh butter tends to be saltier than the butter liked in England. This has been attributed[106] to the need of the miners to replace the salt lost through so much sweating, but a brief investigation would show that the taste reappears in sister regions, like the Isle of Man, with no such prevalence of mining. Salting, in fact, was the normal preservative method till the advent of canning. Only food so treated could be wholly depended on for soundness ('butcher's meat', for example, was a favourite Welsh expression of abuse). Hence the at first sight rather puzzling custom today in South Wales of showing one's respect for a guest by opening a tin of Spam in his honour.[107] In the same circumstances an earlier generation would have brought out a leg of salted pork or, maybe, a well-dried ham. The Welsh, very typically, still persist in rehearsing a race-memory of a world in which food all too easily went bad, a world in which a stranger under one's roof might destroy one's reputation for all time in a single night by falling foul of some impurity – the worst sin of hospitality that could surely be perpetrated in a land where adulteration must have been judged almost as heinous as adultery.

Were we to trouble to trace this concern with purity further and further back, we should find, more than probably, that it is of much more ancient growth than the main wave of fundamentalist religious faith, just as in Scotland rabid self-discipline shows signs of having flourished (if that be the right word) well before John Knox. Puritanism in Wales, in all likelihood, dropped anchor on a pre-existing shoal of purity-worship, a code of milk-white perfectionism conceivably derived, in an exceptionally backward-glancing people, from the age-old mother-goddess fixations. The perfectionism of the Welshman is like that of a mandarin scholar, for ever worrying about the absolute precision of his facts, a form of passionate integrity, seen at its most typical in his struggle to keep the Welsh language pure and untainted, free of all intrusive Anglicisms; it bears but a surface resemblance to the self-denying austereness of the Scot. The Welsh temperament straggles too luxuriantly to tolerate pruning of any comparable rigour. Betting, for instance, the special fever of miners, exposed to the perennial lure of treasure-hunt mania, has stubbornly defied all attempts at suppression – and betting-offices now proliferate as almost nowhere else in Britain (Merthyr Tydfil, the national record-holder, currently has as many as one for every thousand inhabitants.[108]) If throats are harshly punished, with fierce liquids and burning sauces and tobaccos, the culprit is not masochism, but coal-dust. In so far as the flesh is mortified at all, indeed, much of the performance seems a façade, almost convenient. Total abstinence is no great hardship for a people who on the whole seem to have come late to alcohol, chastity no new endurance test for scrupulous preservers of lineages, chapel-going a welcome chance to release oneself in song. Only in an unreal prudery, imposed on a people so warmly curious by nature, have the Welsh seemed to suffer at all severely for their religion. The stern Protestant ethos, originally adopted by and suited to a people that then resembled the stern North Walian in the main, has been made to look exposed and out-of-keeping by the subsequent population explosion in the mining valleys that has made the South Welshman overwhelmingly predominant in numbers. The South Welsh, as we have seen hinted at already, are not the natural stuff of heavy-handed fathers: the sombre mantle of Nonconformism sits uncomfortably on their emotionalism. Underneath the disguise, they are more like the Irish and the Italians, incorrigible matrists. That they ended up as Methodists and Presbytarians, not as Roman Catholics, must be one of history's more remarkable accidents. Perhaps, even, the very exuberance of their emotions owes something to a continuing inner struggle, a long-drawn-out civil war between their basic nature and an ill-fitting system of morals. A Number Nine nation, shall we say, parading for life in Number Eight shoes?

By letting off steam, at any rate, the Welsh certainly do themselves good service. Compared with the English, for one thing, they are far less prone to crack up abruptly: suicides, both successful and unsuccessful,[61] are exceptionally uncommon and most of all in the densely-populated south-east corner – helped in part, perhaps, by the sheltering strength of the 'Celtic' extended family, which must lighten the desolation of the aged. Less tension, too, is suggested by the rarity of those stress conditions vaguely termed 'slipped discs' – outside industry rarer, apparently, than in any English region and diagnosed by doctors in an average year seven times less frequently than in Yorkshiremen.[1] As if to make up for this, they tend much more to slip beyond the plimsoll line of level-headedness. First admissions to mental hospitals in proportion to population, in one year reported on (1957),[109] were 36 per cent above the national average in Cardiff and no less than 53 per cent in Monmouthshire, no city or region in England departing from the norm to anything approaching this extent. The principal culprits were the less destructive disturbances, such as psycho-neuroses and, even more, manic depression, which was virtually double the national rate in Monmouthshire and extremely high also in Cardiff women. Schizophrenia, by contrast, tended to be mercifully scarce. In this same south-east corner spells off work due to well-defined mental disorders are, correspondingly, almost twice as common as in Britain in general.[6] Asthma, another affliction at least partly of nervous origin, is also unusually widespread and severe (necessitating admission to hospital) among both men and women.[1, 6, 61] Even alcoholism – or perhaps merely worry about alcoholism (by no means necessarily at variance with a dominant legacy of abstinence) – seems to be considerably more rampant, for in 1955–6 over three times as many Welsh patients as in England apparently consulted their doctors for this.[1] It looks as if the anxieties of an overburdened conscience only serve to aggravate a natural inborn melancholy. The 'Celts' may come more vigorously and violently alive than the English, but they seem to pay a price for this by plunging more deeply into illusion and depression.

Ill-health as a whole, indeed, is so much more widespread in Wales than in the remainder of Britain, and particularly in the mining areas, that it almost seems as if the Welsh had less all-round resistance, psychological no less than physical. Certainly, it is hard to continue to lay all the blame on the Depression and the malnutrition that resulted, for in the insurance year 1961–2 *all age-groups* of men under 55 had periods off work, requiring medical certificates, 36–40 per cent more than the national average.[6] A check by the Ministry of Pensions and National Insurance failed to find any evidence of lower standards among doctors in Wales in the issuing of certificates – but assuming they are no less ready than elsewhere to issue one when given a fair reason, they only need to be pestered more frequently to give rise to these high figures. Without some temperamental predisposition it is hard to see why Welsh miners should fall off work so much more commonly than miners in, say, County Durham. In any case, though the Rhondda Valley has easily the worst rates for incapacity of any place in Britain, even Swansea, well away from the mining area, had a rate in 1961–2 considerably above the average.[6] Nor is the ill-health by any means confined to men. Welsh women – relatively few of whom, it should be remembered, go out to work – appear to consult their doctors more than women in other regions,[89] and to enter hospital in abnormally high numbers for skin infections and much more, even, for burns.[61] From this last fact it rather looks as if they may be more accident-prone in general, even perhaps more careless. And here the shocking figures for infant mortality[5] are highly relevant. Wales follows hard on the heels of the North West for deaths in and around birth, and actually has the worst rates, significantly, for deliveries at home. A higher proportion of babies die from pulmonary infections than anywhere else in Britain. Stillbirths, too, continually achieve the maximum levels – and especially, again, in the case of home confinements. Are they looked after as well as they could be, one wonders? So recently as 1946 very few births in Wales took place in hospital[99] (in 1937 no more than 2 per cent of those in Anglesey) and it may be that injurious practices, based on old wives' tales, have simply had less chance as yet to be stamped out here by the spread of modern knowledge. Expenditure on baby-wear, it should be noticed, is persistently extremely low, bearing in mind the larger than average number of babies that are born here overall. Clearly, the figures suggest that the whole pattern of infant care in Wales deserves careful study. Poor housing conditions are obviously a big potential source of damage; and although these are probably no worse here than in Lancashire or Scotland, it may be that the damper climate intervenes to render them just that much more lethal.

Atmospheric pollution, however, is the one factor that cannot be invoked to explain Welsh illness in general – despite the high incidence of most respiratory diseases, including bronchitis. Sulphur-dioxide levels in Wales are markedly low, for Welsh coal has a relatively small sulphur content and the coastal towns are well ventilated by sea-breezes. For the present, medical statisticians have to confess to remaining puzzled.

V

The Midlands

The Midlands is the least well known, yet quite the most fascinating, of all the regions of Britain. Midlanders, for the most part inarticulate people, have always been slow to sing its praises. Southerners regard it as part of the North, Northerners lump it with the South. It has no geographical distinctions or traditional notorieties, no Ilkley Moor or Brighton Pier, nothing that would make one exclaim 'The Midlands!' as a kind of reflex action.

In a great many ways the stereotype is true of a featureless 'middle land', a zone of smooth transition. This has tempted people to view the region as nothing other than the national mean – a view further encouraged by its psychologically suggestive central position. In past years, accordingly, it was often picked out as an ideal test market. From certain points of view this undoubtedly makes much sense: it eliminates the extremes. The Midlands is a region, for example, with a marked excess of middle-sized incomes and correspondingly few that are conspicuously high or low;[75] very small and very large houses are also rarer here than in the rest of the country. But even in this role, of the intermediate area occupying the mid-point on the national scales, it can prove deceptive. For when North and South do differ, the Midlands is not always a region of simple overlap, where one characteristic gradually gives out and is equally gradually replaced by another: sometimes it works out an ingenious new compromise all its own. The method of boiling green vegetables is an example. In the North these are put into cold water, which is then heated; in the South, perpetually in a hurry, into water brought to the boil already. The Midlanders, taking a leaf out of both books, impartially content themselves with water that is merely hot.[9] With practices that allow of no such original reformulation, that can only either be accepted or rejected, some intriguing grafting operations tend to take place instead. The best example of this known to the author has, unfortunately, never been quantified, at least in any survey so far published; one cannot therefore be wholly certain of its validity. It has to do with the use of table-napkins. In the South these seem to be brought out more or less exclusively for meals of the dining-room type involving savoury foods (and, by implication, knives and forks); namely, breakfast, lunch and evening dinner. In the North the pattern is the same except that the equivalent knife-and-fork meal in the evening is known as 'tea'. Middle-class Midlanders, infected from the North with the notion that table-napkins must invariably accompany 'tea', accordingly produce them for the four o'clock meal that is the Southerners' version of this word – and so become the only people to introduce them into sitting-rooms for dealing mainly with jam and cakes. This could, of course, affect the potential for paper napkins; it might also lead to the adoption of separate sets of table linen, maybe in different styles and colours, for use in the sitting-room as distinct from the dining-room. In just such a way a small, seemingly trivial new regional departure, perhaps a spontaneous mutation, perhaps a viable hybrid, can throw up an important new market. Occasionally, even, such novelties spread beyond the original regional borders. When this happens, in the case of the Midlands there develops a strikingly distinctive national pattern which may for convenience be termed the 'central bulge': a marked peak across the central belt of England with a fairly sharp fall-off both northwards

H

and southwards. Two examples of this are the frequency of papered kitchen ceilings[69] and the making of damson jam.[44]

To confound the picture even further, the Midlands has an awkward tendency to side decisively with the South in certain respects and equally decisively with the North in others. Thus its weakness for stone fruit, natural cheese, and dining room tables is utterly Southern; its liking for malt bread and vitamin tablets,[8] its avoidance of letter-writing, the lack of interest of its husbands in the decorating scheme of bedrooms,[69] the drawing of blinds after death,[23] are all quintessentially Northern – or, more precisely, North English. It spends as little as the North on insuring its homes, but as much as the South on protecting itself against sickness and accidents. From the front it can pass itself off as a second South East, lashing out, impressively, on rose-bushes[10] and mustard, carrying aspirins around,[8] and even dying of ulcers. From behind it shows itself tied to the North West, far more tautly, sharing Lancashire's excess of small shops, its delight in bootees, its avoidance of jelly-like jams[44] and gladioli,[10] its itch to paper ceilings instead of painting them white,[69] its huge tea consumption. If its face often seems rather dashing, its inner self is yet homely and scarcely modish.

This area, sandwiched uncomfortably between two much more confident parts of the country, consists of two Standard Regions, the West Midlands and the East (or, misleadingly, North) Midlands, with a combined population of nearly eight and three-quarter million, rather larger than the total of Greater London and amounting to roughly one Briton in every six. The West Midlands, with over a million more inhabitants than its associate, packs in its people much more tightly, very nearly half being found in the conurbation centred on Birmingham.

As usual, therefore, the picture presented by sample surveys is predominantly a picture of the people in the cities and largest towns: Birmingham and the Black

Country, the Potteries, Coventry, Rugby, Derby, Nottingham, Leicester, Northampton. This matters more in this region than in most. For the rural population differs from the urban and industrial not only in the predictable range of tastes and habits but, even more markedly, in its very physique. This can be seen most clearly by taking a bus, say, from Birmingham into Worcestershire. To begin with the passengers, in so far as their voices indicate a local origin, will be for the most part typical 'Brummies': small, slightly built, wiry people with dark hair, narrow heads and sharp, almost chiselled, features, their accent a faintly sing-song, often rasping nasal twang. At about Studley a totally new type of person will start to come on board: stocky, muscular, broad-headed, flattish-faced, talking deep down in the throat with a comforting Loamshire burr. The first type, one might say, is a fox-terrier, the second a bulldog. They represent two quite separate racial stocks, which for centuries have kept their identities by constant inbreeding. The bulldogs are the descendants of the Saxon farmers who settled on the rich soils of the river-valleys; the fox-terriers are the modern version of the Saxons' predecessors, the old native British stock, penned up in the vast wedge of forests – Arden and Needwood, Charnwood and Rockingham – that formerly covered the entire central Midlands, their land unwanted by several waves of invaders, because the heavy clay soils made it too intractable for agriculture. The two followed different ways of life and doubtless seldom met or intermarried. Their essential distinctness has accordingly been preserved. That the population of Britain is now so inextricably mixed that all the old racial outlines have been obscured is a vulgar error, comparatively recent in growth: it is merely that we refuse to look. Dr. John Beddoe, the author of the classic work on the races of Britain,[110] published as long ago as 1885 but yet to be supplanted, and one of the very few who have ever stared hard and long at our heads and faces, certainly had no difficulty in spotting this exceptional darkness of features when he came to study the central Midland strip. Hardly anyone else has attended to it since; but the evidence is still there, obvious to any experienced eye.

In going out today into the streets of any central Midland town or city the first reaction of any normally perceptive person can hardly fail to be one of momentary surprise, even shock. Almost everyone, it seems, looks remarkably alike. At least, compared with other areas of this kind in England (Tyneside perhaps excepted) the people do on the whole look distinctly similar, very much of one physical type.

At some point in history, the small fox-terriers, this isolated pocket of the 'Old Black Breed', must have crept out of their forests quietly and all-unnoticed; and from a background as charcoal-burners and tanners they became skilled in the fashioning of iron and leather. From saddles and stirrups they moved on to saucepans and guns, from these on to bicycle parts, and from these on to cars. The story is long and complicated, and the full details can be left to the economic historians and geographers. Enough is known, however, to suggest with some conclusiveness that the industries for which this region became most famed arose naturally more or less *in situ*. It is therefore reasonable to suppose that the population did so too, handing down the secrets of their trades from one generation to another and for obvious reasons hardly welcoming outsiders. Thus, by accident, the ancestral strain ran pure.

That the urban Midlanders really do share a common background in heredity to a most impressive extent has recently been confirmed by some unimpeachable evidence from genetics. Detailed mapping of the blood-groups of the ABO system[111] reveals that a tongue of abnormally high levels of blood-group O protrudes southwards into the central Midlands, down to Coventry and Northampton, from its main area of distribution north of the Humber-Mersey line.[112] High frequencies of this blood-group are characteristic of the Celtic-speaking peoples of Britain and reappear round the coasts of South Europe and North Africa, where much the same physical type recurs: a specialised branch of the Mediterranean Race, one of the three great subdivisions of the 'white' race recognised by anthropologists. The first settlers to colonise Britain in any numbers in prehistoric times, who thereby formed its basic racial substratum, came here from South Europe and were predominantly of this general stock, short and dark and slender-featured – in all essential respects, our Midland fox-terriers.

Without this knowledge of the distinctive racial background, it is almost impossible to understand much that is most important in the Midland personality. Its effects, inevitably, have varied in their straightforwardness. The most readily apparent are, as usual, the bodily ones. Height, for example: the urban Midlander tends on the whole to be lacking in stature, so much so that the pictures in the City Art Gallery in Birmingham are deliberately hung low down. For the same reason Midland women are less keen than elsewhere on wearing heel-less shoes. 'High heels are not meant to add to Woman's beauty, but only to her stature', our leading costume historian[113] has assured us. The women, in fact, are generally petite, with the small hips that this implies, and with little of the Northern tendency to run to fat. They can therefore dispense with the heaviest types of corsets and have figures that look well in dresses, which they buy in specially large numbers at the expense of separates and ensembles. The 'Sack' line is reported to have sold much better in Birmingham than in any other city in Britain.[92] Sallow skins, however, force them, by a small margin, to be the widest users of rouge.

But, more important, this particular type of build also seems to imply a particular type of temperament to go with it. In the terminology of the classification most widely subscribed to, that of Sheldon, the urban Midlanders are decidedly 'ectomorphs', with small-boned, skinny builds; and also, by association, 'cerebrotones', tending to be highly strung and moody and inhibited. This constitutional type, with its wiriness and unusually sensitive reactions, appears to have developed in response to life in cities; certainly it seems to thrive in those of Britain, possibly, it has been suggested, due to a natural selective advantage. It would seem to have, though, obvious weaknesses as well as strengths; in that it cannot, evidently, stand up to too much battering, particularly at critical periods in life like early childhood and adolescence.

In both of these, a good deal of evidence appears to suggest, the average Midlander has suffered disablement; and almost everything that is so special about his behaviour seems interpretable as an attempt, in one way or another, at compensation.

Two root causes of this seem to be identifiable. The first, the older and more profound, resides in the Midlanders' native dexterity, the manipulative skill that makes this a zone of born mechanics, renowned for their love of 'ondling' everything with a craftsman's appreciative finger. That the metal trades first sprang to prominence in Britain in this region has an air about it of historical inevitability, given plentiful iron deposits so happily located by nature in the midst of people accustomed, since at least the fourteenth century, to a self-supporting craft economy[114] and with such a heredity of nimble hands. Today, in the West Midlands, 53 per cent of the workpeople are employed in manufacturing (38 per cent is the United Kingdom average) and three-quarters of these are involved in some way or other with the production or use of metals. Obsessive tinkerers, inevitably they also make excellent home-handymen. 'Do-it-yourself' claims two Midlanders out of every three, as against just under half the population in Britain in general. Electric drills are as popular as would be expected but, significantly, wood-work tends to be avoided: it is machinery that matters, the more complicated the better. The money, fortunately, is usually no problem. A high percentage of the washing-machines are of the twin-tub variety; lawn-mowers are power-driven twice as commonly as usual; vehicles are crammed with awe-inspiring knobs and switches. The region is motor-conscious on an almost transatlantic scale, and for years outpaced the rest of Britain in the extent of owning cars, due to the large numbers that percolated down to manual workers. Those employed in the car factories may have benefited to some extent from discounts, though conditions in this respect have always been more stringent than the outside public tends to suppose. In any case, looking for an explanation for this in economics is quite unnecessary, for cars here have a golden aura and acquiring one has long had exceptional priority. The passion for powerful motor-cycles, ridden earlier than in the South East and abandoned earlier – presumably for that more desirable object, a car – only serves to confirm this. Rather more men than elsewhere, perhaps as a result, die in crashes.

But this connoisseurship of mechanisms, admirable within limits, tends to be taken much too far. A mere skill, just because it prevails so generally here and promises success and prosperity, enjoys a valuation as inflated as it is grossly undeserved. Other, more important things in life, less simply measurable in hard cash, are disregarded or even totally dispensed with. Book-learning, in particular, seems held in low esteem. In every respect the Midland performance in education is worse than in the South. The proportion staying on at school after passing the official leaving-age, especially among girls, is noticeably low: as in London, for the early leaver the lure of easy money is all-corrosive. Little is spent on college or school fees; there are few booksellers per head; and, in a region of lavish present-givers, many more people than one would expect fail to own even a fountain-pen. Few books are read, particularly by men,[31] and markedly few general magazines – especially if, like the *Reader's Digest*, they appear to demand any reasonable mental exertion. Of all the magazines with a sizeable circulation one alone has a disproportionately strong Midland following and that, naturally enough, is *Car Mechanics*. No wonder Birmingham spends so little per head on public libraries[115] and, unlike Merthyr Tydfil or Stoke-on-Trent (not obviously less salubrious places), suffers from a chronically acute shortage of school-teachers.

The Midlander's intelligence, one is tempted to suppose, becomes all too often concentrated in the hands. The risk then is that the personality may become machine-like itself, unable to register feelings with a proper range and depth. 'You can always tell the Midlanders,' a Blackpool hotel proprietor was recently reported as claiming: 'they're the ones who never look as if they're enjoying themselves.'[116]

So much for the first source of trouble. The second, possibly more recent in origin, and related to the too machine-like approach to life, must have made the Midlands a rewardingly fertile field for Puritanism. Gorer[21] found 12 per cent in this region regarding them-selves as Methodists, the second highest proportion in England – and doubtless seriously understated in view of the youthful bias of his sample – and, as in the even more strongly Nonconformist North East, a heavy emphasis on paternal authority. Fundamentalism here has bitten unusually deep. But it is a fundamentalism, as in Wales, of a distinctive type: a grey and joyless faith, a fire with very few distracting sparks. It stresses retribution, not abstinence; it is a religion of gloom and guilt, of The Wages-of-Sin-is-Death, a religion assuring damnation for all infringing its absolute commandments. Through and through can be heard reverberating the tones of an all-powerful, awe-inspiring father-figure, a Jehovah on high, seated eternally in judgement – the projection (surely it is not too far-fetched to suggest?) of the average Midland father, terrifyingly enlarged and distorted; the typical parent in this region that insists most fervently that children should be brought up hard, that most demands for them sterner and stronger discipline,[21] that trusts in the catharsis of 'a good, sound thrashing'. This is a region that favours violent measures and drastic solutions. And far more than elsewhere in England, its working class believes in responding vigorously to marital unfaithfulness and thoroughly approves, if need be, of divorce.[21]

For a delicate nervous make-up such a setting is, to put it mildly, scarcely encouraging. Instead of the gentle reassurance that it properly needs and deserves, it is likely to be crushed and trampled on, brutally and clumsily. All too many Midlanders, therefore, may thus receive unusually severe emotional scars, which they carry with them throughout the rest of life.

The apparent effects of this can be seen today in aspect after aspect of Midland life, evidenced by an all-pervading nervous tension. On the more obvious, purely physical level there are, for example, the abundant difficulties evidently experienced here by the women in childbirth. The West Midlands has the highest death rate in Britain among infants born in hospital,[5] and in one sample year, 1955–6, its general practitioners reported eight times as many consultations in connection with abnormal delivery as in the London and South East Standard Region. Then, too, there is the Midland concern with pain. In a typical survey on how minor ailments are treated[8] no other region harps on the word to anything like the same extent: it is the Midlanders, above all, who insist they would resort to a doctor 'if the pain continued' or 'if the pain got worse'. In surveys about ordinary, everyday domestic equipment it is the Midlanders, time and time again, who without any prompting mention the risk of accidents. For just this reason, presumably, this fear of what might just conceivably happen, they own disproportionately few electric blankets.

The worrying extends as well to health. In an average year the West Midlands tops the national league in visits paid to doctors; to complain of such afflictions as head-aches, rashes, constipation, colds, sinusitis, gout, obesity and what enter the medical records as 'anxiety states without bodily symptoms'.[1] Clearly, Midlanders pester their doctors more than people elsewhere about matters that are largely trivial,[8] and are more inclined to race round to them at the slightest suggestion of trouble. No wonder that doctors (and dentists too), like the school-teachers, are in specially short supply here.[117] Probably the patients have to be rebuffed all too often – certainly they bear telltale signs of a hurt defensiveness, being readier than elsewhere to cite batteries of reasons to justify their visits.[8] More often than not, however, they seem to come away empty-handed, for sales of medicines only to be obtained on prescriptions ('ethicals') are reported to be unduly low here. Accordingly they have to fall back on self-treatment and this they do in no uncer-tain manner. The region, in consequence, is one great pharmacopoeia of patent remedies – the more old-fashioned, one suspects, the more highly regarded.[118] The people here are the greatest tablet-takers in the kingdom, particularly, it seems, for stomach upsets,[8] though this is heavily at the expense of dosing themselves with mixtures from bottles. They treat their bodies as they treat their machines: all the better for a thorough going-over, with frequent oilings and greasings. They revel, so to speak, in 'ondling' themselves and take a morbid delight in exchanging the minutiae of ailments with fellow-sufferers.

'Good for health' is emphasised especially in this region as a reason for eating vegetables.[2] This leads us on to consider the remarkable Midland pattern of eating and drinking. 'Everything they do is done hard', a writer on the Black Country has written;[119] they work hard while they are on the job, and they eat, drink and play hard. In this they display, surely, the peculiarly desperate energy of people who have to function with the brakes half on, who labour under the handicap of nervous overdrive. They need to have someone to tell them to relax, even if it is only the tobacco manufacturers. Those who smoke cigarettes tend to smoke extremely heavily, rather than to savour the finer qualities of tobacco; for the brands they buy are distinctly on the cheap side and, despite the fact that they are usually well-off, they buy the shortest lengths much more than elsewhere.

It is the same with drink. The Midlands spends more on beer and gets through more of it than anywhere else in Britain. In the licensed clubs half-pints are most uncommon and consumption is huge: in Coventry clubs eight to ten pints per head per night is not at all unusual. Nearly all of this is draught mild. Pint bottles of lemonade are often bought to produce a shandy, particularly at lunchtimes, but on the whole the drinking has little variety. Lager, cider, table wines, rum – all find few takers, and the proportion drinking whisky (oddly, very often here with hot water) is only average. Pint after pint, steadily and monotonously: this is the pattern. The Midlanders drink to fuel themselves just as they would their cars at petrol-pumps; not, like the Scots, to grow fiercely drunk. Even so, this is the one region in England that lays particular stress on drink as a cause of unhappy marriages.[21]

One would think that with all this beer in them Midlanders could hardly bear to be faced with a further drop of anything. Far from it. Their heavy consumption of tea has been alluded to already; they also drink a great deal of milk – much of it sterilised, for some reason that has never been satisfactorily explained[120] – as well as the greatest amount of liquid coffee essences in Britain. This last, a Midland quirk of long standing, made the region unusually resistant at first to the onslaught of the instant, powdered varieties. Finally, they still manage to find room for branded milk drinks on a scale comparing well with Southern England.

How, one may well ask, can they possibly absorb all this? It is almost like that classic turn among clowns in which gallons and gallons are poured into somebody down a funnel and not a drop, mysteriously, ever seems to leak out. Part of the answer must lie in the highest incidence here of elevenses (mainly just a hot drink on its own), which in this region, very confusingly, is still often known as 'lunch' – the 'slight repast between morning meals' in the older, seventeenth-century meaning of this word. For the rest, however, one can only invoke a vanishing trick worthy of the cleverest illusionist.

Drinking is the only activity not to have been affected (or so they claim, and they are doubtless right) by the Midlanders' obsession with television.[31] People here scrambled to buy sets from the very first and have stayed glued to them ever since. Compared with other regions, they had 'no particular reason'; they 'just wanted' sets.[31] And having secured them, they have served them with much more devotion than elsewhere, unselectively and indiscriminately. They are possessed, it would seem, by a kind of screen-mania: watching everything and anything that will help to nourish a visual famine, for their root trouble, surely, is a starvation of imagery. They might do better, in view of this, to sample the films at the cinema more often: their audiences, at present, consist of the under-twenties to a more disproportionate extent than anywhere else in Britain.

The pattern that emerges in beer-drinking is detectable again when we come to scrutinise the Midland diet. Basically, this is remarkable only for a rather stodgy unimaginativeness. The staple items, the dreary norm of English cooking, are given ponderous emphasis: great hunks of meat, lavish helpings of peas and cabbage, apple pies[45] by the plateful, interminable quantities of tasteless shop bread. The meat is mainly lamb or pork, seldom beef or the inexpensive mutton – in this respect, as in much else, the Midlands being the precise opposite of Scotland. Pork chops and pork (as opposed to beef) sausages are especial favourites, pastas a pet dislike. Little soup or fish is eaten, rather few eggs – doubtless because they bake so seldom – and, because of the absence of a sweet tooth, fewer cakes and biscuits than anywhere else in the country.

But though the centre of the diet appears drab and monotonous, as if Midlanders scarcely noticed what they ate, the edges, by contrast, are excitingly pungent. Pickles, for instance: pickled onions, pickled cabbage and pickled walnuts are all great Midland favourites; and their acidity – at least in the Black Country – is reported to be twice as high as is customary in London.[121] Strong Cheddar very often accompanies them, eaten in solid chunks, the soft, easily spreading cheeses being traditionally in low demand in this region.[39] Spending on vinegar is the highest in the country, despite the fact that Midland food also tends to be torrentially anointed with gravy, tomato ketchup and intensely acid Worcester sauce – this last, as its name implies, one of the very few (and, in a palatal sense, so eminently fitting) original contributions from the Midlands to the British national diet. Canned tomatoes, for years bought in the East Midlands on a puzzlingly extensive scale, are reputed to owe this popularity to their use as an uncommonly full-bodied kind of sauce. The trend to bitterness even turns up in the beer, the Midland 'mild' being noticeably less so than that drunk in the South. Rum and aniseed (vulgarly 'rum and ani') is one of several liquid concoctions more or less peculiar to the Midlands that might also be mentioned.

The tendency towards sourness is even more general, however, than these few facts suggest, for there is a compensating shortfall in the opposite direction, towards the sweeter end of the taste-scale. Sales are poor of most sweet things, such as cakes, fruit, fruit juices, cider, sweet biscuits, sweet pastry, and all sweet spreads not even excluding jam. The place of sweet spreads is taken partly by meat extracts and partly by cheese and pickles, which in areas like Nottingham are even eaten for breakfast, a meal in the Midlands often quite devoid of jam or marmalade and with an altogether savoury tang to it. All in all, there is probably less sugar in the diet;[122] but calculating the truth in this respect is difficult, due to the fact that the Midlanders use exceptional quantities in sweetening their tea and coffee. In this they resemble at least one other people, the Brazilians, who also over-fill their cups with sugar though they imbibe great amounts of quite sour beer. To complicate matters further, there is evidence that the Midland aversion to alcoholic drinks of any sweetness is not without its exceptions. It has been reported, for instance, that housewives in this region are distinctly partial to liqueurs for elevenses.[123] There are other examples that have yet to be publicly divulged. From this it would appear that it is sharpness, irrespective of whether this is sweet or sour, that is aimed at first and foremost. The primary purpose, presumably – and this would fit in neatly with our general thesis – is to subject the palate to continual convulsive shocks, for it seems that the Midland mouth (like the Midland eyes that stare so fixedly at television) is insensitive and as the penalty for this can taste only faintly. Subordinate to this, perhaps (and tilting the taste-scale so that the sharp stressing falls at the one end much more often than at the other), there may also be a quite separate bias towards sourness. But whether this springs from hereditary biochemistry or from mere conditioning and upbringing or, as is most probable of all, from an inextricable fusion of the two, it is quite impossible to be sure, in the present state of scientific knowledge of this very neglected subject. We certainly do know, however, from study of identical twins living apart, that the degree of taste sensitivity is, at base at least, an inherited character; and it is tempting to suggest, unprovable though the point may be, that this distinctive, sour-biased palate of the Midlanders, so different from that of most of the rest of Britain and so suspiciously similar to that of Mediterranean peoples, may be one more part of their peculiar racial legacy. Whatever the truth of the matter, social or physical causes quite apart, the taste bias is an undoubted fact and clearly deep-seated. Manufacturers ignore it at their peril.

One further feature of the Midland menu that cannot be allowed to pass unnoticed is the ever-increasing reliance on 'convenience' foods of every kind. Cans have no special *mana* in this region, either good or bad; they are merely seen as simple, handy and quick, the obvious answer for any modern young housewife with little enough time to spare to cook. There is little concern about food values, for this is not a region that dedicates itself to 'Good Cooking'. Even before the war Birmingham, out of all the major British cities, showed the least interest in cookery books.[71] There is less home-baking, indeed, than almost anywhere; and even cakes are not very often made from packet-mixes, but bought from shops. Ready-made foods, equally, are rarely condemned for lacking in flavour, for most food here is sadly undertasted: flavour is something poured on later, out of a bottle. Kitchen skills, altogether, are at a discount, illustrated by the lowest interest in methods of preparing and serving vegetables.[2] The only vegetables, in fact, that Midland housewives *are* prepared to take much trouble with are fresh peas, of which the region has the heaviest consumption in Britain. Even this may be accounted for by the fact that the tedium of shelling can so readily be delegated to husbands or children. Salads, typically, are a popular standby for the evening meal,[45] accounting for the high absorption of ham and the above-average intake of canned fish (such as salmon) of a fairly substantial and expensive type.

The reason, of course, is that so many wives in this region have jobs outside their homes. The Midlands has a history of prosperity extending back many years, the industries are highly diversified, and there have long been jobs for married women and no strong bias, apparently, against their taking them. And they themselves have seldom hesitated, for they seem to be less emotionally involved in the cult of domesticity than married women in most of the rest of Britain. They cook little, knit little[90] and sew little,[31] though they are well enough supplied with all the latest domestic gadgets. The home is less sharply identified as the woman's domain, and husbands do rather more of the housework than elsewhere. In return the husband's domain is more widely invaded: wives descend on the garden,[10] elbow their way into the home decorating,[69] join the circle at the pub. They are half in the home and half out of it – and end up by committing themselves to neither world wholeheartedly. Without sufficient concerns of their own they attempt to share their husbands', but too often must succeed only in pestering them or in getting under their feet. One result is that each sex tends to grow tired of the other on a purely social level, and at parties there occurs that curious segregation of the two at opposite ends of rooms, better known as a feature of Australia, the Scottish Lowlands or Dublin.

Ironically, it is less essential here for wives to work than anywhere else in Britain. Basic living costs are nowhere near as high as in the equally prosperous South East, entertainment cheaper (if far less copious), and property prices on the whole much lower. A disproportionately high proportion of families, furthermore, rent subsidised local council housing: 36 per cent in the West Midland conurbation, against 20 per cent in Greater London and no more than 28 per cent even on Merseyside, surely a much more deserving case. The post-war prosperity of the region has attracted immigrants from all other parts of the country; the Midland cities and towns have been expanding rapidly and the pressure on the councils to build has been all the greater in view of the high percentage of the newcomers possessing young families. (The average household, especially in the east of the region, is unusually large in size and council houses in the Midlands have had to be built with three bedrooms on a greater scale than anywhere else.) Earnings, for years, have been substantially above the national average and, what is more, have grown steadily better. Workers in the Midlands are estimated to have doubled their earnings lead of the rest of the country in the period 1957–64. Incomes per household (already above average due to the number of earners they contain) are now higher even than in London and the South East, and no less than 13 per cent above the average for Great Britain. However, these are more dependent on manufacturing than elsewhere and geared to the prosperity of one major industry, which makes them more than ordinarily vulnerable to even minor recessions. All production and consumption, in the West Midlands especially, even down to the birth-rate, tend to oscillate more violently than elsewhere, corresponding exactly to the ups and downs of the motor industry as that in turn, over the last ten years, has moved to the jerkiness of the bank rate. The Midlanders' affluence, vigorously buoyant though it may seem at first glance, is in reality precarious and insecurely based. And this may account for some at least of the frantic strenuousness with which money in this region is both pursued and spent, as though the prevailing mentality, as in Lancashire, has become rigidly attuned to the nerve-racking rhythm of sudden boom and slump, producing a hardened disbelief in the permanence of prosperity and a determination to make the most of it while the chance still exists.

Is this really enough, however, to explain the peculiar intensity of the 'consumption fever' that holds the Midlands in its grip? Is there not perhaps some extra, deeper

I

motive that impels the Midlander to lavish possessions on himself with such inordinate abandon? Life here may have its ups and downs, but prosperity on the whole has been far more continuous than in, say, Lancashire or Scotland. Yet the acquisitiveness goes on, if anything more fiercely than before – and in a chronic atmosphere of strain, with little obvious sign of contentment at the end. There is an irritable restlessness, a furious energy expended in a vacuum, which is seemingly most marked of all in just that section of the community that has been most dramatically enriched and materially transformed: the emergent 'blue-collar' middle class, so graphically depicted in Graham Turner's book *The Car Makers*[124]. If it was solely a hedonistic urge that demanded to be satisfied, to make up for a previous deprivation of sensory pleasures and worldly goods, that phase surely, in all reasonableness, would by now have passed.

There must therefore be, one is driven to conclude, some other kind of deprivation, of a more deep-seated character, which obsesses the Midlander and goads him on. His 'over-consumption', it would seem more likely, is not so much for the concrete gratifications that he thereby purchases but for the internal reassurance that this somehow manages to bring. And to find a reason to such need for reassurance, we do not have far to look if our earlier thesis is right: we can find it in the average Midland upbringing, with its over-dominance by a heavy-handed father. The Midlanders, one might say, remain eternally anxious offspring engaged in continuing open-ended self-justification to long-departed parents. To find themselves, they need to have powerful anti-figures: people against whom to measure themselves, consistently and emphatically.

Unhappily, within the larger social context obtaining in this region clear-cut opposing authority is in awkwardly short supply. The upper and upper-middle classes are seriously under-represented (reflected in the surprisingly low ownership of telephones), whereas the skilled working-class segment accounts for 43 per cent of the households as against only 36 per cent in Britain in general. Prosperity has arrived here within too ill-defined a social framework. There are too many *arrivistes* frustratedly exultant outside too few acceptably superior social doors – more simply, not enough people to flourish one's success at. A great deal that somehow seems wrong today in the Midlands appears to be explicable in terms of this basic hiatus. Because of it, the fruits of effort tend to emerge as empty and illusory; and all the striving runs to waste in a desert of senseless dynamism, no less barren and self-deceiving than the transatlantic cult of hustle.

Lacking a local upper crust that is either obvious or considerable, the Midlanders in recent years have tended to fall back, rather despairingly, on copying the South. But having acquired its latest novelties, they seem at a loss, all too often, to know what to do with them. The new Bull Ring shopping centre in Birmingham is surely typical: erected to great fanfares, but noticeably cold-shouldered by the local populace immediately upon completion. The pleasure seems to lie in the idea of newness, in being seen to be sophisticated, rather than in the actual experience of consumption. The South and its ways are things to be fondled, gingerly but admiringly, in the belief that good somehow or other will result from the mere contact. It is to the far South of England, as a matter of course, that so many holidaymakers from this region year after year now choose to journey, as if there, and there alone, is to be found some vital essence waiting to be soaked up through the pores by some miraculous osmosis. Come summer, a great motorcade leaves for the South Coast in an irresistible downward surge, a massive *Drang nach Süden*, like a collective regression, strewing Midlanders – unsurpassed in their devotion to camping and caravanning – all over an innocent, unsuspecting countryside. The routes are traditional now and the trails, alas, well blazed. In the summer of 1958 a thousand empty milk-bottles every week were cleared from the New Forest, most of them emanating unambiguously from Birmingham.[125] Two seasons later, during the fortnight when the Midland car factories annually close down, anti-litter wardens in Devon reported a sudden trebling in wayside rubbish.[126] This is hardly the behaviour of people on a pilgrimage with a clear idea of what it is they come to worship.

Yet use-and-throw-away is the standard treatment for most material goods in the Midlands. This is decidedly not a region for make-do-and-mend, for hoarding in case of need, for darning or patching. Few factory workers in Coventry, it is said, ever bother to have their shoes repaired: they buy a new pair instead.[127] The Midland housewife, similarly, will throw away her vegetable water, instead of using it for stock or sauces, more often than her sisters to north or south.[9] She will be less ready to decry extravagance,[3] slopping around disinfectants[128] and cleaning chemicals with excessively carefree abandon, and buying ampler measures of food at a time on expeditions to the grocer. Midlanders stock up rather than shop, spending in fearsome lunges. They like to see their purses exploding, revel in tossing notes and coins around and watching them work their effects, unashamedly. Children here receive the most pocket-money[21] and much more than elsewhere is spent on toys. Wardrobes are constantly replenished; cars, naturally, changed for a new model most often;[78] curtains, carpets and linoleum all renewed more speedily. Kitchen ceilings, even, are continually being re-papered:[68] a most revealingly symbolic activity. This is a society of discarders, in which people race to alter outward appearances in default of competitions in subtler refinement. Life is like a screen filled with flickering pictures. It has no depth – and cannot have, just so long as people show so little involvement in their surroundings. There can be no real sense of homeliness while houses are treated like furniture repositories or occupied like waiting-rooms. This is a pathological defect, with a recognised name: 'shallow living'; and it must be both a cause and effect, once more, of the widespread feelings of insecurity.

Behind everything here, behind all the surface glitter, the futile bustling, the restless chopping and changing, signs are evident on every hand of a widespread, even general, sensory numbness. Something, quite simply, is lacking in the Midlanders' powers of awareness. Their perceptions seem to be oddly distorted. Their colour sense, for example: a gaudy rainbow of sickly greens and bilious blues, shocking pinks and lurid purples – hues of a primitive violence, the poster-paints that betray a shrieking unconscious. A generation or more ago, long before the present national reversion to dandyism, Black Country men were famed for their brilliantly checked flannel shirts, their women for glossy satins.[119] Today, as likely as not, the men will turn up to work in yellow shoes; while the women buy more rayon blouses than elsewhere and much the most satin girdles. The situation shows no change; with so much more money around, it is now merely far more obtrusive. For years on end, according to one manufacturer's figures,[15] Midland women have distinguished themselves by a special demand for blue lingerie. Blue, unusually, is a favourite colour too for bedrooms and kitchens – chosen in this region largely by wives; yellow is also popular for bedrooms, but muted greys and creams firmly rejected.[68] Green, on the other hand, is said to be a difficult colour to sell for dresses in Birmingham.[129] Were more to be published on this tantalising topic, we should certainly find that the Midlanders differ from the rest of the country in their choices time and time again. And at least there is this to be said: they are splendidly audacious colour choices and help to brighten up a world that is all too drab and sombre.

In order to account for this, one sometimes hears it suggested that Midlanders have a strong gypsy streak in their make-up. But this is surely over-ingenious, and in any case unnecessary. Tension, once again, is a sufficient explanation in itself. These colours that almost make one gasp, these jazzily unnerving designs and patterns, are merely the shredded remnants of a quite plain and ordinary aesthetic sense that has to be brutally put through a mangle. Their purpose is utterly basic: to shout and attract. We cannot expect subtleties from people who seem so cut off from their deeper selves and so blind and deaf to all nudges and hinting.

Clothes play the same tune, if less staccato. As in the houses, it is the public parts, the areas most often exposed to view and lending themselves to the most rapid and cheapest changes, that win most attention financially. The men spend heavily on ties and socks, on shoes, and on trousers and topcoats; the women on summer dresses and sweaters, on highly styled stockings, on brassières – an unusually high proportion of them stiffened – and seductive slips, though less than one would expect on shoes, and puzzlingly little on coats or jackets.

The end is to strut, flauntingly and provocatively, with the stop-go teasing of human traffic-lights. All the effort goes to the surface. In dark contrast, the nether regions, the areas nearest to the machine room, can be almost equally resoundingly unglamorous. Almost three women out of every four in Birmingham, for example, irrespective of their social class, confess to wearing vests – two out of three of them all the year round.[83]

Most surprising of all is the extraordinary outburst of fashion-consciousness here among women in their early forties. From marriage until the age of 39, dress budgets have to be kept in check or severely trimmed. By 40, however, children for the most part are off their parents' hands and all of a sudden wives find themselves once more temptingly and excitingly flush with money. And to an extent unknown elsewhere in Britain, they spend this on beautifying themselves while there still remain some years in which this continues to hold attractions. Nature, happily, normally proves kind to them: thanks to their racial heredity they tend to preserve their figures or, at least, their legs. Stockings, especially, feature among their purchases; so do slips and nightdresses – in styles of fantastic, unexpected allure and daring. Manufacturers, for years, assumed that the highly *outré* types of slips that sold in this region in such eyebrow-raising quantities were invariably bought by teenagers. They were dumbfounded when it turned out where most of them in actual fact were going: to the teenagers' mothers. Even after 45 the use of lipstick is heavier here than elsewhere. The Midland women, like the matrons of America, go down fighting with conspicuous gallantry, reluctant to accept that youthfulness has passed. Perhaps in consequence, when sex gives way to gender, a disturbing number of them crumble, as if life now holds nothing valuable, worthwhile or achievable. The West Midland conurbation is plagued consistently with one of the highest suicide rates in the country among women between 40 and 65 and the region as a whole has easily the most admissions to ordinary hospitals with 'mental disorders',[61] a term used generally to denote attempted suicides. Both, by comparison, are relatively rare among the men – at least until after 65.

These facts seem to confirm what, on all the evidence already disclosed, we may have suspected: that, with deeper perceptions so generally blocked, a rather desperate sensuality has to do duty all too often here for a truer and fuller sense of womanliness. As Gorer[21] found, the Midlanders' attitudes to sex are – or at any rate were at that time – altogether freer and more expressive than those of the rest of Britain. The people here were the readiest to defend pre-marital experience as 'natural' and 'normal'; and to a quite marked extent they stood out in asserting that women enjoy the physical side of sex just as much as men. But permissiveness is not the same as freedom. It would be wholly in keeping with all that we know of the Midlanders for strenuous over-drives to prevail in the sphere of the erotic as much as they seem to in eating and drinking, in toiling in gardens or in staring at screens. May not the explanation of the tragically high level of suicide lie in the profound dissatisfaction and, ultimately, self-destructiveness implicit in the hectic pursuit of unreal goals in default of a properly-achieved inner fulfilment?

'Unfulfilled', in short, must be our eventual diagnosis. For the whole malaise from which this region seems to suffer springs, surely, from an all-round approach to life that is too flat and shallow. Trapped within a personality emotionally limited and restricting, the Midlander – for all his frantic intake – remains perpetually undernourished. All the time he is restlessly searching for something, without ever knowing quite what this is or where it is most likely to be found. Misinterpreting the pressing dictates of his inmost self, he expands ever-outwards instead of inwards, like a bird fluttering helplessly at the panes of a window that it cannot, or will not, perceive as the wall of a cage through which escape is impossible. To free himself he needs, in effect, to become more introverted. And this is just what, of all things, he is least likely to feel inclined to become – in a region that already, out of all those in England, stops least often, in private, to pause and pray.[22]

VI

The North West

Beyond the Midlands lies that vast stretch of country, the land pre-eminently of tall, belching chimneys and hideous slag-heaps, the home of one Englishman in three, so generally and irritatingly termed 'the North'. Of all the regional vaguenesses none, perhaps, is worse than this. For the North of England, in the sense of a single, monolithic entity with distinctive tastes and customs abundantly in common, can scarcely be said to exist. Only a few traits seem to be shared by the whole area that serve to differentiate it from the rest of Britain with any approach to sharpness, and most of these in some way or other have to do with that most resilient of all fields: food. The whole of the North, one might say, meets together only at mealtimes.

The people of the North of England have, on average, the smallest breakfasts, their midday meals more often than elsewhere in works canteens (if at home, rather small ones), and early teas with a main savoury dish eaten to the accompaniment of slices of bread already spread beforehand with margarine or butter – this last a practice almost unheard-of, for example, in Scotland. Both halves of the North eat large quantities of chips, the most lard, and delight in tripe, cow-heels and pigs' trotters. They have a greater disdain for cookery books and for newspaper recipes.[45] Their kitchens are their power-houses, and the central source of warmth both actual and metaphorical, and this removes much of the need for subsidiary equipment like oil-stoves. They live further back, in the more primitive parts of their homes, tending to turn the front room (the parlour of ancient tradition) into a kind of secular shrine full of ritual objects and reserved almost exclusively for the formal entertainment of visitors,[130] decorating it accordingly with conspicuous extravagance and frequency.[68] Their gardens, when they have them, are mostly tiny and their armoury of tools for use in these smaller than the average.[10] All in all, they live a more cramped life than their actual circumstances warrant.

But in almost all other ways the North is full of internal differences and discrepancies, overshadowing and all but obliterating any impression of a wider, underlying basic unity. All the more reason to regret, therefore, that so many sample surveys still fail to separate North East from North West; for, in Gorer's[21] words, 'the two Northern regions, divided by the Pennines, differ much more dramatically from one another than either differs from the rest of the country'. This is an overstatement, perhaps, when consumption habits are taken into account as well as the ethical attitudes that formed the main concern of Gorer's study, but as a generalisation it has a certain arresting force and value. It deserves to be brandished, at any rate, at those who talk airily of 'The North', showing up as it does the ill-judged presumptuousness of trying to foist on two regions, so sharply individual in character, a pallid and middling standardisation of choice. For beneath the long-played rivalry, the Wars of the Roses game bouncing to and fro – the game which keeps Wensleydale cheese out of Lancashire and Lancashire cheese, for the most part, out of Yorkshire[41] – a much wider and much more decisive dichotomy reveals its existence. North West and North East are like a pair of hands, each neatly complementing the other, permanent partners and opposites, the left one soft and the right one hard – in sentiments and attitudes quite as much as in water supplies. The North West is a mother-centred society, gentler and more indulgent; the North East, father-centred, stern, forceful, unyielding, flinty. In the North West Roman Catholicism is stronger than in any other region of Britain,[132] embracing rather more than a quarter of the entire population;[23] in the North East, in contrast, the second strongest denomination, after the Church of England, is Methodism.

The two regions are roughly balanced in weight of population, each with about six and a half million in total. The North West, however, is much the more densely crowded and easily the most urbanised of all the regions apart from London, the only region, in fact, containing two quite separate conurbations: one, centred on Manchester, with about two and a half million inhabitants; the other, Merseyside, with just over a million and a third – the two together accounting for no less than 58 per cent of the entire regional population. Lancashire has a desperate shortage of elbow-room and, until very recently, the steady decline in her fortunes merely served to postpone the urgently needed scrapping of acre upon acre of obsolete domestic plant. One out of every five houses in this region is either unfit for human habitation or is expected to become so by 1981. In some parts every other house is scheduled to be demolished. Liverpool still has nearly 80,000 dwellings classified as slums, more than in any other British city apart from Glasgow and, on a conservative reckoning, it will take fifteen years just to clear these, on the basis of the present slum-clearance programme, without attending to the many other old, dilapidated buildings. Manchester, by contrast, has a considerably lighter burden: only 50,000 or so, not many more to clear than Birmingham.

This is a region, therefore, where the physical landscape has changed very little, for several generations: a black, smoky region for the majority of its inhabitants, crammed with row upon row of ugly little back-to-back houses, with handkerchief-sized gardens[10] seldom capable of yielding any home-grown vegetables.[2] Some of the death rates (e.g. those of Salford) are the highest in Britain, 20 per cent above the national average, and there is a particularly severe mortality from bronchitis. The Liverpool area stands out for its generally high rate of admissions to hospital for both men and women.[61] Babies, too, die in or around birth in this region in numbers unparalleled anywhere else except in Wales.[5] The moist air current brought by the westerly winds, to which the mill towns of East Lancashire ironically owe at least some of their prosperity (for the exceptional humidity aided the processing of cotton), soaks into the bones and leads to a continual, obsessive search for warmth. Houses, traditionally, are perpetually warmed by fires, however hot the weather. Out of doors, in the old days, a shawl and clogs – especially to cope with so many cobbled streets – were practically essential; and even today the accent in clothes-buying falls noticeably on cardigans and protective covering for the legs and feet: bedroom slippers, half-boots, thick stockings, full-length coats, with the emphasis on warmth and comfort at the expense of styling. As soon as money first began to become widely available for spreading out on non-necessities, in the early 1960s, a quite disproportionate share of this went on shoes and stockings,[131] as if Lancashire women felt a more than ordinary urge to start at the bottom in re-equipping themselves preparatory to working upwards. There is little sign, so far, of the overriding concern of the Midlanders to wage the battle of glamour along the most extended possible front. Even the men have more of their pullovers knitted for them with long-sleeves than elsewhere.[90] The only odd feature is that so little, at least at present, is spent on carpets and rugs.

This is a region where the elements not merely impose their pattern on the people's way of life but, indeed, seem even to become incorporated in it, so that the physical geography, almost uncannily, appears like a mirror of their attitudes. There is the eternally shifting coastline, matching the inward mobility of the typical Lancastrian; there are the dredgers, for ever keeping open the harbours; there is the Tunnel, so central to Merseyside existence, suggestive of connections beneath the surface. . . . For inhabitants so maternally inclined even the very place-names, worn seemingly into the shape of symbols by countless generations of careless usage, sound to the ear appropriately protective (Childwall, Walton) or like echoes of the womb (Formby, Aigburth, Ribchester, Clayton-le-Moors, Makerfield).

What is more fitting, therefore, than that the coastal parts of this county should have served as the great cradle of the old faith through all the years of Protestant perse-cution, invincibly resistant to all attempts at suppression? In the Civil War West Lancashire, loyal as ever to the Earl of Derby, stayed staunchly Royalist; and, in the century that followed, the two Jacobite invasions were routed this way southwards because of the county's well-known reservoir of Catholic and Royalist sympa-thisers. Even today, places like Lancaster, St. Helens and Preston (sometimes nicknamed 'Priests' Town') have an imposing proportion of Roman Catholics, dating from this old, never-extinguished layer that was here long before the invasion of the Irish.

It is Liverpool, none the less, that has incomparably the greatest Roman Catholic concentration – rather more than half a million is the current estimate – in keeping with its traditional role as the main port of entry into Britain for immigrants from Ireland. Even before 1840 a seventh of its population was Irish, many of them labourers employed in building the new docks. The Great Famine of 1847 unloaded 300,000 more in the space of only five months – on to a native population of only about 250,000 – a shock which no other British city was called upon to sustain to anything like the same extent.[133]

133

To this day Liverpool has never really recovered from it, the city's housing and social provision never quite managing to keep pace with the bursting population or the squalor in which so many of its inhabitants are still compelled to live. One Liverpudlian in every three is now reckoned to be of Irish descent; add to these the unnumbered Welshmen, and one arrives at the chastening thought that this is possibly now a more 'Celtic' city even than Edinburgh. This is underlined by the fact that the blood-group composition is markedly different from elsewhere in the North West, abnormally raised frequencies of group O having been definitely shown to be associated with those bearing Irish surnames.[134] The presence of so many Roman Catholics among these Irish shows itself in the exceptionally high legitimate birth-rate on Merseyside to women in all child-bearing age-groups. The average number of children per family is 2·7, a marked departure from the general British norm, and a much higher percentage of the people are under twenty-five than in the other English and Welsh conurbations. The illegitimacy rate, in sharp contrast, is notably low, certainly lower than in south-east Lancashire and despite the role of the city as a rather raffish seaport. It is low, too, in Ireland, which Merseyside copies likewise in the marked infrequency of suicides, particularly among women. A further resemblance to Ireland is the exceptionally high incidence in just this one region in England of anencephaly, a severe type of congenital malformation, which is known to occur more in births to older mothers. The Irish might be charged, too, with much of the passion here for gambling – far more betting offices per head, for example, than in the rest of the county[108] – and with the record of violence, for the most part due to drunkenness, only rivalled among the main British cities by Glasgow. As in Glasgow, too, a powerful, peppery ingredient of long-memoried Ulstermen lovingly prolongs the old Green and Orange rivalries and brawlings, and the city as a whole has to suffer from a tedious, endless private Irish quarrel. The disproportionately strong vote for the Conservatives among Liverpool's manual workers over many years is generally, and no doubt rightly, ascribed to the fervent Unionist loyalties of the Orangemen (though the women's vote in Lancashire in general is said also to be cast unexpectedly heavily to the right). Liverpool did not elect a Labour-controlled local government till 1955, and in general elections the city only began to move with the normal national swing as recently as 1964. Apart from these, there are other special characteristics of the North West in general for which Roman Catholicism can clearly be held responsible, without their having to be specifically Irish in origin. We find in this region, for example, the heaviest readership of Catholic papers like the *Universe*, much the highest belief in the Devil,[23] and the eating of well-above-average amounts of fish, principally hake[103] and the cheap, invariable, omnipresent cod.

There are certain strands in the Lancastrian character that seem to make it pre-eminently well-attuned to Roman Catholicism. There is its love of ritual, for instance, well exemplified by the passion for processions (those at Whitsuntide being a specially deep-seated tradition and a cause of much absenteeism in industry) and for collective orgies like hot-pot suppers and stylish funeral teas involving 'burying them with ham'.[51] The adherence to the Wakes, the old pre-Reformation religious holidays, was sufficiently tenacious for these to survive the early days of industrialism, when so many of the old ways perished. As English regions go, too, this seems easily the most superstitious; belief in the truth of fortune-tellers and horoscopes being both prominent and widespread.[21] Lancastrians are more, shall we say, 'symbol-oriented': exceptionally imaginative, in the most literal meaning of that word. They live closer to the source of things, in the kitchens of their minds. Of all the regions this one is the most open and exposed on the inward side: the one where back doors are used extensively in preference to the front, even by comparatively grand outsiders like doctors in the course of their rounds. The people here are accordingly capricious, tossed around by whims, acting just as the mood takes them. Not for nothing is Lancashire regarded in political circles as a particularly reliable reflector of the underlying national mood. Its voters swing like clockwork, control of the County Council having shifted from one main party to the other with absolute regularity every three years since the war. The particular vice with which Lancastrians tax themselves above all other regions is the vice of procrastination,[21] the weakness peculiar to those with energies that prove at best only fitful. Thinking inwardly comes more easily and naturally than thinking outwardly: rather than submit to the demanding disciplines of empirical tests and proof, they prefer to trust to hunches. It is enough for them to feel themselves correct. The textile industry, as classically structured, perfectly suited and reflected minds of this type: ultra-receptive to the slighter drifts in design; unperturbed by the trades' perpetual inconstancy and fluidity; sheltered from the harsh front of fashion by a calm, protecting tangle of middlemen. A provincial blindness to new themes quite outside their traditional range and experience has been their one great undoing. This is a region that for years has lived and thrived by taking in other people's raw materials and processing them, a land of converters and makers-up. It is inclusive where Yorkshire is exclusive: an absorbing region, one enormous sponge. Consumer research firms have found that the North West is a good deal readier than the North East to give new products a try-out; but it is also much quicker to drop them, should they not prove to its liking. For this reason Lancashire can be a treacherous choice as a test market, if the aim is to gauge the likely responsiveness of the North as a whole and in general. If Yorkshire likes something new, on the other hand, it tends to stick with it; for it has too much pride in the rightness of its judgement to bear to go back on it. Women's shampoos are one published case-history where these two contrasting attitudes can be observed, very neatly, in action.

It is more in the field of food, however, that Lancashire shows off its eternal weakness for experiment, unable, as it were, to resist dipping in its fingers and sucking them. It buys an unexpected medley of canned soups, for example, and has a weakness for obscurer flavours in products like jellies – differing from the South only in the lack of sophistication displayed in its choices. It rather prides itself, in fact, on its readiness to eat almost anything, an all-embracing appetite being merely another facet of its engulfing inclusiveness. This renders the one or two samples of faddiness all the more piquant and eye-catching, as the customary exceptions that prove all rules of this character. One of these, attested by three separate national surveys, is a distinctly lower liking for baked beans, a relatively high percentage of housewives in this region never in fact buying even a single tin. Another pet dislike is tomatoes in liquid form – whereas consumption of the fresh fruits is quite normal. Tomato sauce, tomato soup and the tinned or bottled tomatoes that the East Midlanders utilise so much are all, for some reason, relatively most unpopular (could this conceivably be because of their resemblance to blood?). Raspberries, even more oddly, are singled out for avoidance by many women when purchasing fruit.[3] The region is further peculiar for its almost total rejection of Blue Stilton among natural cheeses.[41]

No clear pattern emerges from the items that rise to exceptional prominence within the regional diet, except that there appears to be some of the Midland fondness for foods that leave a sharp sting in the mouth, if to a rather less accentuated degree. Onions are consistently eaten here in large quantities, being used in the traditional hot-pot and as the standard accompaniment to tripe. Red cabbage is another hot-pot ingredient ordained by long custom, and there is also a high expenditure on pickles. Parkin, a fiercely hot ginger cake, is yet another Lancashire speciality. And perhaps the particular liking for marmalade, which thrusts its consumption well above that of the other regions of the North, is part of this same general trend.

Lancashire, it is reported, also goes for sharper perfumes than its next-door neighbours,[24] illustrating its weakness for effects that are abruptly exciting. Lancastrians are famous for suddenly letting off their brakes, especially for the habit of saving up all year for their Wakes Week holiday and then resolutely spending on it every single penny, as often as not returning broke. They are given to short, explosive bouts of improvidence, recklessly buying things by the houseful instead of patiently acquiring items one by one as they become able to afford them – a phenomenon quite peculiar to this region and wholly at variance with its background of widespread poverty. There is a special exuberant quality in the people and one recent writer,[51] a Lancastrian himself by birth, singles this out as the most sentimental of all the regions of England. Again, after years of interviewing school-children from all parts of the country for positions in the National Youth Orchestra of Great Britain, Dr. Ruth Railton has remarked on a special emotional quality in those from Lancashire; when seeing children from here, she finds, it is advisable to allow for five minutes longer per child in order to speak more slowly.[135]

Despite the bubbling humour that has earned this county its name as an inexhaustible fountain-head of professional comedians, there is also a countervailing current of gloominess and melancholia. Black here tends to march hand in hand with white. Indeed, as though echoing this, black-and-white is said to be always a popular choice for women's clothes in Liverpool;[13] and black as well as white shoes seem to be preferred to other shades rather more insistently by women in the North West than elsewhere. In this up-and-downness, this continual sharp switching of moods, from 'fall' to 'redemption', or between almost any other pair of opposing emotions, we have a behaviour pattern rather 'Celtic' than typically English. According to a leading historical psychologist,[136] such a pattern is 'displayed today by many individuals whose personality has been formed in a Roman Catholic culture; it consists of a zigzag movement between the 'id' and the super-ego, between indulgence and guilt'. This, it is postulated, permits a low degree of inner unity, so that the end-product is a type of personality radically different from that more centrally balanced one, a kind of dynamic compromise, which the English mostly developed in the later part of the sixteenth century and which they have managed to maintain until the present. Of all regions, in fact, the North West perhaps most deeply resembles Wales, more obviously in its fundamentally maternalist character.

Yet for all the heady enthusiasms a volcanic nature of this kind can engender, its possession also implies a certain element of danger. Volcanoes can erupt, catastrophically, with the minimum of warning. Too much turbulence can overwhelm some at least of the normal protective controls. The result, then, may be serious instability, and in bad cases chronic mental illness may succeed in gaining hold. It would therefore not be all that unexpected to find in Lancashire dismaying evidence of widespread, well below-average mental health. Suggestive of this, certainly, are the consistently high rates for suicide in the county, especially in old age and in both sexes (though the women's rate is pulled down overall, and thus partially concealed, by the disproportionately low rate on Merseyside). These rates, however, are difficult to square with the fact that, though the percentage of pensioners who live by themselves is no higher than usual in this region, kinsfolk in general here are, for England, more than ordinarily closely knit.[21] If, as the figures for the 'Celtic' regions clearly seem to suggest, family ties substantially reduce the risk that people will take their own lives, then there must presumably be some basic defect of temperament predisposing Lancastrians to resort to such drastic action with this quite exceptional frequency.

The high propensity to violence and vandalism, seen at its worst on Merseyside but extending throughout the region – producing, for example, by far the highest death-rates from homicide (and primarily among men over 35; not, as in London, among gang-ridden teenagers) – may well be just one further aspect of this. Lancastrians believe in letting themselves go and in paying the price for their follies afterwards. The region, furthermore, has a persistent excess of unskilled manual workers, whom one might expect to be socially less constrained and so more forthright and reckless in their responses. Small wonder therefore that the people here, out of all the regions of England, voice quite the greatest regard for the police.[21] Both externally and internally, their need is greatest for the constant reassurance of their simple physical presence; and it is probably because this is tacitly sensed on both sides that the Lancashire police forces have long had a reputation for the excellence of their morale, helped in turn by exceptionally well disposed and generous local and county authorities, which have made the constabularies here the accepted trend-setters throughout the North.

This is a region, in any case, where protectiveness has high value. Lancashire, one might say, is Britain's night-nursery: an accepting, involuted land, the natural home of *laissez-faire*. Yorkshiremen insist, Lancastrians inveigle. Children here are told to 'Give over!'; elsewhere they are ordered, more tersely, to 'Chuck it!' The difference is between an extrovert's command and an introvert's persistent sapping and undermining. Lancastrians are schooled in insinuating themselves, rather than hacking off ivy with a frontal attack: their prying inquisitiveness, which makes so many Southerners so acutely uncomfortable, is a reaching-out, not an intentionally aggressive intrusion; their enquiries are simply the feelers of mutuality. Intensely sociable people, with a liking for crowds, they develop thinner masks and have that warm frankness that comes so readily to those who dwell close to their deeper, collective selves. They feel less than others the need of a protecting barrier of privacy, and this makes them more than normally well-equipped for coping with communal ventures. Lancashire gave birth to the modern Co-operative movement and had the first municipal free library and the first public baths in Britain. More recently, it has taken to self-service launderettes with quite exceptional abandon.[95] It may, indeed, have been this aptitude for large-scale combination that made the people of this region the natural pace-setters in the formative years of industrialism, so well suited must their native temperament have made them to the strange new world of the factories.

That it was the character of the people that determined the trend of the economy is easier to believe than the reverse. Just because the facts and figures of an economy's development can normally be established with some approach to exactness, while next to nothing – with any precision – is normally known about the character of the people who run it, the search for causes and origins tends too often to be limited to features intrinsic in the economy itself. This may be more safely empirical, keeping to facts and steering clear of fields still troublingly ill-defined and subject to argument, but the view it produces can well be a distorted one. It can encourage the belief that radical changes in economies occur *sui generis*, regardless of the emotional biases or differential energies of the people involved in them. It seems especially important to bear this in mind when considering Lancashire and the influences that led to the rise of the cotton industry; for all that we know of the personality of the people in this region today points to a clearly distinctive pattern compared with the country as a whole, and a pattern moreover that could well have been long-enduring. Could not one powerful pre-existent factor, conducive to easy adaptation to factory methods of working, have been, for instance, the very self-sufficiency of the Lancashire woman? The usual assumption is that this well-known idiosyncrasy of the region is the outcome of the long tradition of abundant employment for women in local industry, the very nature of which has often ensured for them better opportunities of work than for men. (Even as late as the 1930s it was common for salesmen who called on houses in the mill towns during the work-day to encounter only the husbands – unemployed, while their wives were out at work in the factories.) But in view of the strong maternalist slant visible at so many levels in Lancashire's culture, might it not be that the self-sufficiency came first: part of a much older, unchanging social psychology, of which the wide and lasting attachment to Roman Catholicism was, as has been hinted at already, merely the most obtrusive outward manifestation? From what we know of the domestic system that preceded the advent of factories, the women already had a long history of working alongside their menfolk and fulfilling an essential role economically. The father was the weaver, the mother the spinner, while the children did the picking, cleaning, drying and carding. The new machines brought no reduction in demand for spinners, so the women suffered no threat at all to their status. But when the power-loom arrived, many of the men were deprived of their livelihood and after 1825 weaving wages were forced down in general, so that by being compelled to send their wives and children into the factories in greater numbers the men were dealt a double blow to their self-esteem as the family breadwinners.[137] Industrialism thus clearly brought imbalance to the sex roles, but it may merely have exacerbated a tendency by then already in existence.

Today the dominant role of the average housewife in Lancashire is best exemplified by the remarkable degree of control she is ceded over the husband's pay-packet, a practice noticed already among the miners in South Wales. In a survey during the last war 49 per cent of the husbands in a typical town like Blackburn claimed that all their weekly earnings were handed straight to their wives, whereas in other towns in England this figure nowhere exceeded 25 per cent.[138] This results in far more than mere domestic convenience: it means that wives here have much the greater say in what the family's finances should be spent on. And indeed there is every sign that they cling tightly to the purse-strings, showing a peasant shrewdness in shopping and a thoroughly grudging approach to prices. Liverpool is probably the most bargain-conscious city in Britain, Scotland even excepted. When Tesco's first self-service store there started to offer cut prices, it did more trade in three days than it had previously done in three weeks.[139] On average, lower prices over a wide range of products tend to be paid in the North West compared with the rest of the country. Money has always been short in this region, where more men than elsewhere tend to work in poorly paid unskilled jobs and where households are frequently weighed down with more children than the family budget can support in comfort. It may be because of this last factor that cases of cruelty to children turn up here, rather surprisingly, relatively more often than elsewhere[140] – or it may be that, in a region so ardently protective by nature, the people are much more effectively vigilant and their native Lancastrian inquisitiveness is made to serve, in this one respect at least, a commendably constructive purpose.

That the niggling approach to prices springs, quite simply, from a long history of widespread poverty and the general insecurity bred into the bones, at every social level, by the ultra-sharp boom-and-slump pattern of the cotton cycle is easier to accept in this case than in that of Scotland or Yorkshire. The Lancastrians, if they had the money, would more likely throw it around freely and carelessly, like the Midlanders. The tightness of their purses till now has been due not so much to the indulgence of taboos and suspicions or to any obscure guilts about spending as to straightforward financial stringency. By nature an adaptable people, they have had to trim their tastes and usages purely to suit their pockets. And, as is usual in such matters, the habit of years quite easily out-lives the necessity, so that self-denial becomes too blindly acquiesced in. Is it still economically essential, one wonders, that salaries paid to business executives should be so much lower here on average than in the rest of Britain?[76] Is it not more likely that the managements in the North West can simply escape with paying less to staffs who have grown so habitually tight-belted?

Saving, eliminating waste, 'watching points' are traits built deep into the Lancashire character. Anything that might, just conceivably, be used afresh is ruthlessly pounced on and preserved by the average housewife. This is a wonderful region for reprocessing and for utili-sing throw-outs, from the odds and ends of cows and pigs to second-hand clothing and furniture; and sales by pawnbrokers have remained high here considerably longer than elsewhere. Costs are kept down and savings made in all directions possible, certainly in some which other regions could only with difficulty bring themselves to copy. More households than anywhere else, for example, wholly dispense with butter – unthinkable in Wales and unlikely in Scotland. Doubtless the very lack of a butter-eating tradition has made Lancastrians far less perturbed about surrendering themselves entirely to margarine. Cheapness is all that matters: inhibitions of taste or cooking custom are too luxurious to be afforded. Before the war, in much the same way, Merseyside resembled the South East and London in its ready acceptance of frozen and chilled imported meat. The rest of the North insisted on home-killed meat, preferring to pay more on grounds of better quality.[141] In the Midlands today it is difficult to buy that cheap meat, mutton: it all goes, the butchers say, to Lancashire – where it traditionally forms the meat used in making hot-pot.

Another reason why the Lancashire wife may show such a scrimping attitude in her shopping is that she would rather the family money were spent in ways likely to bring more lasting satisfaction. As the purse is held by her, it opens more readily for the various intangibles that contribute to long-term security, the sort of ends too often neglected when the budget remains in the hands of the wage-earning male. One result of this, presumably, is the surprisingly high proportion of families in this under-privileged region whose homes are their own – Merseyside excepted. Another is the large outlay devoted to keeping up a reputable domestic front. It is a notorious local foible that no matter how dirty the house is inside, its outside – up to and including the adjoining pavement – must be kept entirely and completely spotless. This is the test of a family's respectability. Even the curtains, so it is said, are commonly hung the wrong way round, to ensure that the pattern is displayed to the street. It is thus quite in keeping that a survey in 1960 should have found that the outsides of their homes had been painted on average more recently than anywhere else in Britain.[68] The region further showed itself peculiar for its very marked preference for cream or white for the outsides of doors and of blue for drainpipes and guttering, green and yellow being generally avoided. Perhaps living so much in the back regions serves to give Lancastrians a lengthier perspective, so that 'the front' becomes separated in their minds as something apart and rather special. This can be seen in their exaggerated attention to detail when formally receiving guests (that Lancashire love of ritual again): 'the front' is almost, it seems, a disused part of life brought into service, like some treasured tea-set, only on such special occasions. There are echoes here of the lavishly 'Celtic' standards of hospitality, half-oriental in their face-saving. But instead of the tin of Spam that a Welshman might proffer, the Lancastrian regales his visitors with expensive fancy cakes. The 'shop cake', gaudily iced and bulging with synthetic cream, is a long-standing tradition, a gesture that guests can be counted on to recognise and appreciate, if only tacitly. The high consumption of these in consequence aligns Lancashire with Scotland as a primarily cake-eating region, in contrast to primarily bun-eating Yorkshire – which puts bulk before glitter.

By handling the family budget regularly in this way, the Lancashire wife gains an uncommon self-assurance: the self-assurance which comes from seeing the whole household economy in the round, so that she can know precisely where she stands and lay her plans accordingly. She holds what amounts, in effect, to the family tiller. More power and authority are ceded to her inside the family and over the children than in any other region in Britain.[21] And perhaps because of the importance attached to intuition here, she is allowed to trust more to her own views and experience than is, perhaps, always wise and to value these too highly. Very confident in their roles, the wives here run the risk of being tempted into over-authoritarian stances, captivated by the very force of their rectitude and convictions. The result, however, is a sour maternalism, without the rasping quality of the woman who has battled in a man's world and remained dissatisfied. Rather than frontally attacking her husband, the sourpuss wife in Lancashire tends to roll over on him and crush him. The men, in any case, are physically small,[142] the woman very often enormous – a reality all too close to the comic postcards for comfort. Too much reliance on cheap, starchy foods brings here its most massive retribution. There is much the greatest buying of ultra-strong, fully boned corsets. There is also, regrettably, the widest indifference to slimming, more older husbands in this region than elsewhere professing to be happy with (or resigned to?) outsize spouses.[26] The women perhaps, quite simply, eat far more than the men, becoming compulsive gorgers – could it be? – through a displaced longing to devour their families emotionally. The evidence seems to suggest that the typical married woman in Lancashire tends to underplay her role as a wife and overplay that as a Mum, fussing over her children and, unlike her Welsh sister, neglecting her husband – in little telltale ways. When she knits, it is the men's garments, quite noticeably, about which she is inclined not to bother.[91] Husbands are allowed to wander around looking shabby in a way that no self-respecting Welsh or Yorkshire wife could conceivably permit and which conflicts with the Lancashire wife's almost total enslavement to the concept of respectability in public – a concept viewed only in terms of woman-and-home and scarcely envisaged as extending to the outward appearance of menfolk. Worst snub of all, as if betraying a deep-seated difficulty in ever bringing themselves to surrender submissively, a notable number of brides in this region choose to go to the altar dressed in some other colour than the customary white.[143]

The tendency for wives to hold down jobs outside the home has ceased to be the exceptional feature now for which the region has been so famous in the past. Although as recently as 1950, 37 per cent of all its females were to be found in paid employment (40–45 per cent in the cotton towns), a figure then higher than in all other regions, within ten years this had dropped to 33 per cent. The prosperous Midlands had drawn level in this respect and London and the South East had even begun to exceed it. In the North West, however, the women still seem to work in more demanding jobs and on average shoulder a more economically necessary burden on behalf of the family. Emotional involvement in the job is probably also more widespread, in a region where women for so long have taken themselves seriously as wage-earners – and even formed part of an all-woman economic network that emerges as a well-developed local feature, as dressmakers, hairdressers or even, till very recently, washerwomen. This is a region, too, of a superabundance of small shops, offering innumerable further openings for working wives and other older women. Married women, once their children were off their hands, must have always found it easy here to go back to their previous jobs. In the middle of the last century, we are told, between a fifth and a quarter of the women workers in the cotton mills were married.[137] This has been one more factor, no doubt, making for feminine independence.

From this, however, there have nevertheless been losses as well as gains. Girls in the old days went straight to the mills as soon as they were old enough to earn and so missed the chance, it was held, of learning the domestic skills that they would need in marriage. So many wives away from home all day at jobs must also have led to some cutting down on the more laborious, less essential household tasks. Lancashire women today do little home baking (and so have little call for either flour or suet) with the marked exception of apple pies and sponge cakes.[45] Similarly, only a small number make jam.[44] This is the only region where the one substantial meal of the day is eaten more widely in the evening than at lunchtime.[2, 45] Entertaining friends to meals is also confined more to week-ends compared with elsewhere,[45] as also are other routine domestic chores. Rather few women in this region find the chance to knit at all[91] and remarkably few, for years now, have been able to manage even to glance at those trade papers of the wife and mother, the women's weekly magazines. Possibly this desperate shortage of time in the past also helps to explain the unexpected degree of patronage here given to professional hairdressers.

In one respect at least, then, the region is well adapted in advance to the more complicated style of life that greater prosperity will surely bring. The established tradition of the working wife is bound to lead to far fewer dislocations and adjustments than usual to the pre-existing domestic pattern. All the same, in a great many other directions new pressures that will lead to changes have to be expected very soon. More than that of any other region, the North-western way of life has been stunted by poverty. Its people, as we have seen, are alert and receptive, and like those of no other region – unless it be Tyneside – they can be expected to revel in their altered status. Indeed, there are signs in plenty already that the economic saucepan-lid is about to blow off. Already, the men here are the heaviest smokers of any region, despite the thinness of funds that confines them at present mainly to cheaper brands. Already, the numbers drinking wines, particularly the numbers of women – with many years of port-drinking behind them – are close to reaching Southern levels: only the quantity drunk still lies a long, long way behind. Spirits, too, already claim a far wider following among women here than in the other parts of the North, so much freer is Lancashire from puritan repressions.

Survey after survey is now beginning to indicate that the North West is already staring hard towards the South – far harder, certainly, than any of its Northern neighbours. The range of drinks being sampled here is already Midland to Southern in its audacity; so is the level of ownership of portable transistor radios. A new high-price purchasing pattern, way above the traditional low one that still accompanies it, has made its appearance in clothes-buying on Merseyside.[83] Lancashire, as always, it seems, is refusing to take the sensible middle course and is already reaching for the stars.

VII

The North East: Yorkshire and Tyne-Tees

In few parts of Britain does there exist a more clearly marked moral type than in Yorkshire . . . The character is essentially Teutonic, including the shrewdness, the truthfulness with candour, the perseverance, energy and industry of the Lowland Scotch, but little of their frugality. . . . The sound judgment, the spirit of fairplay, the love of comfort, order and cleanliness, and the fondness for heavy feeding, are shared with the Saxon Englishman; but some of them are still more strongly marked in the Yorkshireman, as is also the bluff independence – a very fine quality, when it does not degenerate into selfish rudeness. . . . The mind, like the body, is generally very vigorous and energetic, and extremely well adapted to commercial and industrial pursuits, as well as to the cultivation of the exact sciences; but a certain defect in imaginative power must be admitted. . . .

Thus the great Dr. Beddoe in 1885.[110] A thorough, well-considered report, its accuracy only to be challenged in one or two small and insignificant details. It serves to introduce Yorkshire – the best-known of all the English regions.

First, however, we must look at this area in its wider setting. This chapter is titled 'The North East' advisedly, for in most commercial sample surveys the East and West Ridings are fused with the Registrar General's Northern Region, which consists of the North Riding, the Border counties and the densely populated Tyne-Tees coastal fringe, the two together familiarly designated 'N. & N.E.' This whole area has a certain underlying unity, founded

on a patriarchal family pattern and a prevailing Nonconformism, both of which associate it with Scotland, not
with Lancashire. There are even detectable faint, half-
buried traces of a one-time far wider unity, which we may
for convenience term 'Northumbrian': a rough jumble of
traits that extend across both the Northern Region and
Yorkshire and down into the East Midlands as well, and
that differentiate the three together from the whole of
the rest of the country. Under this head may be mentioned
an exceptionally large ownership of washing-machines
and rediffusion radio sets, the heaviest indulgence in
chips, the widest taste for White Stilton cheese;[41] less
sharing of homes with relatives or in-laws, a weak tradition of overseas holidays (a pointer to xenophobia?) and
a remarkably infrequent need, or inclination, to enter
hospital for varicose veins.[61] This is the area Havelock
Ellis[88] discriminated as the Anglo-Danish District, in
which sense it extends a good way further northwards,
well on into the Scottish Lowlands. Except in the exact
sciences, he concluded, it has not produced such outstanding ability, two chief claims to notice being an
aptitude for mathematics, shared by no other district
comparing with this in size, and a peculiarly stubborn
independence, responsible in history for an undue number
who underwent religious martyrdom.

The county of Yorkshire itself has little of the relative
uniformity of Lancashire. Generalisations about its
character are normally based on a knowledge of the West
Riding – and reasonably so, for this can boast just over
three-quarters of the total population – but even within
the West Riding, fissured with innumerable valleys,
customs, dialects, even the very look of the inhabitants
can vary tremendously from one district to another. As
usual, therefore, it is necessary to begin by apologising
for the roughness of the abstractions that follow. It is
fully accepted that no such person as a 'typical' Yorkshireman can ever be said to have existed. What is put forward

here is merely a broadly impressionistic picture: a statistical average for the county, which those who know the local details with proper precision can adjust accordingly for themselves.

In examining the character of Yorkshiremen the most sensible place to start is, undoubtedly, with their physique. An outstanding number of them, as no one can fail to notice, are big, muscular and burly. Statistics in this matter do more to confuse than to assist, for the average figures for the county as a whole are evened downwards inevitably by the large number of Yorkshire people who, instead, are short, squat and, by comparison, dumpy. One of the few things we *can* say for certain, however, is that the men as a whole are distinctly heavier than in the rest of North England, though easily outweighed in turn in this respect by Highland Scots.[142] It may perhaps be because of this greater massiveness, or the greater strenuousness that it no doubt enjoins, that such an unusually high proportion in this county seem to complain of what the doctors diagnose as 'slipped discs'.[1] The women, especially, are penalised by their build and respond to this challenge in a way that seems distinctive. Unkindly endowed by nature with over-large bones and a tendency to bulk, they find they have to watch their figures scrupulously. Though few of them deteriorate so badly as to need the heavier corsets and girdles so much in evidence in Lancashire, equally few can afford to deceive themselves by dispensing with everything short of just a skimpy suspender-belt. We find here, in consequence, much the greatest demand for roll-ons and for the lighter types of all-in-one foundations.

A great many big and beefy people means, in turn, a great many people with a more than ordinary amount of weight to throw around – and a more than ordinary size of frame in constant need of filling. It naturally follows from this that Yorkshiremen are inclined to pugnacity, to pushing and shoving; and that this is also a county highly famed, deservedly, for trenchermen. Compared with those of Lancashire, the place-names of Yorkshire leave a notably harsher sensation on the tongue: Masham, Spofforth, Riccall, Garforth, Cleckheaton . . . or else seem more ponderous and hefty: Market Weighton, Ampleforth, Burley-in-Wharfedale . . . or simply more brusquely stolid: York, Hull, Leeds, Thirsk, Pudsey, Batley, Ossett. . . . No romanticism here, for sure; nothing that is not grim, downright, straightforward and prosaic.

The pugnacity, quite plainly, is the display-behaviour of cock birds instinctively demarcating their territories. For Yorkshiremen, first and foremost, are essentially individualists with a highly positive sense of their selfness. They are autarchs, with a fortress personality, with battlements bristling watchfully with guns. They have none of the Lancastrians' careless edges – nor will they tolerate them in others or in everyday objects around them, all affectations, anything indeed that can be remotely construed as fanciful or 'nonsense', being quite fiercely and firmly rejected. Quite typical is the extreme disdain expressed here for asparagus[43] – so out of the ordinary, so questionably substantial. Why hanker after the alien, when the cosy and familiar is already so satisfactory? Yorkshiremen, in effect, are true, genuine extroverts – much rarer as a breed than popularly supposed, and a world away in spirit from that other mislabelled kind that parades itself as outgoing while all the time it really flees from a troubling, insecure centre. The Yorkshireman, in contrast to these bogus extroverts, enjoys a complete and absolute self-certainty, a sublimely unflappable quality, which makes it hard for him to sympathise with others less favoured by nature. With a mind unmuddied by all intrusive flows – the source of life's more subtle pleasures, after all, as well as its more tedious indecisions – he has all the devastating literalness of the person who knows no other way than the externalising of energies; that literalness which, misused, litters the world with stiff-necked, unreceptive traditionalists, professional philistines and sceptics. The Yorkshireman's failings are as clear and as uncomplicated as his actions: they are his strengths unimaginatively distended.

The results, in practical terms, are not unpredictable. The superabundant outflowing energies give Yorkshire and Tyneside the highest rates in England and Wales for crimes of violence (exclusive of homicide), and in the decade of sharp deterioration, 1950–60, the rates went up here faster than anywhere.[30] Many more women than elsewhere, both in Yorkshire and on Tyneside, lose their lives in road accidents, which in a region without any marked excess of cars (but with a high annual milage per motorist) points to a culpable amount of furious and reckless driving. Far more people than elsewhere in England troop along to sports grounds,[21] to work off their aggressiveness vicariously. Far more than elsewhere, too, are they contemptuous of harmless mysteries like ghosts and fortune-telling.[21] And perhaps aided by the fact that husbands here exercise so much more control over how their wages are eventually disbursed, there is a great resistance to change in general. A highly rational people, with an over-developed taste for plainness, they refuse to take up novelties just because they are told they are novel; they need to be offered a reason, a good and convincing reason, for switching from something that up to the present has appeared to be perfectly satisfactory. This makes them especially intolerant of new styles and designs: they like neatness and cleanness, gaiety even, anything well turned-out, but their appreciation in general jibs at being asked to extend itself to intangibles. Fashion purely for fashion's sake can only be smuggled in very gradually. Yorkshire has no frustrated love-affair with the South, unlike the Midlands; it is not to be won over by smartness, or to be chivvied or hurried. The men have clung to shaving sticks longer than elsewhere in the country, the wives have been slower to switch to self-raising flour for baking. Fewer shops offer trading stamps,[144] super-markets have made slowish headway[145] – and so have pre-packed vegetables[2] and tinned foods in general. More cookers here are still run on solid fuel, doubtless preserved by so much cheap or free domestic coal available in the mining areas. More women than elsewhere have also tried various of the more out-of-the-ordinary cosmetics but not gone on with them – their ingrained conservatism perhaps only deepened by their having to endure a much fiercer barrage than elsewhere of pointed remarks from their menfolk.

This Yorkshire conservatism arises from a much more positive base than any mere parochial slowness. There is an actual hostility to outside invaders and invasions, and a notoriously cold reception for successful 'comers-in'. A special resentment is reserved for the South, that 'Great Defiler' – for there is something of the anti-foreign-body mania that so forcefully agitates the Welsh (though here it explodes more as a forthright 'Keep out!' than as a rather negative worry about the potential risk of insidious pollution).

It is interesting to note, more particularly, that while the puritan regions of Britain unite in their reverence for the homely, in their quest for purity they sharply divide over that distinctly unhomely object, the tin. For Wales and Scotland tins, it would appear, are emblems of guaranteed intactness: Yorkshire, as we have just seen, tends to distrust and reject them. So great is the pride of the oven here that the general English attitude prevails all-unquestioned; and the Yorkshire wife joins her cousins in East Anglia and the West Country in roundly condemning tins for lacking just that goodness she con-trives to ensure for her family by her own devoted and laborious efforts of processing. The 'Celtic' regions, by contrast, weighed down by a less demanding tradition of home cookery experience no such guilt.

Yorkshire, even so, is as puritanical as can be in another main direction: in its insistence on cleanliness. Along with Tyneside and County Durham it can boast of an extreme abundance of washing-machines – almost three-quarters of housewives in the combined regions in fact possess one – though this is partly due to the heavy representation of miners, amongst whom these have long taken high priority. Vacuum-cleaners, likewise, have achieved a higher diffusion than in the North of England generally. Items of clothing most liable to become overtly unhygienic are renewed more frequently than elsewhere, and in surveys about fresh food there tends to be more emphasis here on the cleanness of both the surface of the food and its wrapping. All the more incongruous, therefore, and surely hard to bear must be the lack in so many homes in the county of either a fixed bath (affecting 26 per cent, a relatively high proportion for Britain) or even a water-closet (15 per cent, or twice the national average, and as high as 18 per cent in the Leeds-Bradford conurbation). Unlike all other urban areas, however, in the Yorkshire conurbation there are far fewer – indeed hardly any – cases of water-closets being shared between two or more separate households, a standard of amenity, perhaps, here found peculiarly unendurable.

As one might expect, early toilet-training for children – in the first six months, if possible – is especially in favour in this region,[21] a view that finds no less vehement support in Scotland. Life in general is lived more rigorously, more ascetically, with fewer frills – Scotland, perhaps, alone excepted. There are various indications that people here revel in denying themselves the more marginal luxuries. Teetotalism is rampant, at least in theory, and certainly declared drinkers of both spirits and wines are impressively few in number, especially among women (a reminder, if one should be needed, that we are now in patriarchal country). Even so, a high proportion of men are extremely regular beer-drinkers and rival even the Midlands in the average quantity consumed: 8·4 pints of draught per week per man, according to one recent survey estimate. Yorkshire, like the East Midlands, also supports a relative profusion of off-licences, indicative of a lot of home drinking, some of it perhaps a trifle furtive. The men in this region, too, are among the heaviest and most numerous smokers in Britain. Thus self-denial, it would seem from this, is focussed mainly on quite bearable deprivations, rather than on fleshly pleasures whose with-holding might give rise to really grievous suffering.

One rather puzzling feature of this region that may be mentioned at this point is the extraordinarily low con-sumption of two chief dairy products: milk – fresh no less than tinned – and cheese, both natural and processed. Cheese rations all through the war here were persistently under-utilised, as in Scotland also, and a prejudice against milk is known to have been in existence already in the 'thirties. This is strangely out of line for people who pride themselves on the wholesomeness of their standard of eating, for one side-effect, inescapably, is that the regional diet is distinctly deficient in calcium. Strong tea is known to be a special taste of this region and this must account for a certain lessening of milk intake; the lower liking for breakfast cereals and, as in Scotland again, a much weaker appetite for blancmange also imply some further savings still. Against these, on the credit side, must be set a well-above-average devotion to milk puddings,[45] which also results in more rice being eaten than is normal for the country in general. So very opposite is the taste of York-shire to the taste of Wales in just these respects that one is tempted to suggest the reverse of the explanation reason-ably put forward for the latter: a shortage of cows over the centuries, instead of, as in Wales, an overabundance. Yorkshiremen (it may perhaps be forgivable to hazard) preferred amassing flocks of sheep in place of the pastoral peoples' herds of cattle. While the Welsh happily slaughtered sheep and gained fame for their lamb and mutton, Yorkshiremen, no less happily, slaughtered cattle and gained fame for ther beef – roasted, of course, and plentifully backed up with their Yorkshire pudding. Slaughtering sheep in such a region must have been a heartbreaking disaster, a sacrifice only to be undertaken as a desperate last resort, for it was equivalent to blowing up one's bank. Sheep meant fleeces, and fleeces were golden. And no true Yorkshireman, of that day or any other, could have allowed himself to disregard his brass, in whatever form it may have existed.

Whatever truth this explanation may possess, it serves at any rate to introduce the Yorkshireman in his original natural setting: in his role as 'lord of the fold'. While place-names in Lancashire frequently end in '–ton', celebrating a hamlet or cluster of homesteads occupied by a joint-family, in Yorkshire they tend instead to end in '–field' or '–ley', celebrating areas of ground – turned, no doubt, into private enclosures and tucked away out of sight behind a forbidding barricade of stone walls. The Yorkshireman's motive, all through history, has been to protect himself by forcible exclusion. For this we describe him as 'clannish' – though the term is not well chosen; for the drives that power him in this way are not the centripetal, clumping drives of the true or 'Celtic' clansman, but the centrifugal, separating ones of the head of a single isolationist family. The West Riding, through the centuries, was one of the strongholds of the small freeholder, all but the poorest effectively self-supporting with a handful of horses and cows and maybe just a few pigs. He was thus independent; 'my own master'. As a result the woollen industry evolved here on quite different lines compared with the West Country or East Anglia.

The town of York, it is known, was an important centre for trading in wool long before A.D. 1000 and weavers' guilds were in being by the twelfth century, if not earlier.[146] The manufacturing industry developed slowly and steadily in the hands of men who were primarily manual craftsmen (as opposed to entrepreneurs), who did not depend on this wholly for their livelihood and who owned both their looms and the material on which they worked, unlike the clothiers and weavers in the other parts of England. Unlike workers elsewhere, too, any wage-earner in the Yorkshire industry had a reasonable chance – and knew he had – of rising to the status of a master. This gave it superior, built-in strengths, and in later years it was to outgrow and overtake its Southern rivals by being free of the genteel pretensions that tended to sap their energies. In addition, by preserving small-scale manœuvrability it was able to introduce vital new machinery the more rapidly for not having to contend with the resistance of large-scale work forces.[147] Even as late as 1856 only half the workers engaged in woollen manufacturing here were employed in factories: the rest continued to work in their own homes, on the domestic system. And down to this day a multiplicity of small to medium-sized firms, each under tight (and often tight-fisted) family control, has remained the basic pattern.

Now, however, this pattern is condemned as a menace. The industry, it is held, urgently requires rationalisation by mergers; but in the way of this stands 'the stubborn independence of Yorkshiremen who would rather be their own bosses, support their far-flung relations comfortably, and live well from a rundown firm than be part of a larger, if more efficient, organisation'.[148] The same yeoman mentality is also identified as the source of a widespread malaise in Yorkshire local government, in which far too many small municipalities, too small to be efficiently viable, insist on retaining their autonomy against all normal sense and logic.[51]

The Yorkshireman, however, is only interested in expansion in so far as this promises direct and foreseeable benefits to himself and his immediate family. The whole trend in his way of life is towards containment, not annexation: he is concerned with bulwarks, not problematical alien forays. While he is not inward-looking, he is none the less firmly based. His home is a barn, a place where he stores himself and gathers in his possessions, a place into which he retires and where he takes unkindly to being disturbed. He has that special resentment of prying that so many psychological studies have found to be often closely associated with a strongly authoritarian personality, and expresses a particularly marked dislike of gossip, to which he shows himself hypersensitive. Wives who gossip, especially, incur his condemnation.[21] Compared with the rest of England, more people in Yorkshire say they prefer the company of their family to that of anyone else and there is greater disapproval of too many interests outside the home.[21] The home constitutes a haven from the rough outside world, and over it the man presides as a strutting paterfamilias while the woman ministers unto him and defers to his wishes.

Hat styles like bonnets, the insignia of retreating womanhood, seem to keep reappearing in this region with more revivalist vigour than elsewhere. It is odd, indeed, in view of this attachment to the home that so many wives in Yorkshire have long held full-time outside jobs, and hard to believe that they have not always been much more difficult to lure away from there than in Lancashire. The domestic system, in which by tradition it was the woman who did the spinning, survived much longer in wool than in cotton. Factory work did not achieve its present scale, indeed, till the textile strike of 1883 and the fact that it was a Yorkshire city, Bradford, that pioneered the municipal crèche at least suggests that rather stronger inducements needed to be offered there to prise the married woman away from her hearth.

Wifely skills are esteemed extremely highly in Yorkshire, certainly more than elsewhere in England.[21] Even so, the wives here are not such all-round paragons as this might seem to suggest. The number of home dressmakers,[91] for instance, proves to be by no means exceptional – though more of the sewing-machines here are electric and more of them modern than elsewhere – those who knit have a rather low output, and an exceptionally small proportion indulge at all in embroidery.[91] Could this perhaps be because none of these activities is appreciated sufficiently by men? By comparison the home itself, which men must and do notice, has lavished on it an almost smothering amount of devoted care and attention. It is decorated internally more often than in all other regions (in contrast to Lancashire, where it is the outside – the social 'front' – that is most attended to), the wife taking part in the painting and papering to an extent only rivalled in the Midlands;[68] and it is furnished richly and snugly, even massively – armchairs and the like being necessarily hefty to hold such hefty bodies – and padded out luxuriously with those special Yorkshire and Tyneside favourites, carpets and rugs, at the expense, sometimes, of linoleum but more generally of exposed polished wood. The North East, it appears, cannot abide the stark nakedness of floors. Fitted carpets here, for years, have formed an important status symbol and on Tyneside, in particular, they hold what must be a dauntingly high position in a normally badly strained domestic budget. The 'pricking' of hearthrugs has a wide and impressive pedigree in Yorkshire, and these in turn go back, perhaps, to a custom for covering floors with fleeces in a county always liberally supplied with these, thanks to its sheep-centred economy. This is the only area in Britain today where bedroom slippers are ordinarily called 'carpet' slippers – implying that their principal purpose is to save the wear on the carpets (trust Yorkshire people to have such a thought for the wool), not to shelter the feet on trips between the bed and the bathroom. They have to appear in public more, and for this reason they tend to be more elegant and altogether more money is spent on them. Backless slippers, which most of the rest of Britain, in the absence of central heating, has inevitably tended to spurn, have proved every bit as popular with women here as in the well-warmed, ultra-stylish Metropolis.

Above all, however, it is as a cook, as a supreme virtuoso of the oven, that the Yorkshire wife expects to excel – and to be recognised and praised for that excellence. For in this region that swaddles itself in a thoroughly Teutonic *Gemütlichkeit* it is only natural that, in similar Teutonic fashion, the heaviest emphasis of all should fall on food and eating. The way to a Yorkshireman's heart, with a vengeance, is through his stomach; and he has such a perpetual voraciousness that keeping him – and herself – satisfied demands a kitchen production-line almost on the scale of a conveyor-belt. As the native conservatism precludes much variety, the conspicuous energies poured into cooking have to be expended instead on stakhanovite achievements in volume and quantity. Yorkshire cuisine is geared, accordingly, to the turning out of batches; it eschews the 'one-off' run of the élite-servicing specialist. Its high-spot, inevitably, is baking: a test of keeping to a time-honoured, regular and almost ritual process, which puts an absolute discount on inventiveness. Yorkshire wives still bake their own bread far more than wives in other regions – and far more of them, too, continue to do this daily. Cakes and scones, as well, are still made at home by a majority.[45] This, of course, saves much money and allows the consumption of cakes and buns to remain as high as ever unaffected by rising prices in the shops. Home-baked food in itself, moreover, tends to be devoured in greater volume, not merely on account of its normally greater tastiness, but in order to do honour to the labours of the cook. The wife can thus take comfort from the threefold thought: that she has saved the family money, that she has persuaded it to eat more and, above all, that she has provided it with more certainly wholesome sustenance. For the home bakers of Yorkshire have the further special trait that they insist much more firmly than elsewhere on using only the 'best' ingredients – which means as far as possible non-synthetic ones, applied in unsparing quantities. To put in fat, for example, is regarded here as a *sine qua non* of home breadmaking, so much so that during the war, when fat grew hard to come by, many wives gave up baking their bread for the duration rather than tolerate a product that was necessarily substandard in quality.[149] This fat itself, moreover, should be, for preference, natural; and accordingly Yorkshire keeps to lard far more than the rest of the North and tends to reject the branded compound cooking-fats. For the same reason packet cake-mixes have met with exceptionally stiff resistance here; and as Yorkshire supplies so large a slice of the country's home cake-makers – and, even more, of their output of cakes – it is not altogether a cause for wonder that one of the leading American cake-mix manufacturers should lately have abandoned the British market for good after only a few years' struggle, thoroughly disheartened. Even self-raising flour has achieved less outright dominance here than elsewhere in Britain, being still considered, one must suppose, a somewhat dubious intruder into this most fiercely ritualised domain in this most traditional of all the regions of England.

This heavy dependence on home baking seems, even so, only partly to blame for the fact that the Yorkshire diet is rather overweighted with carbohydrate. For this there exists as well, surely, a much more basic reason, which is to be found in the whole approach here to the matter of food and eating. Yorkshiremen, quite simply, eat to fill themselves. They eat not just to end a sense of hunger or to enjoy a tasty dish: they eat to make sure that no possible gap in the appetite is temporarily left unplugged. And for this elementary function buns and cakes, puddings and bread present themselves as the simple and obvious candidates. Brown bread, malt bread, baked beans, fish-cakes, rice, suet puddings – all these are

Yorkshire specialities, all typical space-fillers, all rich in carbohydrate.

On top of this tendency to solidness in the kind of items favoured, the meals themselves in Yorkshire tend to be both more numerous and more sizable on average. Breakfast, alone, is of relatively modest dimensions (a shadow of its one-time self, it is said), much more than elsewhere restricted to a single cooked course, without bread or toast to follow and preceded by neither cereals or porridge.[45] (Yorkshire has never taken to modern breakfast cereals to the same extent as other regions and, lying well outside the oat zone, lacks the well-marked tradition for porridge that Lancashire shares, in its own small way, with Scotland.) As the day wears on, the eating steadily increases both in volume and duration. High tea, the climax, is eaten later on average than in either Lancashire or Scotland[45] (why, one wonders?) and is normally a repast so overwhelming in its size as commonly to defeat anyone not bred to it. Yet for many Yorkshire people even that is not enough. Later in the evening, in many cases even as late as 10 p.m., no less than one family in every five sits down to a further hot meal – and a proper meal, be it noted, not a snack – consisting, as often as not,[45] of a large plate of fish-and-chips.

Even in between meals the munching goes on, almost as if the jaws functioned automatically. The people of Yorkshire, as a result, eat a lot of fruit. Though they eat less of this than in the South overall – in other words, less at a sitting – they eat fresh fruit with considerably greater frequency and regularity.[3] This is due to the fact that, like the Scots but unlike the rest of the English (at least those further south), they tend to treat it less as a dessert, or as a substitute for a dessert, than as a sideboard reserve to which all overcome by hunger can have free and continual recourse. And even in this their choice goes to the bulkiest, juiciest kinds, like oranges, which more people here than elsewhere name as their favourite.[3]

To accommodate so much bulk, some other foods inevitably have to suffer. The main victims are fish (as eaten apart from chips or in some form other than fish cakes), green vegetables in general, fresh tomatoes and salads. The anti-processing bias also keeps down consumption of tinned fruit (much more than consumption of tinned vegetables); it also keeps away fish pastes and leads to a wholesale rejection of gravy powders.

All this cooking and baking, along with her other household chores, results in the Yorkshire wife having little enough time for a spirited social existence. Her wings, in any case, are kept quite severely clipped by her husband. She rarely drinks spirits, smokes very sparsely, and uses cosmetics sufficiently lightly to suggest little formal parading of her features in public. These imply that she spends most time in the home – the hen-bird in her nest – and this is confirmed by the specially heavy readership here of the women's weeklies and monthlies. Nevertheless, despite this comparatively secluded mode of life, she is certainly no frump. Yorkshire has a name for good dressing: for smartness, that is, rather than for high style-consciousness; for fashion, as we have seen, is only followed here from a comparatively safe distance. The emphasis falls instead on good materials and cut. Every Yorkshireman is an expert, self-styled or genuine, on cloth; people in Yorkshire can therefore dress to compete on this basis, in a way altogether too rarefied for the less informed *beaux mondes* of other regions to manage quite to copy. There is plenty of money for spending on clothes and, in Leeds especially, plenty of small, exclusive fashion shops for the would-be well dressed to patronise. Even so, in the judgement of fashion experts who have toured the leading British cities, Yorkshire is only remarkable in one simple respect:[150] for its eye-catching parade of obviously expensive, extremely stylish women's hats. Yorkshire women, furthermore, were in the habit of visiting their hairdressers more often than British women in general (and so have required and bought fewer electric hair-driers) well before the habits of teenagers in these matters assumed their present dominance; they also led the remainder of the provinces in the use of the rather more sophisticated cosmetics.

Yorkshire women, one may infer from this, make their main effort to appeal from the neckline upwards, ringing the changes in this conventionally more mobile zone all the more attentively for the restraint they insist on observing further down. For Yorkshire, hard-headed, canny Yorkshire, disapproves of low durability. Clothes have to be bought for hard, continuous wear or for wear on carefully few occasions over lengthy periods. This results in not many garments bought but in high average prices paid for them – a pattern proved to apply to items as varied as stockings, suits and slippers. They buy rather few raincoats, rather more three-quarter-length coats, perhaps because they consider the latter better value for money (and perhaps because they are always inclined to be faithful, if possible, to wool). The overall effect that they aim at, and achieve, is not a forthright sexiness, but a subtler display of womanly charm, an appealing natural simplicity. Some of their tastes, indeed, seem to hint even at a leaning to self-effacement: their special fondness for brown slippers is just one instance. It could be that under forceful pressure from the menfolk in this region, so exceptionally exultant in their manliness, the women feel compelled to accentuate their conventional dispar-ities, fluffing out the more feminine edges to their nature and effecting a tactful withdrawal towards the more modest, less socially straining end of the sexual spectrum. Sat on by their husbands, as it were, they withdraw their personalities in due proportion.

Yorkshire husbands are the most critical in all Britain of feminine frailties and failings.[21] They huff and they puff; they demand to be treated as lords and masters. They clench a pipe in their mouths, belligerently, far more than the men elsewhere in the North or the Mid-lands and their consumption of pipe tobacco is easily the heaviest in the country. This they insist on buying themselves, more firmly than other Northern pipe-smokers, just as they regularly buy gadgets for the house, such as oil-stoves without the presence of their wives, in this respect being quite unlike the Scots. On the other hand, like the Scots and the Welsh, the older men seem to regard buying clothes with apathy, if not distaste; and more often than elsewhere in England the wife buys most or all of her husband's clothes for him in his absence, even down to his shoes and ties. In consequence, as in Wales, wardrobes are kept in smoothly efficient condition and the men themselves flatteringly spick-and-span.[151] To be seen to fuss about their appearance, however, or to indulge in superfluous accessories is, for older men at least, an admission of effeminacy. Umbrellas, in particular, are regarded as the ultimate in the decadence of the South-erner, mollycoddles' playthings. 'A Yorkshireman is more afraid to be seen by his neighbours with an open umbrella than to be seen with another woman', as a writer in *Yorkshire Life* so aptly put it.[152] A man needs no superfluous sheltering here. He is content just to wear a cap or a hat – indeed, he goes and buys these distinctly more often than elsewhere, perhaps due to the influence of his womenfolk, or perhaps, less simply, because Yorkshire people as a whole appear to have a hardly suppressed horror of baring their heads in the open. Their most die-hard native incantation ('On Ilkla Moor baht 'at') stresses, and serves to keep fresh in the memory, the awful fate of someone who dared to go out on to a moor recklessly hatless (and ended up by being eaten by worms, another peculiarly Yorkshire horror: they vehemently opt for cremation, conceivably for just this reason, unlike the Scots, their neighbours spatially and emotionally, who candidly prefer to be buried[23]).

Apart from this there remains one further oddity of the

Yorkshire male's customary outfit that can hardly fail to escape attention: his incurable attachment to the cardigan – so strangely similar to a feminine garment in a region that otherwise goes out of its way to accentuate its contrasts. One can only presume that this owes its charmed immunity to ridicule to some ultra-respectable hidden ancestry: a descent from sheepskin waistcoats, perhaps, from a time when wearing one's wealth round one's middle was rather more the fashion?

These sharp discontinuities between the sexes are reasserted no less vigorously between the younger and the older generations. In recent interviews with teenage girls in Yorkshire and on Tyneside, psychologists have been astonished to find the enormous influence mothers still exercise here on daughters, in comparison with the Midlands or South East. On Tyneside, in particular, girls still tend to dress like their mothers to an extent encountered now nowhere else in Britain,[83] which explains why the market for teenage fashions here has remained so puzzlingly underdeveloped. The children in this region, handicapped by having such positive, role-confident parents and lapped around by a home-life so insidiously adhesive, appear to accept the values of their elders much more unquestioningly, an inclination that must also come more naturally in a society such as this made up so largely of uncomplicated extroverts. It is indicative of this that more school-leavers in Yorkshire than elsewhere are firmly bound into apprenticeships, and that the region as a whole has distinguished itself, at least up to the mid-1950s, by the most conscientious patronage of one-sex youth clubs.[21]

But while the children can be dominated, the grand-parents are less malleable and, Yorkshiremen being Yorkshiremen and unduly prone to 'blow their tops', they receive the necessary incentives to remove themselves and to lead a life apart. A social system which depends for its strength on hard-and-fast rulings and the reign of a single supreme authority must find more than usually uncomfortable the housing of two generations of adults under only one roof. The West Riding, accordingly, has the fewest homes that contain near-relatives of any region in Britain. Correspondingly, it also has a high incidence of elderly single persons or couples who live entirely on their own. This is due also, of course, to stubborn Yorkshire independence. And certainly it does not imply any outright neglect of the old people by their children; for they are visited most religiously, especially on one institutionalised occasion, after Sunday church or chapel, which is made into a splendid excuse for the pouring out of cocktails or, at humbler levels, of home-made wines.

Through all these aspects of Yorkshire life, however crucial or however trivial, it is possible to detect weaving in or out a certain common thread: a liking for definite divisions, sharp social contours, clear lines of separation – between the sexes, between the generations, between the everyday and the special occasion, between the bleakness of the outside world and the warming intimacy of the family. Political divisions in Yorkshire show up unusually starkly, as in East Anglia. And the pattern even breaks through in the one great native art form, choral singing: the polyphonic harmony made up of two marked differences in tone, one high, one low, singled out for mention as a special local characteristic some eight hundred years ago by Giraldus Cambrensis, who suggested the custom came from the Danes or the Norsemen. Yorkshire is a land that puts its trust in sharpness, a sharpness that penetrates to almost everything: of barbed comments and pointed remarks, the home of the knife trade, the county of Ripley, Filey and Scissett. Here, at Halifax, people were still being beheaded, merely for stealing cloth, as late as around 1650, well after this barbarous usage had come to an end everywhere else in Britain.[146] A harsh and ruthless quality still resides here only just beneath the surface. The Yorkshireman has a warm and generous heart. He can also be cold and unrelenting in pursuit of the goals that most immediately concern him. While he makes a rock-like friend, he also makes a highly dangerous adversary.

Despite its great size, however, and despite its forceful and very positive personality, Yorkshire has consistently failed throughout the centuries to stamp its own image on the neighbouring counties to the north. As ever, its energies have gone, rather, into the strengthening of its boundaries – into heightening its definition. Its traditional temper is that of the rooted homesteader, not of the colonising migrant. There thus remains a further, extensive North East still to be considered: part of that wide no-man's-land or buffer state separating England from Scotland that the Registrar General, in an unfortunate lapse, most regrettably allowed to be christened 'the Northern Region'.

Few names, surely, could be more ill-chosen. Others that are used instead, however, are scarcely much better: 'Northumbria' is inaccurate (for the old Anglian kingdom of that name extended from the Humber up to the Forth), 'the extreme North of England' clumsy, 'the North East' thoroughly ambiguous, 'the North, North East' uncomfortably pedantic, 'the North Country' (proposed by two professional geographers) quite absurd. Let us settle for 'the Tyne-Tees area': this is now widely familiar and geographically self-explanatory, even though it fails to extend to what is rightly the western half of this sub-region, under-populated Cumbria. At least it contains the main mass of the inhabitants, Northumberland and Durham between them accounting for six in every ten and the tightly clustered Tyneside conurbation centred on Newcastle for as many as one-quarter. As such generalised terms go, therefore, this one seems conveniently usable.

The whole area that it covers has many features of

great distinctiveness. For a start, as if to emphasise this, it stands out in a blaze of red – for, very curiously, no less than 18 per cent of the people in these Border counties have hair technically classifiable as red, a far greater proportion than in any other British region and over four times as many as in Yorkshire. This is a warning that we are entering 'Celtic' country once more, for red hair is also frequent (though nothing like so strikingly) in Wales and Scotland.[153] Socially and culturally, as well, both halves of this Tyne-Tees area, each in their own separate ways, stand sharply apart. In Cumberland and Westmorland the kinship structure differs from the typical English pattern and tends to resemble that in Devon. Here people trace relationships in detail as far as second cousins and instead of a 'great-aunt' talk of their 'father's mother's sister' – a kind of half-way approach to the more fully-developed 'Celtic' lineage system, appropriate to such an intermediate zone.[154] The same two counties also share a special building style, making use of the local Silurian Shale, quite different from anything found elsewhere.[155] In so far as they look anywhere, they look not southwards, but eastwards, in obedience to physical geography: through the Tyne Gap to Newcastle, the logical capital of the whole area. Carlisle, for example, plays in the North-eastern League in the crucial, allegiance-testing field of football. There is more to this, too, than mere convenience of communications. The dalesmen of Cumberland, Vikings to this day in all but nationality, are the spiritual brothers of the people of the almost equally heavily Norse-influenced Tyne-Tees coastal fringe.

Northumberland and Durham, in their turn, are, if anything, even more idiosyncratic. The county of Durham for five hundred years, up to the time of Henry VIII, maintained itself as an autonomous Palatinate, enjoying self-rule under its bishop. It appointed its own judges, minted its own coinage, even kept its own army. The last of these privileges of the bishops was swept away only as recently as 1836. We are dealing, therefore, with a land that certainly has some justification for the feeling it has, and which it tries to impress on the rest of the country so vigorously, of being somewhat apart, half-foreign even. Its sense of identity, indeed, rivals that of Yorkshire or Cornwall. This has produced, in turn, an admirable cultural resilience. In so primitive a matter as children's rhymes and sayings Northumberland and Durham show themselves abundantly different, time after time, from the whole of the rest of England.[156] The Tees is a historic dividing line. As one crosses it, the haystacks change in shape from the rectangular type of England to the Scottish beehive, the scythes alter in their outline, a new way of constructing dry-stone walls takes over.[155] The boundary fixed between England and Scotland was an entirely political boundary, which made little sense either racially or culturally. To this day the people of northern Northumberland, on the evidence of their blood-groups,[111] are essentially Scottish in their physical affinity. Obviously Scottish traits are interwoven, too, into the everyday life of the area. This is the only part of England, for example, with a preponderance of the three-roomed dwelling, which is so general in Scotland. Most workers, as in Scotland, go home to lunch. There is a tradition of touring vans.[86] A lot is spent on clothes for girls, very little by comparison on clothes for boys. Little is spent on hairdressing. Disinfectants are used in the home extremely sparsely.[128] Relatively few households own cars. In these and many other ways the pattern is Scottish, not English.

The diet, especially, presents an intriguing mixture. At first glance it might be taken to be essentially Scottish: the types of meat and fish most eaten are those most preferred in Scotland, there is the same great liking for both plain and chocolate biscuits, for root vegetables, for butter beans. Then the exceptions start to show up. The biscuits include the greatest quantity of cream crackers, to which Yorkshire is also strongly partial, but very few –

like Yorkshire again – of the Scotsman's savoury varieties.[157] The oatmeal bought is at the English level, implying no particular fondness for porridge. Probing beneath the surface, in fact, we find that the more deep-rooted traditions, such as the whole complex of home baking, are most decidedly English, suggesting that, of the two, it is the Scottishness, rather, that forms the intrusive patina. The area, one might say, is Scotland plus the oven (and plus pottery, for the teapots are entirely English, far more seldom than in Scotland made of metal[13]). As in Yorkshire, there is a heavy usage of both flour and cooking fats; fish-cakes, malt bread and canned tomatoes, all favourites south of the Tees, are also much esteemed. Most kinds of green vegetables find their way on to the table on a far wider scale than in Scotland and there is an equally un-Scottish acceptance of pig products, such as bacon, Spam and pork sausages – the last competing on even terms here with the beef variety, for which the Scots have so marked a preference. The tastes in drink, too, are basically English – much the lowest number of spirits drinkers in Britain, for example – but with a recognisably Scottish overtone; the local ales being famous for their strength and brews from across the Border having long secured a very firm following here. Yet as in that other intermediate area, the Midlands, there are also one or two peculiarities confined just to the Tyne-Tees area itself: the novel products of recombination, perhaps, such as also emerge wherever hybrids between natural organisms occur on any extensive scale. Most striking of these is an astonishing capacity (and presumably liking) for canned peas, a quite exceptional demand for corned beef, and by far the heaviest consumption in the country of brown bread, which here accounts for some 10 per cent of all bread eaten – compared with only about 5 per cent everywhere else in Britain. Milk and cheese, in contrast, have a consumption lower even than in either Yorkshire or Scotland. A deep red colour is traditionally popular for cheese on Tyneside,[25] so much so that some local inhabitants, after moving to other areas, confess themselves quite surprised to have found that cheese can also be cream-coloured.

Certain distinctions of the area have their parallel in South Wales and are clearly due to the massing here of so many miners. A fondness for hot, spicy foods, for example, provoked by dusty throats: hence a heavy demand for cheap and potent sauces and hence, too, that great spare-time interest of miners here, the growing of leeks – a taste for which is also found in Scotland but not, it appears, in Yorkshire.[43] Tea, for presumably the same reason, is preferred very strong, which goes part of the way to explaining the little milk consumed and possibly accounts for the fact that for years the most expensive blends have been bought here on a considerably larger scale than anywhere else in Britain,[13] which is unexpected in an area which has long known so little prosperity. Mining is also largely responsible for the very high proportion of households possessing a washing-machine (now over 70 per cent in the Tyne-Tees I.T.V. area) or, alternatively, a wash-boiler; and for the fact that over 90 per cent of homes still rely on solid fuel as their principal source of heating. Even more certainly, it is responsible for the exceptional extent of betting – on racing between creatures as varied as horses, pigeons and whippets – reflected already in a density of licensed betting-offices second only to South Wales in proportion to population.[108] In the Northern Region there are more families than in any other (nearly 8 per cent) that live in rent-free housing by reason of the husband's occupation, and in almost half of all such cases the qualifying occupation is mining. The typical afflictions, too, of miners – pneumoconiosis, rheumatism, skin diseases, and the like – lead to the typically high amount of absence off work from such causes.[6] In addition, the Newcastle Hospital Area stands out for the great numbers admitted as in-patients with serious burns,[61] which is probably a measure of the high incidence locally of welding and steelmaking.

The dominance of heavy industry on this far north-eastern coast has two effects, both of them entirely predictable. One is the low availability of jobs for women, which results in the comparative rarity of wives who go out to work – at the most just over a quarter, as against a third in Britain in general. The other is an undue preponderance of manual workers, the upper and upper-middle classes being less well represented than anywhere else in Britain, as shown, for example, by the phenomenal rarity of private telephones (in only 12 per cent of homes in the Tyne-Tees Television Area). A very high proportion of homes are rented from local councils and this has as its corollary a low number – only about a third in the industrialised belt – in the hands of owner-occupiers. Detached houses are likewise notably lacking. The shortage of middle-class housing that this implies is believed to be an important factor in discouraging executives from moving to jobs here from other areas.

The middle class in the sense in which this term is understood in the South is probably far smaller even than the bare figures themselves suggest, for the fact that the Labour Party has consistently collected a dispropor-tionately high number of middle-class votes here, as also in Wales, points to a relatively weak association between a higher income and the attitude of social and political dissent normally consequent upon an elevated economic status. This is borne out by the finding that on Tyneside the different income-groups differ less sharply than elsewhere in the styles and standard of clothing that they purchase,[83] as if the better-off deliberately chose to dress 'down'. Admittedly, this is one more area, again like Wales, that is notably backward in general fashion-awareness.[83] Even teenage fashions, if they succeed in penetrating up here at all (the absence of black leather

175

jackets is a case in point), are considerably more muted and regularly, as in shoes,[92] up to six months behind the general trend. Spending on lingerie, that sensitive seismograph of chic, is distinctly lower than elsewhere in the North, and only in the high percentage who make use of cosmetics (a feature shared with Yorkshire) can the women of this area be said to show any noticeable concern for self-adornment.

A further factor contributing to the prevailing political uniformity is, no doubt, the exceptional scarcity here of that usually reactionary figure, the small shopkeeper; for he is crowded out on Tyneside by the extraordinary prevalence of large bazaar-like stores, which succeed in attracting to themselves a large part of the trade normally the preserve of various specialist retailers. These, one may suppose, developed from roofed-in assemblies of market stalls, the old booth-vending system which British department stores are partially returning to, perhaps by accident, in the guise of 'shops-within-shops'. Newcastle, even today, has many markets, open as well as covered. Doubtless they proved such a magnet in days gone by that single-unit shops found it advisable to present themselves on this same general pattern, in order to prosper.

This retailing structure, like the structure of Tyne-Tees industry, is hardly an inducement to bold, adventurous innovation. The larger the shop, at least in an area such as this, the more will it tend to be geared to meeting the lowest common denominator in public demand and the less inclined will it be to experiment. It will avoid, as far as possible, catering for minorities. New trends in buying, as a rule, are started either by the middle classes, who are so small in numbers here that their economic 'pushing-power' in this respect must at best be ineffective, or else by the young, who although numerous enough (for families here tend to be on the generous 'Celtic' scale) appear to be too isolated from national currents and too dominated still by the tastes of their elders to exercise a financially irresistible influence on the overall retailing pattern. There is, in short, too poorly-developed an 'infrastructure' of specialising shops to cater for the odd person out, just as there is too little diversity of industry for proper economic health. And both of these deficiencies arise from, and in turn help to perpetuate, the over-homogeneous social pattern of the area and the consequent stunting uniformity of behaviour that it has for too long – because to its own ultimate disadvantage – helped to foster and sustain.

That this is a poverty-stricken area is a truism; and one finds here, as one would expect, the usual tell-tale signs of widespread depression of the general standard of living, such as little buying of electrical equipment and a very heavy consumption of rice pudding. Housing conditions are often squalid and are the most overcrowded any-where outside Scotland. The death rate is the worst in the country after that of Lancashire, and the stillbirth rate is just about as deplorable. Nearly all households have access to some kind of garden, but the low number of lawn-mowers and greenhouses owned suggests that relatively few of these are of any size. Nevertheless, there are exceptions, as always, to the overall pattern. Tyneside resembles Wales in its wholesale conversion to the handy but expensive tinned and frozen foods. Spending on furniture (apart from the much-desired carpets) is, inex-plicably, a good deal heavier than the economic back-ground would seem to warrant. There is also a surprisingly extensive possession of tape-recorders – shown by two separate surveys (by two rival firms) to be above, and possibly well above, the national average.

A delight in tape-recording fits in well with another feature specially characteristic of this area: a great devotion, evidently of quite long standing, to the various forms of passive light entertainment – listening to Radio Luxembourg, watching television and, above all, visiting

the cinema. As late as 1958, before television had succeeded in securing its present blanket coverage, twice as
many housewives in the Northern Region as in Britain
as a whole paid at least one visit a week to the cinema.
In the early 'fifties, before the real advent of television,
Newcastle cinemas had an average of one visit per head
per week compared with a national figure of one per
fortnight. Admissions per head there were actually
greater in 1954 than four years earlier, despite the
opening of the local television station in the meantime.[159]
Only Scotland has shown itself attached to both the
cinema and the commercial radio to anything like the
same extent, and it seems likely that the unusually high
proportion of children of school age both there and
on Tyneside goes some of the way towards explaining
this.

It is natural, even so, that the cinema should have
proved such a popular outlet in this urban area. Unlike
the Scots, more like the Welsh and the people of Yorkshire, Tynesiders read extremely little. Their readership
is low, even, of the magazines devoted to one of their
greatest leisure interests: 'do-it-yourself'. Far more, men
as well as women, do repair or decorating jobs about the
house here than in Britain in general – two-thirds, in fact,
of all adults, despite the very low incidence of home
ownership. Electric drills, those infallible signs of the
home-handyman, enjoy an unexpectedly wide distribution. In an area with such an abundance of highly
skilled manual workers, a display of deft-handedness
spilling over into leisure hours would perhaps only be
remarkable were it absent. But it suggests, as well, a
certain devoted attention to the home, on a scale not to
be encountered at all in Scotland. And this is no doubt
encouraged, just as in Wales, by the few vehicles owned
here, which might have tempted such attention to wander,
all private transport, and cars in particular, being in
noticeably small supply. Correspondingly, spending on

buses is high, doubtless due to the general habit of going home from work for meals at midday. Apart from this, very little travelling is indulged in and few people, compared with Scots or Yorkshiremen, go away from home on holiday in any typical twelve months. The cinema, therefore, as in the mining communities of Wales, is an obvious beneficiary: the only way out of town, as it were, is to go to a 'Western'.

Drinking one's way out, at any rate, is a firmly closed avenue. The industrial belt here is probably the most obstinately teetotal of any area in the country. The quite exceptional strength of Nonconformism is apparent from the fact that proportionately more Methodist marriages take place in the Northern Region than in any other. There are the fewest declared drinkers of beer and cider and, still more, of table-wines and spirits, the percentage of regular drinkers of these last two in particular being only about half the national average. Home-made wines, as usual, are popular and spending on soft drinks is elevated also. Sales per head are poor at both off-licences and licensed grocers, and even public-houses are scarce – much of the drinking taking place in working-men's clubs. The restrictions imposed by the justices on the number of on-licences, in defence of a sober front in public, has had the effect of setting up in Durham and Northumberland an almost complete alternative retailing system for drink, there being one club almost to every two public-houses.[160] Non-subscribers to the pledge tend to drink, accordingly, with the full-throated abandon so traditional to club clienteles – and to all areas where so many men sweat away all day in mines and in foundries. This is a hard world and a man's world; and we shall not find here, as well we might in the Midlands, a woman at every other drinker's elbow. The place for the women here, very firmly and definitely, is in the home.

VIII

Scotland

'Except in Scotland.'

So runs a favourite escape-phrase of marketing men. And as often as not it is abundantly justified. For Scotland differs from all the English regions in a myriad different ways, as is only to be expected of a land of five and a quarter millions – one Scotsman to every eight Englishmen – that remained a foreign, independent country until as recently as two and a half centuries ago. In many respects it is still half-foreign. The Border may be a boundary in the political sense no longer (except, rather curiously, for the dead, who can be permitted in by law only if provided with an Out-of-England Order), but in a cultural sense it still has very substantial validity.

In some traits, indeed, Scotland resembles the Continent rather than England. With France, in particular, its links were numerous and strong, enduring for many centuries; and to the 'Auld Alliance' an enormous influence has been credited, especially in the realm of manners. In the eighteenth century the general custom of greeting strangers with a kiss and the use of 'friend' in conversation were singled out as specifically French in their affinity.[61] The serving of a dessert course, of fruit and sweets, another French custom, was also well established in Scotland before it reached England. Cooking in general was much influenced by the French until the advent of strict Presbyterianism round about 1650,[162] and one relic of this today, almost certainly, is the relatively large number of

Scots wives who insist on using butter for cooking – a practice mainly to be met with in France and Southern Europe. Even the haggis is of French inspiration, derived from *hachis*, meaning minced meat.

There are also suggestive affinities with the Scandinavian countries. Scotland belongs climatically in the same Nordic Zone as these; and its fishing and farming and therefore food-preparing practices might be expected to have a certain similarity, due to the general environmental resemblances as much as to any cross-cultural exchange of traditions. Such an explanation might cover the wide acceptance of herrings, the shortage of cooked green vegetables, the drinking of milk (especially with meals) by so many adults, and the use of similar methods of breadmaking. The resemblances, however, go beyond just these. A glass of neat spirits with a beer 'chaser' – reputedly the quickest way to get drunk – has exact parallels in Scandinavia, with schnapps replacing whisky. A common taste for lager points to an older, shared tradition; so, too, does the less widely-known fondness of the Scots for drinking 'white' spirits neat, with gin, rum and now even vodka standing in for their Scandinavian counterparts. The cylindrical rolls of meat to be seen in butchers' windows in Scotland turn up in Scandinavia also, as does cheese at breakfast (this in Holland, too, of course), which is a regular custom with one Scottish family in ten,[45] though principally in winter. Perhaps, too, the Scots' weakness for cream cakes was originally due to Continental influence, or their liking for cold drinks with ice-cream, or their system of selling from door to door from touring vans. If so, however, we can only guess at how and when these and their like came in, for documentary evidence would seem to be lacking.

Much more unexpected, perhaps, by comparison, is the discovery that in a surprising number of ways Scotland also resembles London. Even the multitude of Scots who have migrated to the Southern capital[163] (their prevalence well attested by the thirty pages of 'Macs' who now occupy the London telephone directory), can hardly account for the scale of the parallelism that emerges from sample surveys. Both areas sit down, for example, to somewhat similar breakfasts: fruit juices, boiled eggs (in winter, in place of having them fried), sometimes even haddock. The two share the widest amount of lager-drinking among men and the highest consumption, as a whole, of colas; they are also the only parts of Britain where both sexes show equal numbers admitting to drinking gin. Each tends to buy its vegetables more from specialist greengrocers,[2] chooses tomato instead of vegetable when buying canned soups, has a greater liking for filter-tipped cigarettes and for certain kinds of confectionery, more regularly uses hand cream, eats fruit and custard much more often for the midday meal,[45] and spends the most on pastas – all tastes that are more sophisticated, more unfamiliar, in some cases even semi-Continental. The two, in short, display a greater urbanity.

In drawing this conclusion, and others like it, we possibly rate the Scots more highly than in actual truth they deserve. For the habit of more or less confining the sample in so many nation-wide surveys (in the interests of economy) to the densely populated central belt must have the effect of over-dramatising the urbanised character of the country. It is true that this central industrial area, on its own, houses a sizable part of the total Scottish nation, which is even more preponderantly compressed into towns and cities than the English. Even so, the generalisations to be inferred on the basis of survey data are often seriously misleading, for the tastes and usages in the urban areas tend to differ far more sharply from those in the rural areas than is commonly the case in England. The chief reason for this is the enormous contrast in space. Flats constitute roughly two homes out of every three in the Scottish cities, a much higher proportion than even in London, and relatively few households in consequence have the advantage of a garden. Dogs, whatever their size, are only about half as frequent in the cities than in the far north of Scotland and cats are, proportionately, even scarcer, as few as 6 per cent of households in Aberdeen possessing one, compared with over 20 per cent in the rural hinterland. Motor cars, similarly, are half as numerous again as in the cities and private telephones, equally essential props to isolation, far more widely provided. The countryside, moreover, like countrysides everywhere, is more devoutly religious and, in the case of Scotland, this means more dedicatedly puritanical. That ultra-strict fringe, the Free Church, for example, finds most of its support, at least in proportion to population, from Invernesshire northwards. There are many more non-smokers in the rural areas in consequence; two wives in every three in the far north, too, still claim to engage in the laborious business of home baking. It must be remembered, therefore, that Scotland is much more variable internally than is generally thought to be the case in England.

It varies, furthermore, in more than just this one dimension. For there is an East-West dichotomy in the country, which overlaps and is often confused with the far better-known Highland-Lowland one. The East is hard, cautious, taciturn, methodical, seen at its most typical in the granitic Aberdonian; the West is amiable, emotional, expansive, the Scotland of the Gael, the tartan and the bagpipes.[164] The Western Scot is predominantly Mediterranean in race, dark and narrow-headed, descended from the early Neolithic colonists who first settled the west coasts for preference; though there may also be a still more ancient stock in the Highlands, possibly pre-Neolithic in origin, tall, heavy, muscular people who have traditionally supplied the Lowlands with many of their policemen. The Eastern Scot, by comparison, is a latecomer: a descendant of the Bronze Age invaders, maybe, who settled so heavily in Aberdeenshire, or, more certainly, of the Angles.

The racial outcome today is not without its significance for manufacturers.[165] Both shoe and sock firms[16, 28] have commented on the exceptional tininess of the feet of Glaswegians, who besides being so patently Mediterranean in their make-up are doubtless undersized as well due to under-nutrition – suggested further by the fact that the recruits from Glasgow called-up in 1939 had on average shorter stature and smaller chests than those from the rest of Scotland.[142] These are the tiny, terrifying soldiers on whom the people of Minden, in West Germany, have reputedly bestowed the nickname 'Poison Dwarfs'. The feet of Scots in the other industrial cities, however, run those of the Glaswegians fairly close, in comparison with the rest of Britain; but in Inverness, Aberdeen and Edinburgh, in contrast, feet tend to be distinctly large.[28]

In this split between West and East, to some extent even between North and South, one of them hard and the other one soft, Scotland seems like a recapitulation of Britain in miniature. Like England, it suffers from a jammed central corridor with a vast empty hinterland to either side. Like England, too, it looks south-eastwards to its capital. It is misleading, indeed, to think of it as a half-foreign country in the sense of somewhere fundamentally different in spirit from England (for it is less alien in this respect than Wales): it is half-foreign mainly in the sheer multiplicity of its differences. It is part of one and the same single continuum, but with certain English tendencies further exaggerated – tendencies for the most part that we have already noticed as we made our way up through North-eastern England. It has a more elemental texture; it lies on older formations, closer to the national bedrock. Extra layers are exposed to view here, which in England generally lie hidden. All is vast, rock-like, interminable and massive. Solid structures built to last for centuries are the pride, and comfort, of the nation's engineers. An older Britain that has elsewhere all but disappeared is enshrined here, as in Ireland, preserved in a kind of cultural aspic, with archaisms almost everywhere: tiered cake-racks, lace curtains, paper blinds; professorial chairs in sciences with quaint, defiantly non-scientific titles, like *materia medica* for pharmacology, natural philosophy for physics, or natural history for zoology; a much more wholehearted acceptance of bereavement and all the solemn ritual that elsewhere once so generally accompanied it;[23] a more persistent taste for old-time variety, which keeps the theatres more profitable today than their counterparts in the English provinces. Sedan-chairs, very typically, were still in use in Edinburgh and St. Andrews as late as 1850,[166] years after almost everywhere else they had turned into antiques. And just as the Scots are slower to say goodbye to such things, more firmly embedded here in a culture still closer in spirit to that of the Victorians, so also are they slower to welcome innovation. They have been behind the rest of Britain in recent years in adopting non-iron shirts,[167] women's shoes gaping daringly at the back or sides, stiletto heels, girls' and women's slacks.[168] They are not very prone to 'impulse' purchasing and have proved somewhat resistant to supermarkets and self-service.[145] They were also far slower to respond to official increases during food rationing – in the case of tea in 1952, for instance.[13]

Besides being an older Britain it is also a Britain that is rougher, harsher and more violent. The Scots run to self-endangering extremes, oblivious of the compromises of the English: they are prone to sudden bursts of energy which have to be discharged in abrupt and passionate gusts. Their minds match their climate, a climate of greater risks and rigour which forces its way into ordinary living by a hundred different routes: heavier spending on all fuels for heating, easily the most electric blankets, few cotton frocks and many more thick woollen skirts, more twin-sets and sweaters with a heavy accent among home knitters[91] on long-sleeved jumpers, vests worn all-the-year-round more,[83] a longer selling-season for winter gloves and tweeds,[169] hot puddings continuing on a larger scale into summer, constantly the lowest number of refrigerators, and far fewer women's outdoor sandals.

One can blame the climate, furthermore, for some of the wildness of the drinking, though one could probably blame even more the precarious quality of the Scots personality. Spirits, in any case, produce more violent drunks than beer; and whether they intend to or not, more Scots than English succeed in getting drunk – and more are picked up by the police in consequence.[80] Spirits are also more destructively addictive. The Scottish rates for alcoholism, in terms of first admissions to mental hospitals, are up to seven times as high in men and up to five times as high in women as in England and Wales. Deaths from cirrhosis of the liver are up to double the English rates each year, in both sexes. The far higher death-rate from domestic accidents too, otherwise hard to explain, may owe something to this tendency. With all those terrible flights of bare stone stairs, it must be only too easy, in a befuddled condition, fatally to lose one's footing.

One of the troubles is that the Scots tend to drink so much faster, gulping instead of sipping. They make a business of it, talking little and seldom even sitting. Scottish pubs are really bars, having failed to develop as full-scale inns on the English pattern, due to the fact that the native hospitality of old was so bounteous that travellers never lodged for the night except in private houses. They have thus given rise to fewer amenities than those in England, a tendency not helped besides by the smaller number 'tied' to promotion-minded breweries. Outwardly bright and welcoming, they have 'the narrow-eyed look of a den of surreptitious vice, inwardly accoutred as frankly as a petrol-station for tip-up and turn-around'.[170] They offer little inducement to linger. Nor, for that matter, do the Scottish licensing hours, with closing-time at ten (not long ago, half past nine) and little chance of a drink on a Sunday. There must be less room to lift an elbow than in England, too, for the number of pubs and, even more, licensed clubs is, by comparison very low in proportion to population. Much more drinking, therefore, has to be done in the home – and often alone. Canned beer has won exceptional popularity for this reason, as has also, in its own small way, canned cider.[171] Sales of bottled beer are boosted too: in the north of Scotland twice as many men drink beer in this form as ever drink it on draught. Even so, little of this is shared with wives, for more women than in England proclaim themselves teetotal, very few by comparison admitting to touching ale, stout, port, gin and even lager or whisky. Spending on soft drinks is heavy in compensation, the women in Scotland in particular emerging as heavy buyers of, amongst others, fizzy minerals and colas.

Beer, however, is the regular choice of rather few Scottish men and the amount consumed per head is distinctly lower than in England. When the Scots do deign to drink it, they prefer a heavier brew with a higher specific gravity, just as they tend to take the lesser spirits at rather more daring strengths. Whisky goes further down the social scale than in England, but in relative terms there are only marginally more Scotsmen who drink it *at all*: the difference is that far more drink it regularly. They get far more of it, too, for their money, due to the different measures in use in licensed houses – a 'large' whisky, for instance, is $2\frac{1}{2}$ oz. compared with only $1\frac{2}{3}$ oz. in England. Other spirits do not necessarily suffer in consequence. Rum, admittedly, is not as popular as in the North of England, but the amount consumed by those who do drink it is sufficiently vast to make Scotland the best single market in the whole of Britain. According to a report in the *Financial Times*,[172] one recent count in Aberdeen after Hogmanay revealed more empty rum bottles than whisky bottles among the city's refuse. Vodka, too, has proved exceedingly popular here, half the total gallonage sold throughout Britain in 1961 being accounted for by the Scots.[173] Two other drinks that are also noticeably more popular than in England are draught stout and that very sweet liqueur, cherry brandy.

It may be because of more widespread rowdiness induced by this so much more lethal drinking, or simply because of a generalised fear of indiscipline and a liking in Scotland for order, that the police here are a good deal more powerful in numbers. Edinburgh was well and effectively policed long before this became true for London: in 1775 even a woman, it was said, could walk abroad in its streets at midnight in perfect safety.[161] Today the authorised establishment of the regular police in Scotland is 9 per cent above the figure for England and Wales in proportion to population. One could hardly find anything more suitably symbolic. For if there is one feature that the Scots display over and above all others, it is a greater repressiveness, an urge to bury all their passions and indecencies well out of sight.

We can follow this, as a central connecting theme, all through Scottish life. So basic is its influence, in fact, that it is almost no surprise to find unmistakable signs of its presence well before the Reformation and the advent of the Calvinism usually regarded as its inspirer. Calvinism, rather, came as the answer to a pre-existing psychological condition. Already, in the reign of James IV, round about 1500, the Scottish Sunday was observed with a cumbrous piety, the king himself on that day forbearing to ride, under any circumstances, not even to go to Mass. Already, too, there was the Scottish suspicion of pleasure for pleasure's sake – the king decreeing that 'no foot-ball, golf or other such unprofitable sports' be indulged in.[162] The subsequent Reformation merely made this mould tougher and more inflexible. What was being wrought was an extreme example of that system of self-piloting that David Riesman[174] has lately characterised as 'inner-direction': the acquisition in one's earlier years of a clearly-prescribed code of conduct through a rigorous process of authoritarian conditioning, a code which teaches dutifulness and the bearing of temporary hardship and sacrifices on the assurance of greater rewards in an indefinite future.

On to this already severely constrained social character the Reformation, and later still Presbyterianism, piled a further load of purely religious inhibitions. Of these, the one that has had the widest and most enduring effect on life in general is that ultimate in bleak sabbatarianism, the Scottish Sunday. Within the last hundred years it was still customary on that day of days for all games, travelling and even walking to be expressly forbidden. There could be no sewing or watering one's garden. Matters like shaving and letter-writing had to be postponed till noon. Cooking, too, was kept to a minimum – the common trick was to put a singed sheep's head on to boil and leave it there during church hours[175] – and, in consequence, nothing similar to the English Sunday lunch has ever had a chance to develop. The only equivalent in Scotland of such a ceremonial meal is Saturday lunch or Sunday tea. The pattern of leisure, also, has been extensively distorted. The public houses and cinemas, for the most part, have been closed all Sunday; fewer homes than in England and Wales have possessed a wireless set or, in recent years, television (66 per cent as late as 1961, compared with nearly 80 per cent south of the Border – reflected in the very low readerships of the *Radio Times* and the *Scottish TV Guide*); and, in default of these, people have had to read more newspapers. Though relatively few Scots, unlike the English, read any national daily, rather more of them than in England buy a paper on Sunday – and as a rule several. In the middle of the 'fifties, before television had properly arrived and had the chance to affect this habit, 45 per cent of those who bought national Sundays in Scotland read three or more, compared with only 28 per cent over Britain in general. In the field of reading matter Scotland is also peculiar for the great popularity of a special kind of family or women's weekly (*People's Friend, Red Letter, Red Star, Family Star, Secrets*) which has nothing like the same following in England and which seriously eats into the market for the national women's magazines, though how far this type of reading is specially associated with Sunday has never been made quite clear.

Apart from Sunday there was one further casualty of Scottish religious extremism: the celebration of Christmas. This was regarded as Popish and except among Episcopalians and Catholics quite fell into disuse in Scotland till only comparatively recently. Before the First World War it was customary for Christmas Day to be treated as a normal working day and for all the shops to open as usual. Though this has since become steadily more and more uncommon and the rival hold of New Year's Day has steadily loosened – with the happy result that many businesses in Scotland now close down for both festivals in turn – the Christmas market is still discernibly underdeveloped. There is less extra spending on food over the period of the holiday than in any English region;[176] and many of the items traditionally favoured, and indeed relied on, as presents show no exceptional rise in sales at this season, the shortfall so far as necessities are concerned being made good instead at birthdays.

Quite possibly, too, religious fundamentalism and the over-literal observance of the Scriptures that arose from this lie behind another far-reaching Scottish characteristic (though the poorly-developed tradition of roasting may also be to blame in part). This is the very curious avoidance of the pig. Even today almost all pig products here sell poorly. Compared with other regions, Scotland eats much the least pork and bacon, beef sausages preponderate in the ratio 4:1 (against 1:2 in England and Wales), and branded cooking fats are substituted almost entirely for lard. The result is a market so specialised that the

big national firms have baulked at it and left most of the
trade to local suppliers. Traditional tastes have thus
stayed pandered to on what, for these days, is a most
unusual scale. The Scots prefer, and can expect to get,
their bacon wafer-thin, never having taken much to the
more usual Danish types.[39] 'Belfast ham', the normal
gammon, is specially imported from Ireland – and
formidably expensive. To make up for this, beef sausages,
with their lower meat content, tend to be almost a shilling
a pound cheaper in the shops than their pork equivalent.
Yet there seems no sensible, all-embracing economic
explanation; and the natural environment, similarly, can
scarcely be invoked, as it appears to offer no real barrier
to pig-breeding. The only explanation we seem to be left
with, then, is sheer conservatism rooted in a one-time
religious aversion.

The real rigour, however, has long been reserved for
the procedures of upbringing. And these can scarcely be
anything but secular.

They begin their unindulgent progress at the first
possible moment: in the cradle. Scottish infants are
weaned on average earlier than in England. In a survey in
1946, 57 per cent were found to be bottle-fed by the end
of the eighth week after delivery, compared with only
41 per cent in England and Wales, a difference largely due,
it was discovered, to the far greater number of mothers in
Scotland who never began to breast-feed at all.[99] Other
more recent surveys indicate that this pattern still persists.
Indeed, at all the stages of babyhood the pace seems to
be just that little bit more forced. This applies certainly to
toilet-training (so individual informants assert) – though
this may be no earlier than in the scarcely less stringent
North East of England – and the fact that nappies in
Scotland are larger and folded on a different pattern
strengthens the impression that we are confronted here
with a radically different tradition of child-rearing. More
is spent on baby-wear (so unlike the Welsh, in particular)

and the excellence of the shops that specialise in this is often the subject of envious comment by visitors from England. Home knitters, in their turn, concentrate to an exceptional extent on babies' socks, gloves and bonnets.[91]

After the shocks of an abbreviated infancy come a more suppressed childhood than in England and a distinctly more ramrod schooling.[177] The Scots, confirmed patriarchs, seem to pour much of the energy that the English devote to class into the intensification of age barriers. Scottish children are ruled with a heavy hand, discouraged on the whole from speaking their minds in front of their elders, generally rendered gawky and self-conscious. As a result they mature later emotionally – which is evidently to the liking of their parents, many of whom, at least in the past, have tended to keep their sons in shorts, for example, till a considerably later age than in England. Scottish children, indeed, after their hectic start, tend to experience the outward and visible signs of their inward and physical condition a good year or so behind on average – as though Scottish parents, having hustled them through the messier early phases, are determined to enjoy them at this most favoured period and to eke out this enjoyment for as long as possible, before they become half-lost to them in the limbo of adolescence. The move from primary to secondary school takes place at around 12, instead of 11; the highest incidence of indictable offences occurs in the 17–20 age-group, instead of the 14–17 one; the minimum age for Borstal is 16, not 15 (as it has been in England since 1961). The children become more docile and more subservient; some of their natural liveliness is permanently quenched and smothered. The Scots in later life have none of the English frivolity, none of their sprightly childlike sense of fun: they show instead that slow, dry, sardonic turn of humour so nicely characterised as 'pawky'. Their whole personality tends to become more arid and more unfluent, and they find it much harder to let themselves go, in a gentle and easy manner. The Glaswegians, asked in a recent survey[178] what they thought the Scots and the English each respectively excelled in, conceded that the English were better mixers and much better by far at enjoying themselves.

Compared with England the older generation unbends far less, overconscious of its dignity and authority. It prefers to see its children well supervised and following familiar pastimes, if possible *en famille*. Family outings remain more usual than in England, to football grounds (twice as popular per head as in England), to the theatre or the cinema. The Scots accordingly spend more money on cinema tickets than any single region in England, due to this liking for largish family parties, which is reflected in the greater proportions of both women and children in the make-up of the average audience[179] (though we must remember that television has badly lagged here and this pattern may now be on the point of dissolving).

A respect for seniority is all very well – in its proper place. The Scots, however, have made of this something of a fetish and in the process, almost certainly, wrought much harm in their economy, by discouraging the thrusting younger man and often driving him to emigrate, out of sheer desperation. Salaries offered to lower-range executives in business are still well below those in other regions[180] and must function as a strong disincentive to graduate recruitment. Typical is the Scots tolerance, till fairly recently, of the stultifying agency system in their banking, which left many a lucrative branch managership in the part-time and often 'hereditary' hands of some local member of a learned profession or business and thus sadly demoralised the staff at central office.[181]

There is one great benefit, nevertheless, that arises from this reverence for authority: the schoolmaster, like the minister, has long been looked up to and admired, in a way almost unknown among the English. To 'teach or preach' has been many a Scot's ambition for his son. There is therefore a general regard for learning, over and above the more directly self-interested concern for education of a people so dedicated to the effort of 'getting on'. Public expenditure on education is over twice as high as in England in proportion to population (though more is needed, to some extent, due to the much lower amount of private schooling) and the teachers as a whole are better qualified and not in such short supply, the result, almost certainly, of their higher social standing. The ratio of graduate teachers, of each sex, is two to three times that in England. As in Wales, this is the logical outcome in a culture that respects teaching, has relatively few other openings for graduates, and sends such a high percentage of its school-leavers on to universities – twice as many proportionately as in England, as has been the case for many years. Nevertheless, though the intake into the quality 'senior schools' (the counterparts of the English grammar schools) is proportionately almost twice as high as in England – and due to this much more generous provision of places, the average *working-class* boy or girl in Scotland is about as likely to secure entry to a selective course as the average *middle-class* pupil south of the Border – the half-way 'wastage' from these is, unfortunately, far greater. The average Scot, in fact, does not stay on at school as long as the average Englishman; indeed, more boys leave at 15 than in any single English region. Scotland, it thus turns out, is more of a meritocracy than her sister, bringing a rather more finely-sifted élite up just one or two more rungs of the educational ladder.

At the same time lower-level instruction has long been more efficient than in England and has succeeded in producing a more general spread of minimal literacy. As long ago as 1863 the Registrar General found that only 10 per cent of men and 22 per cent of women in Scotland were incapable of writing their names in the Marriage Register, compared with 24 and 33 per cent respectively in England. Though facts and figures on reading habits are hard to come by and not normally reliable, it seems quite likely that the Scots as a whole continue today to consume more print than the English. Certainly, they spend more on average on magazines, newsagents are unusually numerous, and the men give the best reception in the country to *Reader's Digest*. And even the lowest buying of bookcases can be blamed, no doubt, on the reliance that has developed on all the free lending-libraries so generously donated by Andrew Carnegie.

The constraints thus firmly established in early life appear afresh in courtship and marriage. As the Scots themselves are the first to admit, the average male in Scotland hardly shows a devouring interest in women and tends to be ungallant in their presence. Very often he absents himself from female society entirely. In the words of an eighteenth-century Englishman, the discerning Captain Topham:[161] 'A lover in Scotland is the most ignorant Thing imaginable; I mean as to address, compliments, protestations, and endearments, which are so familiar in the mouth of an English *inamorato*.' The French influences, it would seem, did not penetrate to this sphere of behaviour.

The arts of coquetry, accordingly, are notably under-developed. Topham remarked on the fact that, unlike the women in France or London, Scotswomen carefully spurned the use of cosmetics. Indeed, they were altogether most hesitant in adopting the grosser extremes then currently in fashion, seldom using hoops for their skirts and adding very little to their height by means of the heels of their shoes. Much the same could be said of them today. Cosmetics still have less appeal overall than in England and, until the last year or two at least, they seemed to bother very little, even, about their hair, spending little alike on visits to hairdressers or on home sets and 'perms'. They make up for this by a profuse amount of washing, using liquid shampoos in unduly heavy quantities. And though the amount they spend on clothes is, for almost every type, comparatively heavy, they could scarcely claim to be ultra-fashionable – with the conceivable exception of the women in Glasgow. They buy more garments than the average, but one reason for this is that they make so few at home (borne out by the scarcity of sewing-machines: those that do exist being also older than elsewhere), which is explained in turn, perhaps, by their much slighter interest in dresses – for in view of the great output of home knitting[91] this can scarcely be stigmatised as laziness. They buy more garments, furthermore, not, surely, because their turnover is faster, but because they like a wider range in active circulation extending over lengthier periods. Use-and-throw-away may be all right for the Midlanders, but it will not do at all for the Scots. They expect their purchases to last. They buy for quality and durability (not forgetting closer weaves to insulate them against their climate), and this presumably accounts for the high prices per garment paid on average in Scotland – not some quirk in the retailing structure, nor any undue emphasis on exclusiveness in couture.

In so far as they are fashion-conscious at all, Scotswomen, one must suppose, dress largely to impress each other, certainly not to entice or dazzle their menfolk. For as Topham,[161] once again, observed, Scottish men have traditionally scarcely noticed clothes and, indeed, feel awkward when even having to buy their own, preferring even more than in Yorkshire or Wales to delegate this matter to their wives or mothers. Their wardrobes, accordingly, are unexpectedly richly – if dully – furnished, from raincoats inwards to pyjamas. And because Scotsmen (in this land where the old Victorian proprieties have been so much more slowly discarded) still feel sensitive about parading in the streets armed with unsightly packages and bags, women are left with more of the shopping to do than even in the most reactionary regions of England, their versatility as purchasers extending to oil-stoves and even pipe tobacco.

An intriguing tight-lipped note of prudishness also

betrays itself, here and there, in Scottish tastes in clothing. One national outerwear firm reports a perpetual demand, quite peculiar to Scotland, for belted dresses – allegedly for cycling to church in on Sundays.[182] The choice in both lingerie[15] and brassières is also limited to white somewhat more exclusively, perhaps because other colours are seen more as sinfully provocative (or else more prosaically, because a display of white is a better testimony of cleanliness and careful laundering). Quite possibly, too, one can blame as well that powerful obsession with purity that we have seen so often in other regions. There is certainly no denying the presence of this in Scotland, where a special fascination for cream as a colour, or as a substance, turns up repeatedly in one product field after another and where the actual word 'purity' is proffered more than elsewhere as a reason for keeping to one special brand in particular. Like the Welsh, the Scots seem to have a secret fear of being unpleasantly contaminated. Many wives in Scotland refrain from sending their weekly wash to a laundry, for fear of acquiring other people's bugs or germs in the process. As a result they have long led the rest of Britain in the extent of home-laundering by hand,[72] and for years, before the advent of the launderettes, they heavily patronised municipal wash-houses. Were they more prosperous, or merely prepared to give more precedence to new equipment for the home, their possession of washing-machines and wash-boilers would clearly be much more extensive than it is.

As in Wales, too, the far lower death-rate than in England from syphilis bespeaks a much slighter history of promiscuity. The high figures for illegitimacy that so embarrassed Scotland all through the nineteenth century are probably not at variance with this. They occurred primarily in the agricultural communities of the East and South[183] and were doubtless due, as many people claimed at the time, to a greater reluctance to seal more or less permanent liaisons with the formal insignia of marriage.

Even legal marriage, however, seems not to have been an entrancing prospect. Today, though the ratio of men to women is virtually the same as in England and Wales, the proportion of married people in Scotland still continues to be well below average, as it has been for very many years. Marriage began to become more popular, rather rapidly, in the course of the 'thirties and 'forties; and since 1952 the percentage each year contracting matrimony has actually overtaken that in England, due to the greater preponderance in Scotland of teenagers. For despite their greater wariness, when they do marry, the Scots, like the Welsh (and, of course, the mainly Roman Catholic Irish), tend to have distinctly larger families. Over the last six or seven years the birth rate has been some 15 per cent higher than in England, with the result that there are now 20 per cent more children per household. Scotland, it is true, has more Roman Catholics – accounting for 17 per cent of all marriages in 1962 against only 12 per cent in England and Wales, and comprising close on half the population of Clydeside burghs like Coatbridge and Dumbarton (the legacy for the most part of the swamping invasion of the Irish, who over a century ago already constituted every sixth person in Glasgow). But probably no less important is simply a greater liking for children, helped in no small measure by a greater laxity, or perhaps ignorance, about birth control. The Scots, with that love of suppressing potentially subversive knowledge that seems such an invariable accompaniment of an authoritative culture, disapprove of instruction in contraceptive techniques being made freely available much more strongly than the English.[33] They are much stricter, also, in requiring proof of marriage or intention to marry from those consulting Family Planning Association clinics – and these in any case are resorted to far less than elsewhere in Britain.[184] This implies that the initiative for taking contraceptive measures still lies in the hands of the man here, very much more than in

England. In these circumstances more men, almost certainly, insist on their marital rights regardless of the possible outcome – quite apart from the fact that an unduly large number of conceptions must take place, in any case, under a blurring Scotch mist of alcohol. For drunkenness, here, must offer a far greater risk in marriage; and, assuming that the criteria observed by the different legal systems are roughly comparable, it may explain the fact that considerably more of the divorces in Scotland than in England and Wales in recent years have been granted on grounds of cruelty.

Even in marriage, the two sexes, as in Topham's day, still seem to face each other across a greater gulf of incomprehension compared with most of England. As in Wales, Tyneside and Yorkshire, women lead a life of segregation; but here it is even more extreme, as if both sides felt more comfortable and secure with as complete a social dualism as possible. Hence there is much the highest membership, especially in the rural areas,[185] of exclusively female groups, such as Women's Institutes and the multifarious bodies nurtured by the kirk. Both Edinburgh and Glasgow universities have separate unions for men and women students. Edinburgh has even recently introduced the first separate Ladies' Bank. This is on top of the usual wing-clipping common to every patriarchal culture: little drinking, even less smoking, modesty and discretion in dress, relatively few wives in jobs outside their homes.

As always, the women compensate for this worldly constriction by emotionally enlarging the realm specifically assigned to them, showing themselves, in Topham's[161] words, 'peculiarly attentive in their own houses'. Like the Swiss and the Dutch, Scots wives pour themselves into polishing and scrubbing. They bring to this the fierce, one-sided energy of the Celts combined with the stern, self-torturing perfectionism of Puritans. In surveys it is Scottish housewives, far more than any others, who express a positive liking for the generally unpopular domestic tasks. We have noticed already their astonishing keenness to take on all the household washing and to deal with this, if need be, in the most onerous way possible. Their slavish love of drudgery may even be responsible for the rather slower acceptance here of men's drip-dry shirts.[167] They refuse assistance, too, from the rest of the family more often than wives in England, preferring to exercise a sovereignty that is absolute in this, their one special sphere of influence. At one time – it may still be true – the Scottish mother, unlike the English mother, did not expect the men or boys to fend for themselves even to the extent of cleaning their boots.[175] She was the maid-of-all-work and, without question, she revelled in this. It must be remembered, all the same, that her home was generally smaller than an English home and certain traditions of the Scottish diet freed her from the heavy burden of baking borne, for example, by wives in Yorkshire.

The popular sterotype of the Scots wife as a cook without rival is a badly distorted one. True, she still takes great pride and interest in cooking, owns a large number of books on the subject, refers to them a great deal and often tries out recipes published in newspapers.[45] But much of this effort goes into the perfecting of her skill with items like scones, oatcakes and shortbread.[45] She is a pastry-cook, a confectioner, rather than a baker. Compared with wives in the English regions she now bakes, indeed, extremely little, for oven-baked bread was not usual in the 'Celtic' countries due to the general absence of wheat. Most of the bread eaten today in Scotland, even in the remoter parts of the Highlands, comes from large bakeries centralised in towns. The standard loaves produced here differ considerably from the standard loaves of England: they are tall and stately, more crusty, with a silkier texture and a saltier taste (so that many Scots find English bread insipid) and made by a long-fermentation process which ensures much greater keeping qualities and which permits the van man to call in country districts no more than once or twice each week.[186] Furthermore they are generally baked in batches, not individually as in England and Wales. The bread bought is more exclusively white than elsewhere; it is also much more exclusively wrapped and branded, reflecting the dominance of this market by big, impersonal multiples. For her fancy breads, for her hot morning rolls or 'baps' (which are still eaten here for breakfast in enormous quantities despite their considerable expense) and for most of her cakes the Scottish wife tends to patronise, instead, a small local baker whom she knows and trusts. This is no recent tradition, for 200 years ago baking was evidently such a common commercial skill of Scotsmen that a high proportion of those who emigrated proceeded to set up in trade as this. 'The vast majority of London bakers are from Scotland and they do not let the trade go out of their hands', a visiting Danish professor wrote home in 1782.[187] The bakers' shops in Scotland today now often function as a dairy as well (which must help their image for freshness), and it is common to buy special cream from them for adding to cakes back at home. Far more wives in Scotland, one in ten at least, buy cakes or buns every single weekday,[45] inheriting the best – or worst – of both worlds by having to live up to a tradition of cream and icing, as in Lancashire, combined with a tradition of bulkier but plainer bun-food, as in Yorkshire. Thus sitting down for tea in Scotland is like sitting down for tea in the North of England with the Pennines altogether extracted.

The spread at tea-time is extensive as well as varied. The Scots eat almost as many cakes as anyone, but, not content with this, they also gorge themselves on fantastic amounts of Scotch pancakes and scones; they also eat far more chocolate biscuits than the English, treating them as an integral part of the meal. It is not surprising that cake-racks have survived here so much longer. Nor is it really surprising that in so many homes in Scotland *all* the cakes eaten are bought: the wife herself simply has no time to produce such quantities. Even if she did have the time, it would probably not be cakes that we would find her baking for preference. Cake-making is now a little-known art in Scotland, evidenced by the great rarity with which nuts, raisins, glacé cherries and shredded coconut are bought here, compared with the English home-baking regions, quite apart from the very low usage of flour and all cooking fats generally.

Except for jam-making,[44] in fact, there are few other forms of cookery that seem to appeal to Scottish wives. They rely on made-up meats from their butcher to a markedly un-English (and even more un-Welsh) extent; they serve a lot of ice-cream with meals; buy more pre-pared fruit pies; show few qualms about opening certain kinds of tins, such as corned beef, sweet puddings, soups, fruit juices, baked beans and spaghetti, all of which they eat in above-average quantities. Other canned foods – fish, peas, fruit, milk, cream – they tend to avoid, rather mysteriously; while frozen foods have continued to receive the quite exceptionally frosty welcome that the Scots also gave to chilled and frozen meat between the wars.[141] They also have fewer vegetables to prepare than English wives, for all leaf vegetables are eaten singularly little here, their place being taken by peas, beans and root vegetables of almost every kind, including those special Scottish favourites prepared and cooked in a special manner, turnips or 'neaps' (which as long ago as Topham's day were often introduced as dessert and eaten like fruit[161]).

All fruit, whether fresh, canned, bottled or frozen, suffers the same neglect as leaf-vegetables, with the solitary exception of oranges. Much less is grown in gardens, due to the climate, and the kinds brought in from overseas or from England tend to be discouragingly expensive – partly, in turn, because of the weakness of demand, for the Scots have never incorporated fruit on any scale into their everyday diet. One predictable result is a marked shortage of specialist greengrocers and fruiterers.

A further reason for eating so few leaf-vegetables is that roast dishes are far from common, due to the general absence in the past of ovens. The Scots, much more than most Britons, are addicted to stewing. For this reason a lot is spent on beef, and very little, by comparison, on lamb or mutton. Stewed beef, indeed, could be called one of the most typical of all Scots dishes. The very different emphasis that this leads to in shopping for meat means that the popular cuts bear little resemblance to those in England, and meat as a whole is cheaper. (Scottish housewives, it might also be mentioned, show a marked dislike for liver, sweetbreads, oxtails and all other kinds of offal, indicating an almost Grundyish distaste for innards. For some obscure reason, food of this type is considered fit only for animals. This makes it illogical, therefore, that the Scots should deign to touch haggis – which, after all, is little more than a caseful of offals – let alone make such a noisy song and dance about it.) This same stewing-cum-boiling tradition also accounts, one need hardly add, for the Scottish passion for soups and this in turn for the rather heavy use of salt and bones. A good deal of salt, furthermore, must be demanded by their eggs, of which they consume some 20 per cent more than the English, perhaps a relic of the time when eggs had to take over on the meatless days prescribed by the Kirk. The Scots persist in rating eggs more highly for food value than the English, convinced 'they do you good' even more than meat.[36]

An even simpler explanation why the Scots housewife does so little baking is that she has to prepare so many more meals for her family than her sister in England. In Scotland it is still common practice for workers to return home in the middle of the day. This is made easier by the much more compact towns and cities with their slighter suburban sprawl; and it explains the large midday audiences here for television,[87] the lunchtime closing of the Scottish banks and, at least in part, the very heavy expenditure on bus fares. It also means far fewer meals in cafés and restaurants,[2] and by drastically reducing this normally so dependable segment of custom helps to make low-price catering much less profitable and hence, presumably, less adventurous.

It is more than just a matter of more people in to meals, however. The meals themselves contain more courses. This is partly due to the conventional serving of soup (even in summer), which is very rare by comparison in England; and partly due to the Scottish sweet tooth, which makes a dessert all but obligatory. In view of the climate, furthermore, breakfasts, especially, have to be fortifying. This means porridge, obviously, to begin with, in very many homes – though by no means in the majority, for breakfast cereals have now made serious inroads. A cooked course normally follows and after that, more often than in England, toast (hence the rather numerous electric toasters owned). The midday meal also tends to be substantial, being the main occasion for eating the very frequent mince and stews; and, because the children so generally travel home for this from school, there have to be more milk puddings of every kind[45] and (in summer) more jellies, blancmanges and ice-cream than in England. Notwithstanding this the evening meal, most frequently termed 'tea' and commonly begun earlier even than 5.45, is also fairly heavy. Eggs, both boiled and scrambled, are eaten then more widely than in England, as also is haddock. Almost invariably, as well, a late 'snack' follows shortly before bed-time – with not just the usual English hot drink and biscuits or sandwiches, but very often cakes or scones as well.

All of which means, of course, an almost interminable round of food preparing. Little enough time must be left to go out and shop – which, in any event, is a more troublesome procedure than for wives in England, due to the more numerous small children and the often excessive number of stairs to negotiate when returning heavily burdened. It may have been some such considerations as these that have encouraged that specially Scottish phenomenon, the itinerant trader. The best-known of these, the Scotch draper or 'cuddy', has a pedigree that goes back many years, possibly to before 1700. Basing his operations on a well-stocked central warehouse, it was his custom to travel round from this calling from house to house, with clothes, haberdashery and household goods, all offered for purchase on credit. Today this has grown into very big business, so much so that the discount warehouses, selling direct to the public at wholesale prices – and thus long anticipating the discount stores only recently introduced into Britain from America – have badly stifled the growth in Scotland up to now of the specialist retailing of domestic electrical goods; they have also kept for themselves a large share of the trade in various types of clothing. Much the same system of trading, involving the use of travelling vans, is heavily relied on in the field of food as well. Compared with England, in terms of retail trade as a whole, its importance is proportionately about two and a half times as great.[86]

So much, then, for the various processes that conspire to oppress and restrict the Scottish character. Let us look now at some of the more obvious outcomes.

First: an over-addiction to minor sensual pleasures. The Scots, as we have already partially seen, have an insatiable love of all things sweet: cakes and pastries, biscuits (particularly if coated with chocolate), jam, jellies, ice-cream, puddings of all descriptions, well-sugared drinks both alcoholic and otherwise. . . . To this list we can now add treacle and, even more, sweets and chocolates, in particular fudge, fondants, truffles and candies. The amount spent at sweet shops is twice the English level and, not surprisingly, there are far more of these outlets than anywhere else in Britain. They are not patronised just by children: adults in Scotland, even manual workers,[63] have for long eaten sweets and chocolates on a scale quite unknown below the Border. The Scots palate, in fact, is so attuned to sugar that sweet products, for example jellies, are chosen more than elsewhere on finer, rarefied differences in flavour, with little concern for brand or colour. The whole stress, it is interesting to notice, falls on quite the opposite end of the taste-scale compared with the Midlands; the consumption of specially sour foods like pickles and vinegar being the lowest of anywhere, in neat compensation

Nutritionists term people with such a rabid craving for carbohydrates 'carboholics'. It is a sure sign, according to psychiatrists, of some deep-seated anxiety, a nagging drive to make up for a loss that happened in early childhood. The same explanation possibly applies as well to the tremendously heavy consumption of cigarettes, all the more remarkable for the high number of women (70 per cent) who claim to be non-smokers and the relatively few men in the rural districts who admit to lighting even so much as an occasional pipe.

An extension of this is what has been called – or so the dictionary assures us – the 'Scotch douche': a handy term for that specially violent alternation from one savage temperature extreme to the other, to which the palate here is so frequently subjected. The Scots eat not only more ice-cream than the English; they also eat a lot of ginger, as well as sausages that are heavily spiced. Their tobaccos, too, tend to be hotter to the palate – hence, for example, the heavy sales (in contrast to England) of the well-known Player's Capstan. It all seems very masochistic, as if the aim is to chastise the palate rather than to soothe and caress it. Perhaps the sweet-eating and the smoking, by their very excess, reduce it to such a state that the stimuli have to be applied in steadily stronger and stronger doses, as with some habit-forming drug.

Next: a severe disciplining of the flesh. The Scots are treated, and treat themselves in turn, more roughly than the English. They stop short, it is true, of hair shirts and beds of nails, but they clean their teeth with harder brushes[188] and rub themselves with coarser surfaces. They also submit to harder and drier food: more toast, much the heaviest consumption of crispbreads like Ryvita, and a most impressive intake of the crunchier types of biscuits. Scotland eats about 40 per cent more biscuits than Britain in general, which accounts for the fact that such a high proportion of the best-known manufacturers are Scottish. Their tastes in these, however, are abundantly different, some of the best-selling English kinds being almost completely absent – and replaced by other kinds rarely encountered in England. Biscuit-eating here is also stepped-up in winter, much more than further south, as if crispness in the air brings on an accompanying urge for crispness in biting.

These are but the mildest forms of this tendency to self-torture. A good deal more stoical is the widespread tolerance of pain. More people in Scotland than elsewhere refrain from bothering their doctors with minor complaints or even from attempting to treat themselves, preferring to grin and bear it. They relent mainly for headaches and colds[8] – though, oddly, rather few Scots ever seem to suffer from headaches or ever have migraine badly enough to force them to stay off work.[6] Mothers in labour less often than in England receive either inhalational pain-killers or sedatives[5, 99] – an omission already noted among the Welsh. Rather little is spent on medicines and fewer National Health Service prescriptions than in England are dispensed per head (just as there are fewer N.H.S. sight tests). The taking of tablets is frowned on and the use of throat pastilles, in particular, is minimal,[8] for the feel of burning in their throats is something they are fully inured to and, perhaps, may even enjoy.

Edinburgh is often likened to Athens: it would be more

appropriate, surely, to compare it with Sparta. For the Scots admire and cultivate frugality. Their household goods and vehicles have fewer optional attachments that help to make life, marginally, easier; their clothes and draperies have less trimming, their homes contain less furniture, their cities offer scantier amenities. They like drawing in their horns, tightening their belts, living with the ultra-simple sparseness of the Scottish student of tradition with his solitary bag of oatmeal – the process of *Abbau* or 'de-building' that so appealed to that great Scotsman, Sir Patrick Geddes, translated into personal terms: an internal streamlining to test and prove oneself and one's negative capabilities. Along with this goes a great pleasure in scraping and saving, a cult of the tight purse, which is not necessarily related to any actual shortage of funds.

Though they are nowhere nearly so prosperous, the Scots save more than the English[189] – and have probably always done so. To this simple fact they owed the development of a highly sophisticated banking system at a remarkably early date.[181] [190] For the Scottish clearing banks, able to depend on a financially far less volatile public than, say, in England, were permitted to expand rapidly to a quite unusual degree by the straightforward expedient of attracting deposits at interest from the public. One result of this today is the excessive profusion of branches, especially in the smaller country towns. At the same time it has left the average Scotsman exceptionally canny in the matter of shopping around for the best possible return on idle money. Simply by offering a higher rate of interest to the man-in-the-street, the trustee savings banks, in turn, from 1835 onwards, won for themselves a far larger following than in England, to the extent that today – here alone in Britain – they offer quite severe competition to the clearing banks and number as many as two adults out of every five among their customers. They have benefited, as well, from the low popularity of home-ownership in Scotland, which has left building societies weakly developed and traditionally disregarded as a first-resort savings medium.[189] Outlets for savings which carry no assurance of steady interest, such as National Savings Certificates[189] [191] and Premium Bonds,[191] also perform unfavourably, as one would expect, compared with the rest of Britain. The Post Office Savings Bank, too, with its very meagre interest rate, attracts only one-tenth as much annually in deposits as the trustee savings banks – a pattern unmatched anywhere else in Britain.[192]

Either cause or effect of his keenness for depositing his money at interest, the Scotsman also tends to keep a great deal more in his savings bank account than the Englishman[181] – just as his holdings of National Savings Certificates also tend to be larger[189] and just as the Scottish clearing banks, for no apparently logical reason, have long maintained larger capital reserves than their English counterparts. Scotsmen as a whole, it would seem, like to have their money stacked away in nice, big, concentrated masses, not spread around with uncomforting diffuseness. They like their banks to feel like banks – and to look like impregnable strongholds, as the vast, majestic buildings of the Bank of Scotland so reassuringly exemplify. They also dislike being liquid; and to meet their wishes the Scottish clearing banks allow the depositing or withdrawal of considerably smaller sums than in England, often down to as little as a shilling. In former days many of the savings banks purposely devised a most complex procedure for withdrawal, with the aim of discouraging depositors from taking out their money; and the fact that the standard charges levied on current accounts are freely published in Scotland, unlike the practice in England, perhaps still betrays a fondness for deterrents that will assist in keeping money immobile.

We are now on somewhat delicate ground and must be careful to tread warily. Scottish frugality – sometimes misindentified as parsimony, a rather more pejorative word – is not, let us be quite clear, a mere matter of penny-pinching: it goes far wider. Nor, even more important, is it a matter of meanness (as the English jokes would have it), for the Scots can be most hospitable and generous in their spending on others. It is wholly directed at themselves: self-stinting, economising, re-trenchment. It is almost a natural reflex and would still be in operation even if every Scotsman owned a million. Its practical effect is that in almost every aspect of daily life the Scots sally forth armed with a mental pruning-hook, ever on the look-out for a bargain. There is greater seasonal variation in the consumption of potatoes than in England and Wales, for example, because demand is more responsive in Scotland to seasonally low prices. There is greater shrewdness, too, about the advantages of bulk-buying. The larger sizes of baked beans and canned garden peas, for example, tend to be bought more than elsewhere in Britain – and there is even a discernible penchant in the learned societies of Scotland for life subscriptions.[193] More often, however, cool, rational calculation in such matters is swept aside by a more visceral, instantaneous urge to petty cheeseparing; and the result of this is that over a wide range of products it is the smallest possible sizes that tend to be unduly favoured – necessitating much more frequent purchases, if these should chance to be products in constant use, like custard powders – or, at least, as in the case of toilet soaps or patent medicines,[194] the larger-than-average (i.e. more apparently expensive) sizes that are shied away from. Where the purchase is not measurable by pack-size but purely by price, then the Scots again, compared with other parts of Britain, tend to buy more cheaply, though they are far less prone than the Lancastrians to do this quite irrespective of quality. They pay least on average in this way for items as varied as quantities of tea[13] and fresh-cut flowers.[195] They eat the most, too, of the cheapest kinds of white fish[196] (though many types of fish tend to be much more expensive than in England) and in past years, at any rate, paid less for their seats at the cinema than anyone except their neighbours on Tyneside.[37]

Naturally, too, the Scots make their products last – up to their full intended life, and maybe sometimes even further. They are renowned, indeed, for what is politely known in trade circles as 'stretching': the men make their razor blades last out longer, their women their brassières and girdles – one reason why they buy expensively when shopping for clothes, in the belief that higher prices carry assurance of longer wear. This greater reluctance to discard also leads to a greater readiness to pass things on. A high proportion of the radio sets in Scotland are second-hand, chiefly bought from friends,[197] and an abnormal number of women's clothes change ownership as 'gifts' – skirts, blouses, dresses, but not, significantly, coats, which are much less easy to alter. On the other hand, radio[197] or television rental, always a speculative form of expenditure, tends to be avoided: the Scots prefer their savings to be certain.

As prices are weighed up so carefully and used so generally as absolute criteria of value, it is not unreasonable, therefore, that Scottish housewives should express a far greater preference for fixed retail prices[198] and that Scottish shopkeepers, in deference to this, should abstain so much more from price-cutting. It is just because they offer a disguised avenue to bargains within a carefully regulated price structure that the co-operative societies, it has been suggested,[199] have met with such success in Scotland, enjoying an extremely good return (up to 55 per cent per annum on capital investment), a very heavy patronage per member (one-fifth higher than the next highest area in Britain) and the means to pay out the most enticing annual dividends.[200] The Scots love of a return on their money, acquired from their experience of deposit banking, may also be a contributory factor.

Last of all: the Scotsman's cramped accommodation.

The average home in Scotland is much more often a flat than a house; and even when a house, it tends to have fewer rooms. The two-roomed house, made up of a single living-room and a kitchen, is a Scottish speciality, common in the Highlands; it is virtually non-existent, by comparison, in rural England. At the same time, the two-roomed flat is a common feature in the industrial towns and cities. As a result one household in every four in Scotland lives in either one or two rooms – and as many as one in three in the Clydeside conurbation, compared with only one in seven in the County of London, England's area of greatest congestion. In view of the fact that the average family is considerably larger, this means, inevitably, a great deal more overcrowding. This situation is of very long standing: the Census of 1821, for instance, found an average of 1·31 families per dwelling against only 1·20 in England. Today, 22 per cent of Glasgow's households are 'overcrowded' in the technical sense of having more than $1\frac{1}{2}$ persons per room, which is more than twice as bad as the figure for Birmingham. Glasgow is reported also to have 140,000 unimprovable slum dwellings, 11,000 of them unfit for human habitation. Conditions rival Lancashire's in their foulness. Many of the buildings are old and badly built, inadequately lit and poorly ventilated; far more households than in England, almost one in three, have to share a W.C., often located on the stair-head of the tenement; more infants die at and around birth – or slightly later, from pneumonia – and many more people, of both sexes and apparently at all ages, die from respiratory tuberculosis.

The Scots themselves are a good deal to blame for all this. Throughout recent times they have constantly jibbed at spending as large a proportion as the English on their housing. Given the option, they prefer to pay quite uneconomic amounts in rent and put up with the resulting inferior conditions. In the past, this has had the effect of discouraging builders from providing replacements when old buildings were demolished (or fell to pieces). More recently, it has tempted local authorities into the danger-ous practice of heavily subsidising council rents – as low as 7s. 3d. a week on average as recently as 1960 (under pressure from Westminster, they have since been raised). Whether due to this far greater inducement to rent, or simply to a lower insistence on absolute security of tenure, the ratio of private owners to council tenants is more or less exactly reversed compared with England: only one Scottish home in every four is owner-occupied, a proportion that varies startlingly little (unlike in England) between countryside and city.

Even without the artificial inducement to rent, in economic terms, however, home-owning is hardly likely to be a prime preoccupation with Scots, due simply to their lower degree of interest in space and comfort. For here, again, we see the liking for sparseness: bare, gaunt stone, seldom disguised or hidden and very often, even, incompletely carpeted. The Scots buy furniture less frequently – except for beds and mattresses, rendered necessary by their larger families – and when they do buy, they buy it to last, strong and solid like their shoes and clothing. They also decorate less frequently, resulting in smaller sales of paint and wallpaper.[68] They need less of such things, it is true, as their homes on average are so much smaller. Far more than in England they live, as we have seen, in flats (nevertheless, just to confuse matters, universally known here as 'houses'). These have a far longer history than those south of the Border and are inhabited alike by all classes, so that the term 'tenement' here has no derogatory slum-like connotation. They are not the product of economic necessity, as is usually the case in England, but a conscious choice – of a more constricted milieu. As a result, Scotland displays to a marked extent all the various limitations attendant upon living in high flats, already noted in London. There is little provision of garages, which greatly reduces the numbers of cycles and cars and, even more, of scooters and mopeds; few pets of any size; less use of coal, far more use of gas. Oddly enough, however, though gas is used more widely for cooking than in any part of England except London, gassing oneself (usually the preferred method) is the only form of suicide substantially less popular than in England: instead, the Scots opt for drowning or else (high-livers to the last) for lethal jumping.

Yet living in flats, in place of full-scale houses, is by no means the end of their self-imposed domestic restriction. For the flats themselves tend to have fewer rooms. Admittedly, if the building was erected before 1920, like most buildings in Scotland, these rooms will be larger than in England, certainly in height and probably in area as well, maybe by as much as 20 per cent. The kitchen, in particular, will be substantially more spacious, used also as a scullery and with the sink (generally double) tucked away in one corner, abnormally small and with all its accessories, such as the draining-boards, reduced in proportion. Far more than in England kitchens are used for both eating and living in.[45] [47] A separate 'dining-room', specially so-called, is rare in Scotland, rarer even than among the similarly kitchen-dwelling Lancastrians and Yorkshiremen.

As an explanation of why the Scots spend less on their homes none of this, however, is quite enough. The much lower readership of magazines like *Do-It-Yourself*, *Practical Householder*, *Ideal Home*, *Homemaker* and *Homes and Gardens* are sufficient in themselves to give the game away: the simple truth is that the Scots are basically less home-conscious. They do not exhibit to anything like the same extent the constant, strenuous, ingoing concern of the English with adorning and strengthening their nests.

It is, perhaps, their most dangerous failing. Reluctance to improve the domestic environment has brought, besides ill-health, much dirt and general unsightliness, a menacing paralysis to the whole of their economy. In its now famous report of 1961, the Scottish Council singled out the heavily-subsidised rents as one of the principal reasons for Scotland's stagnation. The average local authority in England draws two-thirds of its housing revenue from rents: the average one in Scotland, thanks to its own deliberate policy, can count on no more than one-third from this source. To meet the shortfall, the rates on business premises have had to be raised to a point now that is making certain kinds of trade in Scotland no longer economic. The disproportionate share of rates devoted to housing, moreover, means that standards throughout the rest of local government are permanently depressed in consequence. A further result is that Scottish manpower has an obstructively low mobility, both actual and potential. Scottish manual workers, pampered with these Lilliputian levies on their incomes, are loath, understandably, to move to less favoured areas. At the same time, the greatly lessened inducement to build and buy has also led to a serious shortage of what non-Scots would regard as suitable 'middle-class' housing. Less than 20 per cent of total construction is now for private owners (it was only 33 per cent between the wars), compared with anything from 40 to 80 per cent in England and Wales. And this makes it more than ever difficult for firms in Scotland to attract or retain key technical staff or managers from other parts of Britain or even from overseas.

Thus, like the North East, Scotland makes a weakness of her strengths. Her stolidness is allowed to become a hindering rigidity; her carefulness deteriorates into a self-destructive skimping. The forces that mould her personality, in short, have set too hard. Alone of all the regions of Britain she is handicapped as well, perhaps, by too great a weight of difference. A slight dose of standardisation might, for once, prove more beneficial than injurious. Scotland, alone is robust enough to stand such usually dangerous treatment, too self-sufficient to be seriously thrown off balance by an inrush of harshly discordant novelty. And in saying merely that, we pay her the very highest compliment we can.

IX

The End of Difference?

The different parts of Britain are still far from uniform in a great many of their everyday tastes and attitudes. This much, at least, the data assembled in this book surely affirm. There is, it is true, much surface sameness; and this grows steadily greater day by day. But deeper down, beneath the pall of homogeneousness imposed by a modern, mass-consumption economy, there can still be detected quite substantial amounts of difference; and these, there is every reason to believe, are unlikely to be drastically modified in the foreseeable future, much less extinguished.

The picture of the regions presented in these pages is not a mere snapshot, recording the state of affairs at a single fleeting moment in our history. It is, on the contrary, a picture of some permanence, at least in its broad outlines. For it is the details, in the main, that change – and it is the details that we tend to notice most, in our over-concern with novelty and our delight in all those trivial alterations that help to give spice to the otherwise boring sameness of so much of daily life. Just as the glass of fashion concentrates our gaze on the ups and downs of hems or heels and leaves us blind to the fact that the basic shape of skirts or shoes keep essentially the same over relatively long periods, so the influence of advertising and design, of window-shopping, of simple gossip produces an impression of never-ending flux in which one new line of goods or one new trend in behaviour scarcely establishes

P

itself before being swept away and replaced in turn by another. This impression, of course, is deceptive. The colours, the decorations, the packaging alter: the goods inside and, still more, the ways in which they are bought and used mostly continue as before, substantially the same. The speedy reach of fashion, the unselective beaming of a myriad promotional campaigns and – least noticed but perhaps most influential of all – the growth in centralised buying accompanying the spread of nation-wide chains, have combined to thrust upon the public a face which more and more today appears monoton-ously the same: high streets with the same few familiar fascias, shops with the same familiar labels belonging to the same few leading brands, newspapers and magazines with the same stories, television sets with the same programmes, records and radios with the same few tunes. Wherever we go now, in West Hartlepool or Walsall, in Ipswich or Inverness, the same sights confront us and the same sounds come at us across the air. The one thing that never changes, however, the one thing that can never be rendered uniform, is the mind behind this face. The human receiving-sets – thank goodness – vary in their functioning: the regions still differ, as ever, in the degrees to which they respond – in the strength of their desires, in the looseness of their purses, in the keenness of their eyes and palates, in the hold of their traditions. The same range of choices may be offered, but the items chosen by each region may still form on the average appreciably different mixtures; and even when the same, they may still be cooked or eaten in slightly different ways and worn or used in subtly different manners. The regional sur-roundings change, but the regional personality stays obstinately fixed.

Any who doubt the truth of this need look no further, to be convinced, than the long series of National Food Surveys, started in 1940 by the Ministry of Food and ever since conducted yearly. Since these began to be analysed geographically, in 1955, the broad pattern of regional differences in both household consumption and expenditure has remained, in the Ministry's own words, 'remarkably consistent' year by year, over a very wide variety of foods. The twice-yearly surveys of expenditure on branded food products, instituted more recently by Odhams Press Ltd., tell essentially the same story. (There have of course, as well, been important recent *additions*, such as convenience foods and broiler chickens; but these, at least for the most part, have not required the abandonment of tastes already established.) The fact is that over long periods of years – over decades, certainly, and probably over far lengthier periods still – basic tastes remain the same, and with them the particular likes and dislikes of one part of the country compared with another. In many fields even the brands retain their respective positions long undisturbed, the producers keeping their promotional energies roughly in permanent proportion and having the sense not to tempt providence by introducing newness to a contentedly somnolent public. The notion of rapid and continuous change in anything but superficial aspects – minor variations on previous designs or formulae (as opposed to the introduction of entirely new habits or completely new types of goods) – arises in part from an optical illusion, in part from a professional myth of the marketing fraternity.

To account for this stability, three reasons can be advanced. Firstly, and most simply, there is the sheer force of habit. The ordinary human being prefers what he is used to: changes, except of the most superficial kind, tend to unsettle him, to demand too much in nervous effort. Always, therefore, a powerful bias operates in favour of inertia.

Secondly, within each region, as we have seen, there exist certain long-enduring tendencies, the combined legacy of biological inheritance, of physical environment and of social and economic circumstances: partly predetermined, partly induced by life-long processes of conditioning – or, at the least, imperceptibly assimilated over a more or less lengthy period. Over the years these tendencies have naturally grown together, becoming steadily more and more interwoven, so that they now form a fabric of remarkable resilience and tenacity. This fabric, in essence, is what the social scientist means by a 'culture': the sum of the actions and values of a certain community of people, the particular patterns of which in turn channel and constrain its behaviour. Such cultural patterns, Ruth Benedict[201] has reminded us, 'are not fortuitous congeries of traits. . . . They hold together, and any one item must be taken in conjunction with the whole structure or it has no relevance. Each item is, as it were, a brick of a total structure; and tearing out the bricks indiscriminately, however inconsequential they seem, may bring the whole structure down in ruins.' It follows from this that every region, inasmuch as it constitutes a distinctive culture, has far greater built-in strengths, to help it retain its own essential identity, than we are often inclined to imagine. Odd, adventitious novelties, forcibly promoted, stand little chance of the ultimate success of permanent incorporation, if they fail to accord with the region's particular character. There will, simply, be no cultural niche or socket able to receive them. As the science of genetics has taught us (if a biological analogy be permissible), a foreign intrusion, unless overwhelmingly preponderant in its size, is in due course 'bred out' of a population; its genes, so to speak, do not mesh with the more numerous ones of its associate, and the forces of natural selection operate that much more severely to eliminate the entities that bear them. So it is with a regional culture. Newcomers need to be multitudinous indeed to be able to foist new tastes on any sizable proportion of their receiving communities. They need, moreover, to be more than ordinarily confident, convinced of the complete superiority of their own personal preferences, to persist in the face of, at worst, hostility and, at best, indifference and apathy.

Local shops tend to stock what the majority expect and buy, and are generally loath to pander to the wants of a small and awkward minority. Newcomers soon accept and grow accustomed to what is immediately obtainable, being mostly, in any case, anxious to 'fit in' and not to parade themselves as unconforming outsiders. And so before long they succumb, slowly and inexorably, to the subtly moulding influences of their new social habitat, progressively adapting their usages and attitudes in innumerable small ways almost without noticing. The claim so commonly made that massive inter-regional migration is swamping regional difference and is well on the way to destroying it altogether is thus a much exaggerated one. Were there much truth in it, we should no longer find, surely, anything particularly distinctive about that most invaded provincial region, the Midlands whereas, in point of fact, we still find copious difference, much of it clearly of long standing.

The third factor making for stability is more deep-seated still. Far more than we tend to appreciate, the regional differences that often seem so slight and trivial are in reality the mere surface portions of far greater, reef-like complexes of drives and reactions founded in the most enduring and immutable layers of the human personality. These may sway under commercial pressure, but they will not permanently shift, for they are anchored too deeply down. They are the puzzling discrepancies round which commerce learns to steer, with awed respect – and maybe after spending millions. For the most part their base is instinctive and genetic: differences in taste thresholds, in physical build, in disease susceptibility, in nervous constitution, each giving rise to certain special predisposing trends in behaviour which, in accordance with the normal cultural process, become interlocked with traits and tendencies of shallower, purely social origin and thus help to fix the regional pattern still more firmly. Thanks to past racial movements or to the selective influence of the natural environment over many centuries even so small a country as Great Britain can produce countless cases of regional difference attributable to this factor. Many more, almost certainly, remain to be discovered. The detailed mapping of hereditary traits has barely been started, experimental psychologists still seldom test for regional disparities the perceptions and reactions that form their principal concern. One of these latter which *has* been extensively investigated from just this point of view, the preference in feminine facial beauty, has proved to show no significant regional variation at all in Britain.[202] But not all these basic human responses can safely be assumed to have so universal a distribution. If, as we have learned just recently, some two-fifths of the population of one of the counties of Britain cannot properly taste a certain common acid,[165] who knows what sizeable and extraordinary discrepancies may yet turn up in still more fundamental features?

It is for such reasons as these that so much emphasis has been placed throughout this book on historical continuity. Each region in its present-day behaviour is to a great extent the product of its past. To endeavour to lay bare this past is more than just antiquarian trifling: it is one sure way in which we can hope to diagnose in advance the malleable from the rock-hard, the transient and fleeting from the immovably secure. To devote energy and resources to trying to change the unchangeable is not merely foolish; it is grossly wasteful economically. Regional tastes demand to be studied with patience and with care, to be examined with an intellectual scalpel instead of being battered, pointlessly and crudely, with a series of commercial bludgeons. Britain, beneath its skin, is a highly varied country – and is going to remain so. We must learn to value and accept her differences, not try to stamp them out or, even worse, pretend that none at all exist.

Notes and References

Of the many statements on the subject of regional differences that appear in the popular Press, which constitute no inconsiderable proportion of the items cited below, the majority can be fairly safely assumed to derive from particular firms' sales figures (and may thus not necessarily be true for the whole industry in question) or from confidential sample surveys carried out by individual companies or trade associations. Unfortunately, the precise nature of such sources is seldom made clear, and the time and effort required for attempting to establish this in each case does not normally prove worthwhile. In some cases, increasingly rare, the source of the statement is no more than some vague piece of trade lore, unsupported by any quantified evidence. Though obviously none too reliable, even this type of information usually has some basis in fact, albeit imprecise or outdated. For these reasons it has seemed on balance more sensible to include press statements than to reject them.

1 General Register Office, *Morbidity Statistics from General Practice*, Vol. III (H.M.S.O. 1962). The period covered by this survey was 1955–6.
2 Consumer survey by The Economist Intelligence Unit Ltd. for the Horticultural Marketing Council, 1962.
3 Consumer survey by The Bureau of Commercial Research Ltd. for the Horticultural Marketing Council, 1962.

4 R. F. H. Pinsent, quoted in *The Guardian*, 29 December 1964.

5 N. R. Butler and D. G. Bonham, *Perinatal Mortality: First Report of the 1958 British Perinatal Mortality Survey* (E. & S. Livingstone, 1963).

6 Ministry of Pensions & National Insurance, *Report on an Enquiry into the Incidence of Incapacity for Work, Part II* (H.M.S.O., 1965).

7 P. A. R. Puplett, *Synthetic Detergents* (Sidgwick & Jackson, 1957), pp. 134–7.

8 Consumer survey by National Opinion Polls Ltd. for Aspro-Nicholas Products Ltd., 1965.

9 Consumer survey on methods of cooking vegetables by the Wartime Social Survey, 1942. Though over twenty years old, this is probably not unduly outdated, for of all the elements of a culture, cooking methods are well known to be among the most deeply resistant to change.

10 Consumer survey of the gardening market by Contimart Ltd., 1964.

11 J. T. Coppock, *An Agricultural Atlas of England and Wales* (Faber, 1964).

12 E. Estyn Evans, *Irish Folk Ways* (Routledge, 1957). Many of the broader statements made about 'Celtic' culture in this book are based on this source.

13 Annual consumer surveys by S. H. Benson Ltd. for the Tea Bureau, 1951–7, fieldwork by Social Surveys Ltd. The first of these were published in *Tea Times*, January 1952, no. 43, and November 1952, no. 53. Regional breakdowns published vary from report to report.

14 Buyers for women's fashion stores, quoted in *Woman's Own*, 3 October 1959, pp. 10–13.

15 Sales figures of a Kettering lingerie manufacturer, quoted by T. Ireson, *Northamptonshire* (Robert Hale 1954), p. 226.

16 Sales figures of I. & R. Morley Ltd., quoted in the *Evening News*, 24 September 1959.

17 *Yorkshire Life*, April 1963, p. 53.

18 Malcolm Bradbury, *Stepping Westward* (Secker & Warburg, 1965).

19 The results of this are seen at perhaps their most extreme in the marked South of England bias in the intake into the older professions, in which family tradition has long played a more than ordinarily active part. Out of 472 candidates recommended for ordination in the Church of England in 1965, for example, 368 (or over three-quarters) came from the Province of Canterbury and a mere 89 from the Province of York (according to the Second Report of the Advisory Council for the Church's Ministry). Much the same pattern makes its appearance in the recruitment of officers to the Army. According to a recent survey by S. H. Benson Ltd. (reported in *The Times*, 18 March 1966), over half the applicants for regular commissions are Southerners – or more than twice as many as there should be in strict proportion to population. Immediately after the war the Army experienced great difficulty in finding enough officers of local origin for staffing Northern regiments; as a result it often had to resort to injecting Southerners into them, doubtless to mutual discomfort. At the same time the Army below the officer level has become much more predominantly Northern in make-up: the London District and Southern Command together were producing only 21 per cent of all regular recruits by 1958, compared with as many as 33 per cent in 1937 (War Office statistics, reported in *The Times*, 5 October 1959). If this trend is permitted to carry on indefinitely, we shall finally end up with an army completely stratified geographically, in which the North will be being ordered around almost exclusively by the South.

20 R. Smith, *Advertiser's Weekly*, 2 December 1960, p. 34: an analysis of variance carried out by Dr. M. Quenouille on the results of the Newspaper Society's first Regional Readership Survey showed that, for a given sample, it is more efficient to take fewer informants from

sampling points in the North of England than in the South. Translated into human terms, this seems to indicate that in the North people tend more closely to resemble their neighbours. Perhaps an obvious fact to any casual observer, but not all that easy to prove scientifically.

21 Geoffrey Gorer, *Exploring English Character* (Cresset Press, 1955). This large and important work has been criticised, not unreasonably, for its seriously biased sample, consisting mainly of readers of the *People* energetic enough to write in for, complete and post back a dauntingly long questionnaire. The younger age-groups, in particular, were much over-represented. Despite these limitations, however, the *regional* figures are probably not unduly distorted. Indeed, because of the relatively specialised class composition implicit in the readership of the *People*, the true magnitude of the differences may well be understated. Certainly, the findings of this survey tally well with all that we know from other sources.

22 *Sunday Times*, 29 March 1964.

23 Geoffrey Gorer, *Death, Grief and Mourning* (Cresset Press, 1965). Based on a national survey by Research Services Ltd., 1963.

24 *Retail Business*, February 1959, p. 476; *Financial Times*, 22 September 1959.

25 J. G. Davis of the Express Dairy Co. Ltd., in *The Modern Grocer and Provision Dealer*, Ed. 5, ed. W. G. Copsey (Caxton Publishing Co., 1951), vol. 3, pp. 50–65.

26 Consumer survey by a Sandwich slimming foods firm, quoted in the *Evening Standard*, 16 March 1965.

27 Body Weight Survey for the Ministry of Food, fieldwork by Social Surveys Ltd., 1943, published in W. F. F. Kemsley, 'Weight and height of a population in 1943', *Annals of Eugenics*, 1950, vol. 15, pp. 161–83. The sample comprised 27,500 men and 33,500 women.

28 Sales figures of Wm. Timpson Ltd., quoted in the *Guardian*, 10 September 1964.

29 *Drapery & Fashion Weekly*, 24 January 1964, p. 18.

30 Crime statistics are notoriously unreliable, due to inconsistencies in detection, reporting, sentencing and definition. The items cited are taken from two recent works in which the available figures have been carefully sifted: F. H. McClintock *et al.*, *Crimes of Violence* (Macmillan, 1963), pp. 12–16; L. Radzinowicz (ed.) *Sexual Offences* (Macmillan, 1957).

31 Survey on television's effect on leisure by Research Services Ltd. for the *Sunday Times*, commentary by Geoffrey Gorer, 1957.

32 Opinion survey by Social Surveys (Gallup Poll) Ltd., quoted in the *Daily Telegraph*, 1 April 1963.

33 Survey by Social Surveys (Gallup Poll) Ltd. for the Family Planning Association, published in *Family Planning*, October 1963.

34 A research chemist specialising in the colouring and flavouring of food, quoted in the *Observer*, 19 August 1956.

35 *Liverpool Echo*, 30 December 1965.

36 Consumer survey by Mather & Crowther Ltd. for the Egg Marketing Board, 1961.

37 H. E. Browning & A. A. Sorrell, 'Cinemas and cinema-going in Britain', *Journal of the Royal Statistical Society*, Series A (General), 1954, vol. 117, pp. 133–65.

38 One cannot go on to say, however, that the one is 'other-directed' and the other 'inner-directed' – to seize on the handy terms lately put into currency by David Riesman and his collaborators (*The Lonely Crowd: A Study of the Changing American Character;* Yale University Press, 1950). For though the North as a whole still behaves in obedience to an internal piloting system originally installed in childhood (in Riesman's words 'a psychic gyroscope set going by the parents'), much of the South, and certainly the South West, continues to function along these same basic lines as well. Neither is the Midlands, despite the surface existence it has so blatantly surrendered to, 'other-directed' in the true sense, at least as yet; it displays, rather, an 'inner-direction' pathologically addled.

It is only in the London area, and even there not at all in the rigid circles that still dominate such spheres as the City, that the signs are becoming definite and widespread of the emergence of the altogether new type of character: the stock of responses to one's social peers and contemporaries substituted for the firmly implanted code of personal behaviour; the keener, more anxious tuning-in to the values and opinions of the groups in which one moves and has one's being; the gyroscope of the previous individualism replaced by a questing social radar. We do not know for sure yet whether this is a final, long-enduring new creation, called into being by the new era of mass abundance, or merely a temporary expedient while society takes new bearings in the fundamentally altered situation in which it finds itself. We can, however, be sure that, having now begun to appear in Britain, it will inexorably spread. But, like everything else, it will not spread to each region at a uniform pace, but only so fast as happens to suit the pre-existing pattern of each one in turn. Scotland and the South West, almost certainly, will be the last two to succumb.

39 *Financial Times,* 1 August 1963: article on regional tastes by the commodities staff.

40 Leslie Adrian in the *Spectator,* 20 December 1957.

41 Retailer survey by Contimart Ltd. for the English Country Cheese Council, 1962, abstract in the *Food Trades Directory,* 1965–6, pp. 310–11.

42 Reply to a Parliamentary Question, 28 March 1945, reported in the *Ministry of Food Bulletin,* no. 289, p. 4.

43 Opinion survey by Mass-Observation Ltd., 1962, published by R. Harper, 'Some attitudes to vegetables, and their implications', *Nature,* 1963, vol. 200, pp. 14–18.

44 Unpublished consumer survey on home jam-making by Odhams Press Ltd., 1960.

45 Unpublished consumer survey on home cooking and baking by Odhams Press Ltd., 1960.

46 Edmund B. Bennion, *Breadmaking: Its Principles and*

Practice, Ed. 3 (Oxford University Press, 1954), p. 140. They were originally the product of the Chelsea Bun House, mentioned by Swift as early as 1711 and still popular in the early nineteenth century, according to R. J. Mitchell and M. D. R. Leys, *A History of London Life* (Penguin Books, 1963), p. 266.

47 Consumer survey by Mather & Crowther Ltd. for the Coal Utilisation Council, 1951.

48 *Financial Times*, 9 November 1965.

49 Consumer survey by the Electricity Council, 1955.

50 Sales figures of Great Universal Stores Ltd., quoted in the *Daily Mirror*, 18 June 1964. Direct selling, in contrast, might be expected to have a greater appeal to Southerners for this reason. Since starting with this method in 1959, however, Avon Cosmetics Ltd. (quoted in *Retail Business*, January 1966, p. 20) have met with most success in the North – though this could be due to the special field in which they operate.

51 Geoffrey Moorhouse, *Britain in the Sixties: The Other England* (Penguin Books, 1964).

52 Consumer survey by Sales Research Services Ltd., reported in the *Financial Times*, 24 February 1964; *Nielsen Researcher*, September–October 1963, p. 4.

53 Sales figures of Rossdale Products Ltd., quoted in the *Sports Trader*, December 1960. These garments came in as wear for ski-ing, then pre-eminently a southerners' sport.

54 *Financial Times*, 22 June 1960.

55 *Financial Times*, 24 April 1958.

56 Sales figures of Boots The Chemists Ltd., quoted in the *Financial Times*, 23 March 1961.

57 *Sunday Times*, 29 March 1964.

58 Radcliffe N. Salaman, *The History and Social Influence of the Potato* (Cambridge Univ. Press, 1959), pp. 479–81, 493–517; and 'The influence of food plants on social structure', *Advancent of Science*, 1950, vol. 7, pp. 200–11.

59 Anon., 'The Beatles and the balance of payments', *Barclays Bank Review*, February 1964, p. 12.

60 Stanley Cramp and A. D. Tomlins, 'The birds of Inner London 1951–65', *British Birds*, 1966, vol. 59, pp. 209–33; and quoted in the *Sunday Times*, 22 May 1966.

61 Ministry of Health and General Register Office, *Report on Hospital In-patient Enquiry for the Year 1961. Part II.* (H.M.S.O., 1964).

62 P. J. Chandler, 'Diurnal, seasonal and annual changes in the intensity of London's heat-island', *Meteorological Magazine*, 1962, vol. 91, pp. 146–53; and *The Climate of London* (Hutchinson, 1965).

63 Survey by the Wartime Social Survey for the Ministry of Food on the diet of selected groups of manual workers, 1942.

64 Michael Schofield, *The Sexual Behaviour of Young People* (Longmans, 1965), p. 44. This was based on a nation-wide sample survey.

65 Analysis of borrowers by the Co-operative Permanent Building Society, 1963.

66 Edward Newman, *Magazine of Natural History*, 1840, vol. 4 (new series), p. 175.

67 Consumer survey for the Potato Marketing Board, abstract in its Annual Report for 1957–8, p. 10.

68 Unpublished consumer survey on home decorating by Odhams Press Ltd., 1960.

69 *Evening Standard*, 20 July 1964. This cannot, of course, be more than a wild guess.

70 Sales figures of Marks & Spencer Ltd., quoted by Margaret Wray, *The Women's Outerwear Industry* (Duckworth, 1957), p. 162 footnote.

71 Consumer survey by Sales Research Services Ltd. for W. S. Crawford Ltd., 1936–7, published in Sir William Crawford and H. Broadley, *The People's Food* (Heinemann, 1938).

72 Consumer survey by Sales Research Services Ltd., 1949, published in the *Bulletin of Marketing Facts*, August 1949.

73 National Youth Survey by Market Investigations

Ltd., quoted in the *Financial Times*, 29 January 1960.

74 B. E. Coates and E. M. Rawstron, *Guardian*, 26 July 1965; and in much fuller detail in the *Westminster Bank Review*, February 1966, pp. 28–46.

75 Annual survey of salaries by Associated Industrial Consultants Ltd., December 1964, abstract in the *Sunday Times*, 3 January 1965.

76 Opinion survey by National Opinion Polls Ltd. for the Location of Offices Bureau, 1965.

77 R. F. Heller, *New Society*, 23 January 1964, p. 19.

78 Consumer survey by The Social Survey, 1961, abstract in *Economic Trends*, June 1963.

79 One production engineer has estimated that, for dress output, the efficiency rating of the typical operative in London is 75, against 68 in the North East and only 60 in Wales (Margaret Wray, op. cit., p. 223).

80 Susan Chitty, *Observer*, 20 October 1963.

81 Consumer survey by Social Surveys (Gallup Poll) Ltd. for the British Travel and Holidays Association, extract in *Advertiser's Weekly*, 29 May 1959, p. 31.

82 Leslie Paul, *The Deployment and Payment of the Clergy* (Church Information Office, 1964).

83 Unpublished consumer surveys by Fashion Trends.

84 *Sunday Times*, 8 November 1964.

85 *British Shoeman*, May 1957, p. 21.

86 *Board of Trade Journal*, 19 July 1963: special analysis from the 1961 Census of Distribution.

87 Viewing figures of Television Audience Measurement Ltd., quoted in the *Financial Times*, 2 May 1960.

88 Havelock Ellis, *A Study of British Genius*, Ed. 2 (Constable, 1927).

89 *Registrar-General's Review of England and Wales for the Two Years 1950–1951: Supplement on General Morbidity, Cancer and Mental Health* (H.M.S.O., 1955).

90 *Sunday Times Magazine*, 24 April 1966, p. 39.

91 Unpublished consumer survey on knitting and home dressmaking by Odhams Press Ltd., 1960.

92 Managing director of Lennards Ltd., quoted in the *Sunday Times*, 27 September 1964.

93 The Welsh are said to attach great importance to shoes and to taking special care of the feet. They are reputed to be horrified, in particular, by the very idea of chiropody. Do any Welsh-born chiropodists in fact exist?

94 Richard Llewellyn, *How Green Was My Valley* (Michael Joseph, 1939). Reproduced by permission.

95 Installation figures of Bendix Ltd.

96 *Sunday Times Magazine*, 17 November 1963.

97 Calculated from figures provided by the Public Service Vehicle Advertising Committee.

98 The influence of this demographic factor is largely discounted (surely somewhat cavalierly?) by John Spraos in his extremely penetrating study, *The Decline of the Cinema* (Allen & Unwin, 1962), p. 51.

99 Survey by the Royal College of Obstetricians and Gynaecologists jointly with the Population Investigation Committee, 1946, published as *Maternity in Great Britain* (Oxford University Press, 1948).

100 27th Annual Report of the Central Joint Advisory Committee on Tutorial Classes (1937), p. 42.

101 *The Times*, 11 October 1959.

102 Advertising supplement on Guinness in *The Times*, 10 November 1959.

103 *The Times*, 7 September 1957.

104 Anon., 'Peculiarities of purchasing in South Wales', *Scientific Marketing* (Colman, Prentis & Varley Ltd.), 1953, vol. 1, pp. 91–102.

105 F. J. North, Bruce Campbell and Richenda Scott, *Snowdonia* (Collins 1949), p. 343.

106 *The Grocer*, January 1963, Supplement, p. 10.

107 Verbal information from J. G. Jenkins, of the Welsh Folk Museum, Cardiff.

108 House of Commons, *Betting, Gaming and Lotteries Act 1963: Permits and Licences* (H.M.S.O., 1965).

109 General Register Office, *Area of Residence of Mental Hospital Patients* (H.M.S.O., 1960).

110 John Beddoe, *The Races of Britain* (Arrowsmith, 1885), pp. 251–5; Havelock Ellis, op. cit., p. 39.

111 Unpublished maps compiled from all known sources at the Anthropological Blood Group Centre of the Royal Anthropological Institute, under the direction of Dr. Ada C. Kopeč, to whom I am indebted for assistance in studying them.

112 A similar lobe-like extension from further north, though in this case rather more to the eastward, occurs in the pattern of deaths from 'strokes': G. Melvyn Howe, *National Atlas of Disease Mortality in the United Kingdom* (Nelson, 1963). Possibly this reflects a racial factor involved in their occurrence.

113 G. Willett Cunnington, *Feminine Attitudes in the Nineteenth Century* (Heinemann, 1935), p. 290.

114 W. G. Hoskins, *Midland England* (Batsford, 1949), p. 71.

115 *Public Library Statistics, 1962–3* (Institute of Municipal Treasurers & Accountants and Society of County Treasurers, 1964).

116 Quoted by Dennis Barker in the *Guardian*, 10 April 1965.

117 It could be that the Midlands accounts for an undue share of the current disenchantment with the National Health Service among general practitioners. It is certainly suggestive that the one well-publicised breakaway movement so far to have taken place has been in Birmingham. In this region the pressures from material ostentation are at their most insidious, the patients at their most bothersome and querulous. The two combined must make general practice seem sensibly less rewarding here than elsewhere.

This recalls a thesis that someone has propounded that an unusually virulent strain is kept alive in English politics largely through the influence of emigré Welshmen.

Q

Forced by the Depression to uproot themselves from their mining valleys, they took with them, it is suggested, a rancorous resentment nursed with a peculiarly un-English persistence and venom.

Whether accurate of not, both theses illustrate how grievances with a strong regional focus may masquerade as universal and national, unless scrutinised with care. In the same way national pressure-groups in politics may prove to be plugged into specially regional power-points: mitigate the 'little local difficulties' and sweeping political adjustments may conveniently turn out to be superfluous. Most probably we much underestimate the workings of 'regional error' in our civic and political life.

118 Typical of this preference for old-fashioned formulae is the use of glycerine and rose-water as a hand-lotion, which finds easily its strongest following in the Midlands.

119 Phil Drabble, *Black Country* (Robert Hale, 1952), p. 21.

120 According to Professor E. L. Crossley (quoted in the *Observer*, 25 November 1962), over 60 per cent of all milk sold in Birmingham is sterilised. An explanation confidently advanced in the *Evening Standard*, 24 May 1961, is that the taste originated in the Depression, when milk was scarce and the sealed, sterilised variety would stay fresh, though unrefrigerated, for seven days. This sounds unconvincing. Surely other regions suffered much more severely in the Depression but acquired no such taste in the process? More probably, Midlanders just like the flavour – or, at any rate, find it less objectionable measured against its practical advantages than people of other regions.

121 Verbal information from V. Selwyn.

122 The remarkably low rate of coronary heart disease among men in the Black Country towns – indicated or suggested by three separate sets of medical statistics – perhaps lends some support to the theory that has been lately advanced that the great increase in coronary attacks is

due to too much sugar in the diet. A definite association between coronary disease and heavy smoking in men appears to have been established, yet Midlanders are notably heavy smokers. Conceivably, the addition of excessive amounts of sugar is the extra contributory factor that serves to tilt the scales.

123   *Financial Times*, 5 September 1961.

124   Graham Turner, *The Car Makers* (Eyre & Spottiswoode, 1963).

125   *The Times*, 31 July 1959.

126   *Evening Standard*, 25 August 1960.

127   *The Times*, 31 March, 1959.

128   *Retail Business*, April 1964, p. 31.

129   Miss E. Zelker of Polly Peck Boutiques, quoted in the *Evening Standard*, 10 May 1965. A superstition against green clothing has long been known in parts of the North of England as well.

130   The sociology of the parlour is examined at some length by Dennis Chapman, *The Home and Social Status* (Routledge, 1955), pp. 112–15.

131   Stockings, it seems, have long been a means of rather brazen display by women in Lancashire. In his book on *Lancashire* (Robert Hale, 1951), p. 148, Walter Greenwood records that at the end of the last century in towns like Salford, where warfare between street gangs was a common occurrence, the womenfolk attached to each gang wore distinctive stockings, ringed in different colours like those nowadays worn by footballers.

132   Relatively speaking, there are actually more Roman Catholic marriages each year in London than in the North West, but London's popularity as a place of marriage for non-residents must artificially inflate this figure. The large families in the North West must still mean a far greater preponderance there of Roman Catholics in terms of individuals.

133   Cecil Woodham-Smith, *The Great Hunger* (Hamish Hamilton, 1962), pp. 272–9.

134 Ada C. Kopeč, 'Blood-groups in Great Britain', *Advancement of Science*, 1956, vol. 51, pp. 200–3; and verbal information.

135 Quoted in *The Times*, 26 August 1965.

136 Zevedei Barbu, *Problems of Historical Psychology*, (Routledge, 1960), pp. 205–6.

137 Neil J. Smelser, *Social Change in the Industrial Revolution: An Application of Theory to the Lancashire Cotton Industry 1770–1840* (Routledge, 1959). In this otherwise exhaustive study no account is taken of distinctive features of the regional personality. An unduly generalised picture is accordingly drawn of the roles of the sexes, the severe pressures on which, brought about by successive technical changes, the author sees as a central cause of the various phases of industrial unrest.

138 C. Madge, *War-time Pattern of Saving and Spending* (National Institute of Economic & Social Research, 1943).

139 *Financial Times*, 16 February 1961.

140 Unpublished statistics of prosecutions by the National Society for the Prevention of Cruelty to Children, kindly communicated by Miss W. D. Timmis.

141 J. B. Jefferys, *Retail Trading in Britain, 1850–1950* (Cambridge University Press, 1954), chapter VI.

142 W. J. Martin, *The Physique of Young Adult Males* (Medical Research Council, 1949). Recruits from Lancashire called up for the forces just before the outbreak of war in 1939 had the lowest mean height and weight of any in Great Britain. Poor diet may have largely contributed to this. Feet in the North West are also usually shorter and broader than the English average, according to Wm. Timpson Ltd. (quoted in the *Guardian*, 10 September 1964).

143 A leading firm of wedding-dress manufacturers, quoted in the *Daily Herald*, 13 March 1964.

144 Retailer survey by Mass-Observation Ltd., abstract in *The Times*, 18 July 1966.

145 Based on numbers per region published in *Self Service and Supermarket* Annual Directory.

146 Herbert Heaton, *The Yorkshire Woollen and Worsted Industries*, Ed. 2 (Clarendon Press, 1965).

147 E. Lipson, *A Short History of Wool and its Manufacture* (Heinemann, 1953), p. 191.

148 'New pattern for wool', *Sunday Telegraph*, 19 April 1964. Another example of the effect of petty isolationism in Yorkshire is the failure of the county's local authorities, alone of those in Britain, to work together sufficiently to set up a Regional Library Bureau, to act as a central clearing-house for the area for all inter-library exchange-loans of books. Doubtless there are other, similar instances of self-inflicted wounds from this cause.

149 Lettice Cooper, *Yorkshire West Riding* (Robert Hale, 1950), p. 279. A possibly even greater blow, however, was the ending of supplies of 'white' flour (of 75 per cent extraction) by government order in April 1942. The dramatic decline in home baking in the North East as a result of these wartime hindrances is best shown by the figures for flour consumption, which plunged from 120 per cent above the national average in 1943 to only 50 per cent above by 1949 (Ministry of Agriculture, Fisheries & Food, *Studies in Urban Household Diets 1944–49* (H.M.S.O., 1956), p. 87).

150 Teenagers' shoes are, however, one exception, if Lennards Ltd. (quoted in the *Sunday Times*, 27 September 1964) are to be believed. Fashions in these in Leeds are said to be the fastest of any other city to follow those in London.

151 In an area-by-area report on the general standard of men's appearance, contributed by members of the Wholesale Clothing Manufacturers' Federation in 1959, the men of Leeds were judged second only to those of London. All they were lacking in, it was held, was boldness and imagination.

152 Patrick Ryan, *Yorkshire Life*, January 1966, p. 19.

153   E. Sutherland, 'Hair-colour variation in the United Kingdom', *Annals of Human Genetics*, 1956, vol. 20, pp. 312–33.

154   W. M. Williams, 'Kinship structure in an English village', *Man*, 1952, vol. 52, pp. 143–4.

155   Edmund Vale, *North Country* (Batsford, 1937).

156   Iona & Peter Opie, *The Lore and Language of School-children* (Clarendon Press, 1959), p. 26.

157   Trade sources quoted in *Retail Business*, August 1965, p. 19.

158   In Northumberland bacon is often mixed with fish to form special traditional dishes such as Halibut Bake (*Sunday Times Magazine*, 22 May 1966). This suggests that pig products are no recent intrusion into the diet of this area.

159   'Cinema-going in London and the provinces', *Board of Trade Journal*, 19 November 1955, pp. 1106–12.

160   John Vaizey, *The Brewing Industry 1886–1951* (Pitman, 1960), p. 124.

161   [E. Topham], *Letters from Edinburgh, Written in the Years 1774–1775* (London, 1776).

162   Janet Adam Smith, *Life Among the Scots* (Collins, 1946).

163   Twelve per cent of the population of England, over 630,000 persons in all, were found to be of Scottish birth in the 1961 Census. Proportionately, this was over two and a half times the size of the English-born element resident in Scotland.

164   Remarkably few writers on Scotland seem to have recognised this other, possibly more far-reaching dichotomy. A. S. Fraser's *Vision of Scotland* (Elek, 1948) is one of the exceptions.

165   It has recently been found that the Orkney Isles have unusually high proportions of people (about 38 per cent), compared with most of the rest of Britain, possessing the hereditary factor that inhibits the tasting of phenylthiocarbamide, the acid which produces, for example, the

bitter tang to grape-fruit (E. Sunderland, 'The tasting of phenylthiocarbamide in selected populations in the United Kingdom', *Eugenics Review*, 1966, vol. 58, pp. 143–8). This may merely be a chance outcome produced in a small, isolated population; alternatively, similar levels may prove to occur over much of North Scotland. In most of Northumberland, in contrast, the proportion unable to taste this acid is unduly low (down to 24 per cent), which is 'very remarkable and difficult to explain'. These are examples of a single racial difference that in certain circumstances might conceivably have an important influence on local food preferences – and so on consumer demand. Many more like it may well turn up in the future.

166 H. G. Graham, *The Social Life of Scotland in the Eighteenth Century*, Ed. 4 (A. & C. Black, 1950).

167 Unidentified consumer survey quoted in the *Director*, April 1961, p. 104.

168 *Daily Express*, 8 September 1960.

169 An executive of Lewis's Polytechnic, Glasgow, in *Advertiser's Weekly*, 2 September 1960, Supplement, p. 6.

170 Ian Finlay, *Scotland*, Ed. 2 (Chatto & Windus,1957). p.17

171 *Financial Times*, 12 August 1961.

172 *Financial Times*, 19 September 1964.

173 *Financial Times*, 11 November 1961.

174 David Riesman, with Nathan Glazer and Reuel Denney, *The Lonely Crowd: A Study of the Changing American Character* (Yale University Press, 1950).

175 Elizabeth S. Haldane, *The Scotland of Our Fathers* (Maclehose, 1933).

176 Ministry of Agriculture, Fisheries & Food, *Domestic Food Consumption and Expenditure: 1960*. (H.M.S.O. 1962), p. 147: analysis of additional Christmas spending.

177 At the age of eight, for example, Scottish children score very significantly higher than English or Welsh children in tests of reading and sentence completion, a

lead which they have lost by eleven (J. W. B. Douglas, J. M. Ross, S. M. M. Maxwell and D. A. Walker, 'Differences in test score and in the gaining of selective places for Scottish children and those in England and Wales', *British Journal of Educational Psychology*, 1966, vol. 36, pp. 150–7). This reflects the fact that Scottish schools begin the systematic teaching of letter sounds – as well as formal, written arithmetic – at a significantly earlier age than those in England (M. L. Kellmer Pringle, N. R. Butler and R. Davie, *11,000 Seven-Year-Olds* (Longman's, 1966), pp. 51–5.

178 Opinion survey in the Craigton constituency of Glasgow for the Department of Politics, University of Strathclyde, reported in the *Guardian*, 5 August 1965.

179 Audience survey by the Screen Advertising Association, 1960, published as *The Cinema Audience*.

180 Survey by the Graduate Appointments Register, January 1965.

181 Maxwell Gaskin, *The Scottish Banks: A Modern Survey* (Allen & Unwin, 1965).

182 Joint managing director of L. Harris (Harella) Ltd., quoted in the *Sunday Times*, 14 October 1962.

183 G. Seton, 'On illegitimacy in Scotland', *Royal Society of Edinburgh, Proceedings for 1882–3*, vol. 12, pp. 18–24.

184 Lafitte Report to the Family Planning Association, summarised in *The Times*, 30 May 1962.

185 Consumer survey by Research Services Ltd., 1947, published as *The Rural Market*.

186 John Scade, 'Local loaves', in Ronald Sheppard & Edward Newton, *The Story of Bread* (Routledge, 1957), pp. 128-156.

187 J. C. Fabricius, *Briefe aus London vermischten Inhalts* (Dessau & Leipzig, 1784), 8th letter. In just the same way immigrant Sicilians have lately taken control of the fruit and vegetable markets of Milan. Such regional expatriates, not regarding themselves as aliens, may have much less compunction about – or much less conscious

awareness of – imposing their special tastes on the public they serve. This subject deserves fuller study.

188 Consumer survey by a toothbrush manufacturer, abstract in the *Manchester Guardian*, 8 February 1957.

189 Consumer survey by the Oxford University Institute of Statistics in collaboration with The Social Survey, 1952, published in H. F. Lydall, *British Incomes and Savings* (Blackwell, 1955).

190 H. O. Horne, *A History of Savings Banks* (Oxford University Press, 1947).

191 Consumer survey on unit trusts by Marketing Trends Ltd., 1966.

192 Scottish Savings Committee figures, re-worked, in George T. Murray, *The United Kingdom: An Economic and Marketing Study* (Marketing Economics Ltd., 1964), pp. 50–2.

193 Averil Lysaght (ed.), *Directory of Natural History and Other Field Study Societies in Great Britain* (British Association for the Advancement of Science, 1959), p. x.

194 *Nielsen Researcher*, 1960, no. 1.

195 Retailer survey by Produce Studies Ltd. for the Horticultural Marketing Council, 1962.

196 Ministry of Agriculture, Fisheries & Food, *Studies in Urban Household Diets 1944–49: Second Report of the National Food Survey Committee* (H.M.S.O. 1956), pp. 87–8.

197 Consumer survey by Stats (M.R.) Ltd. for the Economist Intelligence Unit Ltd., published in *Retail Business*, December 1964.

198 Opinion survey by Sales Research Services Ltd., quoted in the *Drapers' Record*, 20 August 1960.

199 David Granick, *The European Executive* (Weidenfeld & Nicholson, 1962), p. 342.

200 Co-operative Union figures, reproduced in *Retail Business*, May 1966.

201 Ruth Benedict, 'Recognition of cultural diversities in the postwar world', *American Academy of Political & Social Science, Annals*, 1943, vol. 228, p. 102.

R

202   A. H. Iliffe, *News Chronicle*, 8 April 1958; and 'A study of preferences in feminine beauty', *British Journal of Psychology*, 1960, vol. 51, pp. 267–73. The basis of this study was a postal ballot by 4,355 *News Chronicle* readers on twelve head-and-shoulders photographs.

Index

Aberdeen, 187
Aberdeenshire, 184
aerosols, 41
agnostics, professional, 60
agriculture and horticulture,
    comparison, 23
alcohol, 66
alcoholism (*see ill-health*)
anaemia (*see ill-health*)
Anglia television survey, 70
Anglicisms, 100
angling (*see sport*)
aniseed, 34, 117
anoraks (*see clothing*)
ante-natal treatment, 81
anxiety states (*see ill-health*)
apples (*see fruit*)
artistic professions, 57
asparagus (*see vegetables*)
aspirins, 106
asthma (*see ill-health*)
atmospheric pollution, 45, 103
attitude to life, 29, 33
'Auld Alliance', the, 180
Australian (*see cheese*)

Babies, 103, 191
bacon (*see meat*)
baking (*see cooking*)
bananas (*see fruit*)
banking, 193, 208
barley zone, 23
barter deals, 75
bachelor girls, 53
baths, 54, 59, 91, 156
beans (*see vegetables*)
Beatlemania, 42
Beddoe, Dr. John, 107, 150
'Bed-sitterland', 48

beef (*see meat*)
beer, 23, 30, 32, 76, 78, 94, 96–8,
    115–17, 156, 173, 179, 181,
    186, 187
Beeton, Mrs., 36
Benedict, Ruth, 220
Bentley, E. C., on geography, 3
Bermondsey, 54
bicycles, 22, 74, 214
bikinis (*see clothing*)
Birmingham, 63, 106, 107, 109, 123,
    212
birth-control, 32, 198
birth-rate, 121, 198
births, 103, 113
biscuits, 23, 66, 87, 117, 118, 172,
    205, 207
    chocolate, 84, 172, 205
    cream crackers, 172
    marie, 84
Black Country, 115, 117
blackberries (*see fruit*)
Blackburn, 143
blancmange, 34, 87, 204
blankets (*see electrical appliances*)
blood-groups, 108, 109 134, 172
blouses (*see clothing*)
Blue Stilton (*see cheese*)
bonnets (*see clothing*)
bootees (*see footwear*)
boots, rubber (*see footwear*)
Bradford, 160
brassières (*see clothing*)
bread, 23, 24, 67, 69, 76, 77, 117,
    129, 162–4, 173, 181, 200, 201
    brown, 173
    French, 57
    fried, 69
    malt, 34, 106, 163, 173

bread—*cont.*
  rolls, 57, 201
  rye, 57
  Ryvita, 207
  wholemeal, 69
breadmaking, 91, 163, 181
Bristol, 70, 78, 83, 86
  footwear, 74
bronchitis (*see ill-health*)
brown bread, 173
brushes, 30, 207
Budleigh Salterton, 73
building societies, 209
buns (*see cakes*)
bungalows, 83
buses (*see transport*)
butter, 34, 77, 98, 129, 144, 181

Cabbage (*see vegetables*)
Caerphilly (*see cheese*)
cafés (*see restaurants*)
cakes, 36, 57, 66, 77, 87, 91, 105,
  117, 118, 146, 148, 162, 163,
  181, 201, 202, 204
  making, 202
  mixes, 163
  racks, 185
Calvinism, 188
Cambrensis, Giraldus, 169
camping, 123
car accommodation, 55
Car Makers, The, 122
Car Mechanics, 112
caravans, 26, 83
Cardiff, 88, 101
cardigans (*see clothing*)
carpentry, 66
career women, 53
carpets (*see furnishings*)
carrots (*see vegetables*)
cars, 55, 60, 64, 68, 74, 93, 110,
  154, 172, 178, 182, 214
  vintage, 60
Catholic, Roman, 101, 131-5,
  139, 142, 190, 198
cats, 71, 77, 183
cauliflower (*see vegetables*)
celery (*see vegetables*)
Census, 14, 50, 212
central heating, 26, 162
cereals, 77, 164
cerebral palsy (*see ill-health*)
Channel Isles, 16, 77

chastity, 100
Cheddar (*see cheese*)
cheese, 34, 98, 106, 117, 118, 137,
  157, 173, 174
  Australian, 34
  Blue Stilton, 137
  Caerphilly, 98
  Cheddar, 34, 117
  Danish, 34
  Double Gloucester, 98
  Gorgonzola, 30, 34
  New Zealand, 34
  White Stilton, 151
Cheltenham Spa, 75
cherries, glacé (*see fruit*)
chest conditions (*see ill-health*)
chicken (*see meat*)
childbirth, 103, 113
china, 84
chocolate (*see confectionery* and
  biscuits)
Christmas, 190
  market, 190
church going, 71, 77
Church of England, 77
cider, 23, 76, 115, 118, 179, 187
cigarettes, 40, 41, 63, 115, 182,
  206 (*see also smoking*)
cinemas, 33, 66, 75, 93, 178, 179,
  189, 193, 211
city life, 50
Civil War, 132
Clean Air Act, 45
clothing, 37, 38, 47, 88, 126, 156,
  195, 196, 197, 205, 208
  anoraks, 41
  baby-wear, 103, 191
  bikinis, 41
  blouses, 63, 125, 211
  bonnets, 192
  bootees, 106
  brassières, 35, 126, 197, 211
  cardigans, 25, 59, 132, 168
  clubs, 77
  coats, 41, 126, 132, 166, 211
  corsetry, 31, 41, 147
  dresses, 26, 126, 196, 197, 211
  frocks, 185
  girdles, 125, 211
  gloves, 186, 192
  jackets, 26, 35, 41, 47, 126, 176
  jumpers, 196
  lingerie, 125, 176, 197

mackintoshes, 22
millinery, 89
nightwear, 26, 127
    second hand, 144
    shirts, 125, 185, 200
    skirts, 63, 185, 195, 211
    slacks, 185
    slips, 126, 127
    socks, 26, 126
        babies', 192
    stockings, 59, 73, 126, 127, 185
    suits, 26, 30, 47, 59, 66, 166
    sweaters, 35, 59, 126, 185
    ties, 126
    topcoats, 126
    trousers, 126
    vests, 72, 89, 126, 186
    waistcoats, 168
    wedding dresses, 41, 147
cliques, 50
clubs, 93, 115, 179
    clothing, 77
    licensed, 32
    working men's, 179
Clydeside, 198
    conurbation, 212
coal, 55, 56, 74, 92, 214
Coatbridge, 198
coats (*see clothing*)
Cockney, 49, 50
cocktail parties, 66
cocoa, 77
coconut (*see fruit*)
cod (*see fish*)
Co. Durham, 102, 156
coffee, 60, 87, 115
coke, 68
colds (*see ill-health*)
colours, 32, 59, 80, 88, 125, 138,
    145, 197
commercial pressure, 221
commercial television areas, 17
community, sense of, 29
commuters, 44, 70
commuting, 43, 44
comparison of arbitrary regions,
    13, 14
confectionery, 30, 32, 87, 182, 203,
    206
Conservative Party, 82
Conservatives, 135
conserves, 76, 118, 148, 202
constipation (*see ill-health*)

Continent, the, 55, 180
conurbations, England and Wales,
    facing p. 13
cookers, 75
    pressure, 23
    solid fuel, 155
cookery, Continental, 57, 72
cooking, 23, 35, 65, 75, 91, 148,
    162, 180, 189, 200, 202
    comparison, 23
    fats, 75, 163, 173, 190
    habits, 23, 35
co-operative societies, 211
corned beef, 173, 202
Cornwall, 70, 74, 80
corsetry (*see clothing*)
cosmetics, 59, 63, 109, 127, 165,
    176, 195
coughs (*see ill-health*)
country life, 73
Covent Garden, 56
Coventry, 107, 108, 115
cows (*see livestock*)
cream, 80, 96, 97, 201, 202
crèche, municipal, 160
cremation, 167
cricket (*see sport*)
crime, 31, 47, 154, 192
Cumberland
    dalesmen, 171
    kinship structure, 171
currants (*see fruit*)
curtains (*see furnishings*)
custard, 57, 182, 210
Cypriots, 54

Dance halls, 66
Danish (*see cheese*)
dairy products
    butter, 34, 77, 98, 129, 144, 181
    cheese, 30, 34, 98, 106, 117, 118,
        137, 157, 173, 174
    cream, 80, 96, 97, 201, 202
    eggs, 32, 65, 77, 87, 98, 117,
        182, 203
    milk, 23, 46, 77, 80, 96–8, 115,
        116, 157, 173, 174, 181, 202
death rates, 132, 140, 177, 187,
    197, 212
    infancy, 79
dentists, 114
department stores, 60
depression (*see ill-health*)

Derby, 107
detergents, 22
Devon, 70, 72, 74, 76, 124, 171
Dictionary of National Biography, 79
disinfectants, 124, 172
divorce, 52, 199
dogs, 56, 183
'do-it-yourself', 110, 178
Do-it-Yourself, 214
domestic appliances, 59, 88, 111,
    174, 196, 205
domestic tasks, 199
dormitory towns and villages, 65
Double Gloucester (*see cheese*)
dresser, 24
dresses (*see clothing*)
dressmakers, 148
dressmaking, 35, 87, 196
driers (*see electrical appliances*)
drills (*see electrical appliances*)
drinking, 66, 94, 179, 186-8
drugs, 41
drunkenness, 31, 48, 115, 186, 199
dry-cleaners, 38
Dumbarton, 198
Durham, historical background,
    171
Dutch, 74, 199

East Anglia, 17, 65, 70, 71, 72,
    74, 75, 78, 80, 81
  clothes, 73
  eating, 75, 96
  focus of intellectual ability, 79
  food, 72, 75, 79, 80
  grouping with the South East, 70
  habits, 71
  housing, 75, 83
  livestock, 79
  political studies, 82
  sewerage and plumbing, 74
  television, 78
East Anglians,
  characteristics, 78-9
  eating, 78
  healthiness, 79
  physique, 78
East Midlands, 17, 196
East Riding, 17
Eastern Region, 17, 65, 71
  eating, 30, 34, 75, 77, 78, 85,
    96, 129, 147, 164, 190, 201,
    205, 206

Eden, Sir Frederick, on diet, 23,
    42
Edinburgh, 63, 133, 184, 188, 199,
    207
education, 38, 51, 68, 94, 95, 110,
    111, 192, 194
eggs, 32, 65, 77, 87, 98, 117, 182,
    203
elections, 38, 82, 94, 135, 136
electrical appliances, 75
  blankets, 114, 185
  driers, 110, 166
  drills, 178
  immersion heaters, 22
  kettles, 35, 75
  sewing machines, 161
  shavers, 40, 72
  toasters, 72, 204
  washing machines, 84, 91, 111,
    151, 174, 197
electricity, 56, 68
  heating, 36
Ellis, Havelock, 79, 151
entertaining, home, 66
entertainment, 44, 93, 159, 177,
    178, 192
environment, 49
Episcopalians, 190
Europe, Central and Eastern, 54
Exeter, 83
Exploring British Character, 82

Fabrics, 25, 26
family gatherings, 29, 84
Family Planning Association
    clinics, 198
fares, 68
farmers, affluent, 74
fashion, 35, 41, 59, 67, 154, 165,
    185, 196
  teenage, 175
Financial Times, 187
fires, gas, 56
fish, 37, 97, 117, 165, 172
  cakes, 163, 165, 173
  chips, and, 87, 164
  cod, 163, 165, 173
  haddock, 182, 204
  hake, 97
  herring, 69, 181
  kippers, 69
  paste, 84, 165
  salmon, 96, 97, 120

shell, 46
tinned, 202
white, 210
flavours, 34, 35, 37
flour, 42, 75, 91, 98, 148, 173
self-raising, 155, 163
flowers, 87, 210
food, 26, 30, 32, 34, 35, 43, 46, 57,
65, 67, 69, 72, 75, 79, 80, 87,
96, 116–20, 137, 144, 146,
156, 157, 172–4, 181, 182,
190, 191, 200–7, 210, 219
canned and frozen, 57, 65, 71,
72, 96, 117, 119, 155, 165,
173, 177, 202
Chinese, 57
Indian, 57
invalid, 83
purchases, 75
ready-made, 119
special vagaries, 69
spicy, 174
supply of, 56
Foods We Eat, The, 6
football (*see sport*)
footwear,
bootees, 106
boots, rubber, 22
sandals, 26, 41, 47
shoes, 73, 109, 125, 126, 132,
176, 183
slippers, 132, 161, 166
Free Church, the, 183
frocks (*see clothing*)
fruit
apples, 76, 116
bananas, 65, 75
blackberries, 76
cherries, glacé, 202
coconut, 202
currants, 75
fresh, 56, 164
grapefruit, 75
greengages, 76
juices, 40, 118, 182, 202
nuts, 75, 202 (*see also coconut and
walnut*)
oranges, 8, 31, 34, 75, 164, 202
peaches, 96
pears, 96
pies, 148, 202
pineapples, 96
raisins, 75, 91, 202

raspberries, 137
tinned, 57, 165
tomatoes, 30, 75, 117, 165, 173,
182
walnuts, 117
fuel, solid, 174 (*see also coal, coke*)
funerals, 29, 84, 135
furnishings, 59, 84, 91, 92, 161
carpets, 41, 87, 91, 124, 161, 177
curtains, 124, 145, 185
linoleum, 87, 91, 124, 161
tiles, 91
furniture, 87, 177, 208, 213
beds, 87, 213
kitchen, 24
second-hand, 144
Fylde, the, 24

Gadgetry, household, 87
gambling, 31, 83, 100, 133, 174
game (*see meat*)
garages and filling stations, 81
gardening, 23, 75
gardening equipment, 41, 56, 66,
75, 177
gardens, 37, 66, 75, 130, 132, 183
gas, 75
appliances, 56
heating, 56
Geddes, Sir Patrick, 208
geese (*see livestock*)
general stores, 76
geysers, gas, 56
gin (*see wines and spirits*)
ginger, 206
girdles (*see clothing*)
gladioli, 106
Glamorgan, 86
Glasgow, 54, 130, 133, 198, 199,
212
glass, 84
Glaswegian feet, 184
gloves (*see clothing*)
Golden Circle Theory, 40
Gorer, Geoffrey, 81, 82, 112, 127,
130
Gorgonzola (*see cheese*)
gout (*see ill-health*)
grapefruit (*see fruit*)
gravy powder, 165
Great Famine (1847), the, 132
Greater London, 65, 120
atmosphere, 45

Greater London—*cont.*
  conurbation, 15, 44
  heat, the, 46
  population complex, 44
  social life, 48
Green Belt, the, 65
greengages (*see fruit*)

Haddock (*see fish*)
haggis, 181, 203
hairdressers, 38, 84, 148, 149
hairdressing, 87, 165, 172, 195
hake (*see fish*)
ham (*see meat*)
Hampstead, 50
hard goods, 84
headaches (*see ill-health*)
heaters, electric immersion, 22
heating
  central, 26, 162
  coal, 55, 56, 74, 92, 214
  electric, 36
  gas, 56
  oil, 56, 130
  paraffin, 68
herb doctors, 96
herring (*see fish*)
Highland Zone, 22, 23, 26, 28, 87
Highlands, 76, 183, 212
Hogmanay, 187
holidays, 68, 71, 81, 83, 151
Homemaker, The, 214
Homes & Gardens, 214
homicide, 140
  rate, 47
horses (*see livestock*)
horticultural expenses, 75
hot-pot, 138, 145
houseboats, 26
household appliances, 91, 156
housing, 54, 67, 75, 83, 92, 103,
    104, 120, 131, 132, 156, 174,
    175, 177, 182, 212, 213, 214,
    215
How Green was my Valley, 89
Humber–Mersey line, 109

Ice-cream, 26, 46, 181, 202, 204, 205
Ideal Home, 214
ideological radicalism, 40
illegitimacy, 51, 95, 197
  rate, 51, 133
ill-health, 22, 39, 102

alcoholism, 102, 186
anaemia, 22
anxiety states, 114
asthma, 45, 101
bronchitis, 103, 132
burns, 103, 175
cerebral palsy, 77
chest conditions, 45
colds, 26, 114, 207
constipation, 114
coughs, 26
depression, 48, 101
gout, 114
headaches, 114, 207
malnutrition, 102
manic depression, 101
mental disorders, 101, 127, 139
nervous illness, 101
obesity, 31, 114, 147
pneumoconiosis, 174
psychological illness, 102
pulmonary infection, 103
rashes, 114
respiratory diseases, 103, 212
rheumatism, 22, 174
schizophrenia, 48, 101
sinusitis, 114
skin diseases, 103, 174
slipped disc, 101
stomach upsets, 114
ulcers, 65, 106
varicose veins, 60, 151
venereal diseases, 51, 95, 197
illness (*see ill-health*)
immersion heaters (*see electrical
    appliances*)
impulse buying, 72
income, 121, 193
  level, 61, 72
  economics of, middle-range, 62
  London girls, 62
individual freedom, 33
industry, 136, 159, 175
infant mortality, 22, 81, 103, 132,
    212
infrastructure, 28, 177
  cause and effect of, 28
innovation, historical corridor of,
    40
insecticides, 26, 75
inter-regional migration, 221
inter-relation of areas, 8
interwoven attitudes, 8

Inverness, 184, 218
Ipswich, 218
Ireland, 81, 99, 133, 135
Irish, the, 54, 100, 132, 198
Isle of Ely, 74
Isle of Man, 16, 99
Italians, the, 100
itinerant trader, 205

Jacobite invasion, 132
jackets (*see clothing*)
jam, 35, 77, 105, 106, 118, 148,
    205 (*see also marmalade*)
  damson, 106
  making, 66, 148, 202
James IV, 188
jellies, 34, 137, 204, 205, 206
jewellers, 68
Joad, Professor, 65
Joneses, keeping up with, 64
jumpers (*see clothing*)

Kensington, 50
Kent, 65, 66
ketchup, tomato, 117
kettles (*see electrical appliances*)
kidney (*see meat*)
kippers (*see fish*)
kitchen, 24, 36, 129, 212, 214
  tables, 24
knitting, 83, 148, 192, 196
Knox, John, 99

Labour Party, 175
Ladies' Bank, 199
Lake District, 76
lamb (*see meat*)
Lancashire, 13, 95, 103, 121, 122,
    130, 137, 145, 151, 164, 210,
    212
  east, 132
  family respectability, 145
  housewife, 143
  superstition, 135
  test market, 136
  west, 132
Lancaster, 132
Lancastrians, 61, 210, 214
  humour, 138
  traits, 138
lard, 190
launderettes. 91, 141
laundries, 38, 60, 197

leeks (*see vegetables*)
Leicester, 107
library borrowing, 75, 112
lighting, 38
lineage system, 28
lingerie (*see clothing*)
linoleum (*see furnishings*)
liquorice, 34
liver (*see meat*)
Liverpool, 131, 132, 133, 134, 138,
    143
livestock, 78, 79
  cows, 144, 157, 158
  geese, 24
  horses, 140
  pigs, 78, 144, 158
  sheep, 152, 157
Llewelyn, Richard, 89
Llywelyn ap Gruffydd, 98
London, 40, 71, 78, 95, 111, 131,
    140, 145, 181, 213, 214
  cellular pattern, 50
  clothes, 47, 58
  County of, 52, 54, 55, 212
  crime pattern, 47
  East End of, 50, 57
  executive, 62
  fashion, 59
  food, 46, 65, 67, 69
  housing, 54, 67, 83
  inflation leader, 61
  Inner, 51
  men, 58
  non-UK population, 50
  population, 44
  service expectation, 59
  social fabric, 51
  social pattern, 63
  tempo of life in, 65
  West End of, 57
  women, 58
London & South East, 121
London & South Eastern Region,
    113
Londoner, way of life, 49
Londoners, 43–66
Lowland Zone, 22, 23
Luton, 71

Mackintoshes (*see clothing*)
mail-order shopping, 38
malnutrition (*see ill-health*)
malt bread, 34, 106, 163, 173

249

managerial groups, 27
Manchester, 131
    conurbation, 131
manic depression (*see ill-health*)
manual workers, 27, 94, 206
margarine, 128, 144
marmalade, 34, 77, 118 (*see also jam*)
marriage, 29, 52, 53, 63, 79, 198
    childless, 53
    rate, 79
    unhappy, 115
mattresses, 87, 213
meat, 116, 172, 181, 202, 203
    bacon, 34, 36, 65, 173, 190, 191
    beef, 87, 157, 173, 202, 203
    corned 173, 202
    chicken, 30, 77, 219
    extracts, 118
    game, 77
    ham, 79, 99, 191
    home-killed, 145
    kidney, 30
    lamb, 87, 117, 157, 203
    liver, 87, 203
    mutton, 117, 145, 157, 203
    oxtail, 203
    pork, 79, 99, 117, 190
    rabbit, 77
    Spam, 79, 99, 146, 173
    sweetbreads, 203
    tinned, 96
medical goods, 68
medicines, 26, 95, 114, 207, 210
    ethicals, 114
    indigestion, 30
    pain killing, 207
    tablets, 114, 207
menswear (*see under clothing, anoraks, cardigans, coats, jackets, shoes, slippers, socks, suits, sweaters, ties, topcoats, trousers, waistcoats*)
mental disorders (*see ill-health*)
Merseyside, 42, 120, 133, 139, 140, 145
    conurbation, 131
Merthyr Tydfil, 100, 112
Methodism, 112, 131, 179
Methodists, 101
middle class(es), 27, 53, 68, 73, 81–3, 105, 122, 175, 194, 215
    publications, 68

Midlander, the, 61, 132
    attitude to sex, 127
    colour taste, 125
    gipsy streak, 126
    heredity, 108
    manipulative skill, 110
    personality, 109, 110, 112
Midlands, 13, 17, 22, 40, 70, 71, 86, 173, 221
    basic living costs, 120
    clothes, 109, 126
    concern with pain, 113
    'consumption fever', 121
    drink, 115
    employment, 110
    extravagance, 124
    food, 117, 137
    health, 114
    housing, 104
    incomes, 104
    kitchen skills, 119
    north-south affinities, 105
    physique, 107, 109, 110
    population, 196
    post-war prosperity, 120
    religion, 112
    television, 116
    wives, 120
milk, 23, 46, 77, 80, 96–8, 115, 116, 157, 173, 174, 181
    canned, 96, 97, 202
    malted, 34
millinery (*see clothing*)
Monmouthshire, 86, 101
mopeds, 74, 93, 214
mortgages, 63
motor cycles, 22, 71, 74, 93, 111
motoring (*see transport*)
    rythm, 64
multi-car households, 74
mustard, 106
mutton (*see meat*)

National Food Surveys, 218
natural reserves, 49
natural unity of areas, 13
'neaps', 202
nervous illnesses (*see ill-health*)
New Forest, 124
New Towns, 71
New Zealand (*see cheese*)
nightwear (*see clothing*)
nonconformism, 93, 100, 112, 171

Nordic Zone, 181
Norfolk, 70
North, the, 70, 73, 86, 104, 129
    dichotomy of, 130
North East, the, 112
    clothing, 156, 165, 166, 167, 168
    eating, 164, 165
    fashion, 165
    food, 155, 156, 157, 172-4
    housing, 156, 174, 175
    patriarchal family pattern, 151
    television, 177, 178
    upbringing, 191
North Midlands, 17
North of England, 129, 210
    eating, 129
north-south gradient, 21, 25
    personal attitudes to, 26
North West, the, 86
    affinity to Wales, 139
    character, 135
    clothes, 132-47
    coastal areas, 133
    eating, 129, 147
    family economics, 143
    food, 144, 146
    housing, 131, 132
    pensioner percentage, 139
    population, 130
    psychology, 138
    violence and vandalism, 140
    working wives, 147-9
Northampton, 70, 107, 108
northern character, 31
Northern Ireland, 16
northern pattern, typical, 37
northern society, 25-42
    Freudian undertones, 30
    social background, 29
northerner, 25-42
    eating, 30
    physique, 31
    traits, 171
Northumberland, 171, 172
Northumbrian traits, 151
Nottingham, 107
nuts (*see fruit*)

Oatcakes, 24
oatlands, 23
oatmeal, 173
oat zone, 164
obesity (*see ill-health*)

occupations, 37, 57, 58, 62, 63
Offices Bureau, Location of, 62
office-work, 37, 38, 63
off-licences, 66, 94, 157, 179
oil-stoves, 130, 167
'Old Black Breed', 108
onions (*see vegetables*)
Orangemen, 135
oranges (*see fruit*)
'Orpington Man', 64
Oxford, 70
Oxfordshire, 63
oxtail (*see meat*)

Paddington, 50, 51
paint, 145, 213
Pakistanis, 54
paraffin stoves, 68
parks, 45
pastas, 57, 117, 182
pawnbrokers, 144
peaches (*see fruit*)
pears (*see fruit*)
peas (*see vegetables*)
People, 82
perfumes, 30
personal autonomy, 33
'personalisation', 36-7
pets, 92, 214
photography, 41, 71
pickles, 117, 118, 137, 206
pigs (*see livestock*)
pineapple (*see fruit*)
place names, 158
plumbing, 74
Plymouth, 83
pneumoconiosis (*see ill-health*)
pocket money, 89, 124
police, 140, 188
population, 106
    annual return of, 16, 86
    drift, 25, 82
    foreign intrusion, 220
    taxable, 61
pork (*see meat*)
porridge, 23, 87, 164, 173, 190
potatoes (*see vegetables*)
Potteries, the, 107
pottery-making, 24, 173
poverty, 39, 88
Practical Householder, 214
pregnancy, 79
prejudices, 41

Index

Presbyterians, 101, 180, 189
pressure-cookers, 23
Preston, 132
price-cutting, 85, 211
privacy, 82
professional classes, 27, 81, 83
professional services, 69
Protestantism, 90
    persecution of, 132
psychological illness (see ill-health)
public-houses, 32, 93, 179, 189
public libraries, 112
publications, 165, 178, 190, 195,
    214
puddings, 78, 163, 202
pulmonary infection (see ill-health)
pulses (see vegetables)
puritanism, 29, 31, 99, 112, 156,
    183, 199

Rabbit (see meat)
radios, 151, 177, 189, 211 (see also
    transistors)
Radio Times, 72, 189
rail travel (see transport)
Railton, Dr. Ruth, 138
rainwear (see mackintoshes and boots,
    rubber)
raisins (see fruit)
rashes (see ill-health)
raspberries (see fruit)
rates, 63, 73
Reader's Digest, 112, 195
reading, 38, 112, 148, 189, 195
records, gramophone, 41, 42, 63
Reformation, the, 188, 189
refrigerators, 26, 56, 186
regional cultures, 8, 9
regional personality, 10
regional stability, 217–22
Regions of Britain, 15, 18
Registrar General, 14, 194
Registrar General's Standard
    Regions, 14
    list of, 15
    origin of, 14
religion
    Anglicism, 100
    Calvinism, 188
    Church of England, 77
    Free Church, 183
    Methodist, 101
    Presbyterian, 101

Roman Catholic, 101, 133, 134,
    135, 139, 142, 198
replacement pattern, 84
respiratory diseases (see ill-health)
restaurants and cafés, 57, 81, 204
retired element, 83
rheumatism (see ill-health)
Rhondda Valley, 102
rhubarb (see vegetables)
rhythm of life in the rural
    south, 71
rice (see vegetables)
Riesman, David, 188
rolls, bread, 57, 201
roses, 23, 106
Rugby, 107
rural habits, 71
rural life, 84
rustic compromise, 66
rum (see wines and spirits)
rye bread, 57
Ryvita, 207

St. Albans, 70
St. Helens, 132
Salads (see vegetables)
Salford, 132
salmon (see fish)
salt, 203
sandals (see footwear)
sample survey, 1, 9
sassafras, 34
sauces, 34, 100, 117, 174
    tomato, 137
    tomato ketchup, 117
    Worcester, 117
sausages, 34, 79, 117, 173, 190,
    191, 206
saving, 209, 211
savoury spreads, 34
schizophrenia (see ill-health)
schnapps (see wines and spirits)
scholarship successes, 39
scones (see cakes)
scooters, 71, 74, 93, 214
'Scotch douche', 206
Scotland, 16, 55, 87, 90, 93, 94,
    95, 96, 103, 117, 122, 143,
    144, 151, 164, 178
    affinities with Scandinavia, 181
    bread baking, 200, 201
    clothes, 73, 185, 196, 197, 211,
    212

comparison with England, 184
eating, 191, 201, 205, 206
east-west dichotomy, 183, 194
effects of climate, 186
fashion, 185, 196
food, 181, 190, 191, 200–7
highland-lowland dichotomy, 183, 184
housing, 83, 182, 212–15
law and order, 188
links with France, 180
manpower, 215
pattern of leisure, 189
religious extremism, 190
specialised market, 190
stagnation, 215
television, 189, 192, 204, 211
women, degradation of, 199
Scots
characteristics, 183
courtships, 195
discipline, 207
drinking habits, 186
frugality, 208–11
hospitality, 210
laundering, 197
personality, 191
physique, 184
reading, 195
reverence for authority, 192
sociability, 192
thrift, 208, 209, 210
Scottish Council, The, 215
Scottish Lowlands, 151
Scottish Sunday, 188, 189
Scottish TV Guide, 189
sedatives, 207
seeds, 56, 87
self-service, 38, 59, 185
sense of family, 29
sewerage, 74
sewing machines, 161, 196
sex-ratio, 52
shavers (*see electrical appliances*)
sheep (*see livestock*)
shellfish (*see fish*)
sherry (*see wines and spirits*)
shirts (*see clothing*)
shoes (*see footwear*)
shopping, 208
habits, 60, 97
mail-order, 38
shops, 85, 176

local, 221
mobile, 76
Shoreditch, 54
Sidmouth, 73
silent Southerner, the, 37
sinusitis (*see ill-health*)
skin diseases (*see ill-health*)
skirts (*see clothing*)
slacks (*see clothing*)
slimming, 31, 67, 147
slipped disc (*see ill-health*)
slippers (*see footwear*)
slips (*see clothing*)
slum clearance, 131
slums, 39, 130, 212
smoking, 63, 83, 87, 115, 165, 183, 206
cigarettes, 40, 41, 63, 182, 206
tobacco, 77, 100, 167, 206
sociability, 35, 192
social classes, mingling of, 37
social iron curtain, 27
socks (*see clothing*)
soft drinks, 30, 94, 115, 187, 205
Somerset, 76
soups, 23, 26, 87, 117, 137, 182, 202, 203
sources, 5, 6
South, Rural, 71, 73
South, the, 87, 93, 123, 137
South East, the, 13, 17, 70, 71, 74, 75, 81, 94, 145
clothes, 45, 58
food, 46, 65, 67, 69
grouping with East Anglia, 70
South Eastern Region, 65, 70, 75
dress, 67
social occupations, 66
way of life, 68
South West, the, 95
South Western Region, 70, 86
Southern Region, 65, 70, 75
southern society, 25–42
complexity of, 33
southerner(s), 25–42, 104
eating, 30
traits, 39
spaghetti, 57, 202
Spam (*see meat*)
specialisation, 36
spinach (*see vegetables*)
spirits (*see wines and spirits*)
sport, 87, 193

sport—*cont.*
  angling, 37
  cricket, 87
  football, 171, 193
Standard Regions, facing p. 13, 15, 16
  changes in, 17
  East and West Riding, 15, 16
  Eastern, 15, 16
  London and South Eastern, 15, 16
  Midland, 15, 16
  North Midland, 15, 16
  Northern, 15, 16
  populations, 16
  Scotland, 15, 16
  Southern, 15, 16
  South Western, 15, 16
  Wales, 15, 16
status symbols, 41
Stepney, 54
stockings (*see clothing*)
Stoke-on-Trent, 112
stomach upsets (*see ill-health*)
strokes, 21
suet, 148
  puddings, 163
Suffolk, 70, 79
sugar, 118, 206
  icing-, 32
suicide, 48, 79, 127, 128, 133, 139, 214,
suits (*see clothing*)
supermarkets, 32, 76, 155, 185
Surrey, 65, 66
Sussex, 65, 67
Swansea, 94, 102
sweaters (*see clothing*)
swedes (*see vegetables*)
sweetbreads (*see meat*)
sweets, 30, 32, 34, 205 (*see also confectionery*)
Swiss, 199
Swiss rolls, 36

Table napkins, 105
tables, 24, 106
tape recorders, 177
taste-sets, 50
tastes, 30, 32, 34, 69
  middle class, 82
  rarified, 60
tea, 22, 39, 66, 115, 157, 185, 210

teapots, 24, 173
teenagers, 61, 168, 175
teetotalism, 94, 100, 156, 179
telephones, 63, 68, 71, 123, 175, 183
television, 37, 72, 78, 94, 116, 177, 178, 189, 193, 204, 211
  Anglia, 17, 70
  ITV, 86
  Tyne-Tees, 17
  Wales and West, 17
Television Audience Measurement (TAM), 17
temperature traits, 25
test marketing, 2
textiles, 39
theatres, 193
thrift, 68
ties (*see clothing*)
tiles (*see furnishing*)
toasters (*see electrical appliances*)
tobacco, 77, 100, 167, 196, 206 (*see also smoking*)
toilet requisites, 40, 41, 67, 68, 137, 210
toilet-training, 30, 156, 191
tomato (*see also fruit*)
  ketchup, 117
  sauce, 137
topcoats (*see clothing*)
Topham, Captain, 195, 196, 199
tourists, 44
toys, 124
trading stamps, 40, 155
trains (*see transport*)
trait gradients, north v. south, 21
transistor radios, 94, 149
transport, 63, 93, 178
  buses, 64, 74, 92, 107, 179
  motoring, 64
  private, 62, 93, 178
  trains, 68, 92
  Underground, the, 64
travel, 68, 83
  retired people, 73
trousers (*see clothing*)
Turner, Graham, 122
turnips (*see vegetables*)
TV Times, the, 72
Tyne-Tees,
  affinities with Wales, 174
  area, 90, 170–1
  depression, 177
  reading habits, 178

retailing structure, 176
working wives, 175
Tyneside, 93, 108, 149, 156, 199

Ulcers (*see ill-health*)
umbrellas, 26, 167
underground, the (*see trains, post*)
underwear (*see under clothing,
    brassières, corsetry, girdles,
    lingerie, slips, vests*)
United Kingdom, 16, 56
Universe, 135
unskilled population, 27
upbringing, 191
upper class, 122, 175
urban influence, 71

Vacuum cleaners, 46, 156
varicose veins (*see ill-health*)
vegetables,
    asparagus, 75
    beans, baked, 137, 163, 202, 210
    beans, butter, 172
    beans, kidney, 80
    cabbage, 75, 116, 138
    carrots, 24
    cauliflower, 75
    celery, 30
    green, 24, 56, 105, 165, 173, 181
    leeks, 174
    onions, 21, 34, 75, 117, 137
    peas, 116, 117, 173, 202, 210
    potatoes, 23, 42, 56, 67, 98
    pre-packed, 155
    pulses, 23
    rhubarb, 56
    rice, 67, 98, 163
    root, 172
    salad, 26, 46, 67, 87, 165
    spinach, 34
    swedes, 24
    tinned, 165, 173
    tomatoes, 30, 75, 117, 155, 173,
        182
    turnips, 24, 202
venereal diseases (*see ill-health*)
vests (*see clothing*)
vices, 31, 82, 136
villages, drift from, 83
vinegar, 34, 117, 206
violence, 47
vodka (*see wines and spirits*)

Waistcoats (*see clothing*)
Wakes Week, 138
Wales, 24, 68, 77, 80, 112, 191,
    197, 198, 199
    clothing, 88
    discipline of children, 94
    eating, 96
    fashion, 88
    food, 87, 96
    housing, 92, 103
    housewives' shopping habits, 97
    housework, 91
    husband-wife relationship, 89
    population, 86
    regional employment, 90
    South, 62, 86, 93, 94, 99
wallpapers, 213
walnuts (*see fruit*)
Walpole, 79
Walsall, 218
wash boilers, 174, 197
washing machines (*see electrical
    appliances*)
wassailing, 76
water closet, 156, 212
water, fluoridation of, 97
water heaters, 22, 75
wedding dresses (*see clothing*)
weddings, 29
Welsh, 198, 207
    characteristics, 88
    earnings, 88
    mental stability, 101
    nationalists, 86
    perfectionism, 100
    temperament, 100
West Country, 13, 24, 27, 62, 63,
    65, 70, 72, 73, 75, 78, 80-2, 85
    clothes, 72, 84
    eating, 75, 77, 78, 85
    food, 72, 75, 79, 80
    housing, 75, 83
    television, 72, 78
West Hartlepool, 218
West Indians, 54
West Midlands, 17, 93, 102, 120
    conurbation, 127
Westmorland, kinship structure,
    171
West Riding, 17, 151
wheatlands, 23
whisky (*see wines and spirits*)
wholemeal bread, 69

Index

wines and spirits, 23, 32, 34, 41,
  60, 83, 94–8, 115, 117, 149,
  156, 165, 173, 179, 181, 186,
  187
  cherry brandy, 188
  gin, 34, 181, 187
  port, 149, 187
  rum, 32, 60, 115, 117, 181, 187
  schnapps, 181
  sherry, 32, 34
  vodka, 181, 187
  whisky, 23, 115, 181
Wolsey, 79
women's clothing (see under clothing)
wool trading, 158
Worcestershire, 107
working classes, 27, 50, 74, 82, 193
writing, 38, 84

York, 158

Yorkshire, 13, 62, 79, 80, 91, 93,
  136, 144, 199, 201
  conurbation, 156
  discontinuity between sexes, 168
  generalisations about character,
    151
  male independence, 166
  manual workers, 158, 159
  maternal influence, 168
  wifely skills, 160
Yorkshire and Humberside, 17
Yorkshire Life, 26, 167
Yorkshire pudding, 78, 158
Yorkshiremen, 78, 214
  character, 152
  characteristics, 150
  headwear, 167
  psychological studies, 160
  pugnacity, 152, 153